BERNARD OTOPAH APPIAH

I0146105

A SOCIO-THEOLOGICAL APPROACH TO
MIGRATION
AND INTEGRATION

Perspectives of African Church Communities in Britain

A SOCIO-THEOLOGICAL APPROACH TO MIGRATION AND INTEGRATION

Perspectives of African Church Communities in Britain

Bernard Otopah Appiah

IngramSpark

Milton Keynes, UK. LaVergne, TN

ISBN: 978-1-78972-719-7

Printed in the UK.
Lightning Source (UK) Ltd
Chapter House
Pitfield
Kiln Farm
Milton Keynes,
Buckinghamshire
MK11 3LW, United Kingdom

Ingram Content Group
1 Ingram Blvd
La Vergne, TN 37086
United States

Design (Cover & page layout) : *www.print-innovation.com*

This book is printed on paper suitable for recycling and made from fully managed forest sources. Logging, pulping and manufacturing processes are expected to conform to the environmental regulations of the country of origin.

A catalogue for this book is available from the British Library.

A catalogue of this book is available from the Library of congress.

Control Number: 2019917259

CONTENTS

DEDICATION

To the Late Ebenezer Atta Otopah and the Late Florence Agyen Frempong; Mum and Dad, thank you for your inspiring roles in my life.

And to all who play diverse roles in the complex reverse mission agenda in the global north, your labour of love would not be in vain.

ACKNOWLEDGEMENTS

I am very grateful to Emeritus Professor Allan H. Anderson, of the University of Birmingham, and my former PhD supervisor whose affirmation of the quality of my initial and follow-up research has led to this book.

I have also immensely benefited from the pioneering research work of Prof. Kingsley Larbi, the Founder and Chancellor of Regent University of Science and Technology into Pentecostalism and the inspiration I caught to pursue academic research to this level over two decades ago.

I am also equally indebted to Prof. Afe Adogame, the Maxwell M. Upson Professor of Christianity and Society at Princeton Theological Seminary, who was also my former supervisor at the University of Edinburgh for his support and encouragement.

Many thanks to the many African migrants and church leaders who opened their doors to me as an observer and researcher; with their insightful perspectives to many social, cultural and theological issues within 'minority' African and 'majority' British communities.

INTRODUCTION

The last few decades have witnessed an unprecedented flow of migrants from parts of Africa and sub-Saharan Africa particularly to Western European countries. These migrants bring their religions with them, creating religious communities in the diaspora and 'resulting in the remapping of old religious landscapes' (Adogame, 2005). These migrants have included adherents of indigenous African Religions, Muslims and Christians. Like the migrants of the other religions mentioned above, the Christians among them come from different Christian denominations such as the mainline historical churches to include the Methodists, Presbyterians, Evangelical Presbyterian; the Pentecostals; and the African Initiated Churches. Significant number of members of these denominations upon arrival congregate themselves together and request a pastor from their place or origin, or in some instances plant their own church with ties to their parent church or churches at the place of origin. The motivation for this phenomenon is that Africans are religious no matter where they find themselves (Kalu, 2000).

One important feature of these churches is that the predominant nationality of the members is in most cases determined by the nationality of the leader or pastor in charge of the churches, apart from the factor of the origins of the church itself. So for instance a church may be designated as a 'Nigerian Church' such as Matthew Ashimolowo's Kingsway International Christian Centre (KICC), Glory House led by the Odulele brothers or Christ Faith Tabernacle led by Apostle Alfred Williams; a 'Ghanaian Church' such as the International Central Gospel Church led by Dr Mensa Otabil, or Victory Bible Church International or the Dominion Centre; a 'Kenyan Church' such as Bishop Climate Irungu's Kingdom Church; or a 'Congolese Church' such as London Fire Church led by Pastor Jean Bosco Kanyemesha; a 'Zimbabwean church' such as the Spirit Embassy Good News Church led by Prophet Uebert Angel (Chike, 2011). In each case the church can be described as such because of its predominant membership, the country of origin of the church and the nationality of the pastor who leads the congregation (Olofinjana, 2010). However, these African churches described as such by scholars and the public in general, do not describe themselves with tags relating to their ancestry or national origins, but as international, due to its networking outside of the place of domicile. One could count many African-led churches that meet in school classrooms, former bingo halls, leisure centres, amusement centres and many other kinds of buildings around cities in Britain. These churches come in varying sizes, and differ in terms of their social composition, influence, liturgy styles, belief systems and practices. Scholars like Asamoah-Gyadu (2004) and Philip Jenkins (1970) believe that the rise in African Christianity generally in the West is the outworking of an observation made in empirical terms and echoed by Barrett, that by AD 2000 the centre of gravity of the Christian faith would have shifted markedly southwards' (Barrett, 1970). Statistics show that Africa, in particular, contributed to the huge surge of the growth of Christianity, showing an increase from only 10 million Christians in 1900 to 360 million at the end of 2000. Considering these developments, it is estimated there could be over 600 million Christians in Africa by 2025.

As at 1980, Christians in the Southern hemisphere were more numerous than those in the North for the first time in a millennium. In 1900 over 80% of all Christians lived in Europe and Northern America, however, by 2005 this proportion would have fallen to under 40% and will likely fall below 16% before 2025 (Johnson, 2012). However an update by Jenkins in 2002 of the distribution of world Christianity is not as grim as Barrett's projections, in 1970. According to Jenkins (2002) by 2025, 50 percent of the Christian population will be in Africa and Latin America, and another 17 percent will be in Asia, leaving the rest of the world with a share of 33 percent: double the projected figure by Barrett. Future projections show that the Christian churches of the Global South (Africa, Asia, Latin America and Oceania) are likely to increase their percentage share of membership of global Christianity (Johnson and Kim, 2012).

As Mkwaila (2009) puts it 'the image of Christianity can no longer be thought of as being defined primarily by its recent history in Europe and America but equally by its present and anticipated future vitality in Africa, Asia and Latin America'. Not only is this vitality resident in these continents mentioned by Mkwaila but also African migrants export it to the global north generally. As a residual effect, one of the thriving Christianity in the global north is African Christianity. Christianity described as African because of the African cultural nuances it carries in its belief and praxes. Hanciles (2008), in his observation of the phenomenon in the United States, notes that these 'immigrant churches are the most dynamic, and act as agents of new spiritual vitality and help initiate forms of outreach to multi-ethnic communities'. Similar to the American story, in Britain, these churches continue to expand their presence in various cities and suburbs among the African migrant communities. They are generally referred to as black majority churches, which include the African-Caribbean originated churches. It is estimated that there are more than 500,000 Black Christians in over 4,000 local congregations in the United Kingdom, the majority of which are in London *(British Minority Churches Directory, No date)*. The 4,000 local congregations are those registered with the African and Caribbean Evangelical Alliance, and the Minority Ethnic Christian Affairs (META) department of Churches Together in England and the number could significantly be more. Indeed, it is worth noting that these African churches have people from a few tens to thousands in attendance every Sunday. In some instances, these churches have satellite branches around the country, and may not have not registered with any of the above-named umbrella bodies as yet.

As these churches spring up, the major challenge they are confronted with is how to move from the immigrant communities and engage their larger host community in their quest to spread their kind of spirituality and vitality and still be able to maintain ties with their homeland. Within the context of the reverse mission agenda, it has been the desire of these churches to re-energise the Christianity of their host community through the process of integration, contextualisation and the carving of a transnational status for themselves. In the process, the churches not only provide a community for belonging, they also embark on wider social, economic and religious programmes. These programmes and initiatives not only mitigate the pain of being 'removed' but assist in integration in the place of settlement and directly or indirectly promote the sustenance of transnational ties (Fumanti and Werbner, 2010).

Thus they adopt a socio-theological approach which is a sociological action situated within a theological framework to understand a community and participate meaningfully through interventions. In other words, these African churches perceive and consider it serious, the religious dimension of social reality and subsequently respond appropriately (Bellah, 1957; Berger and Langman, 1967). Ultimately, the churches have taken a "sociotheological turn" in giving their membership a particular sociological posture in their communities. There has been attempts to socially analyse their migrant-membership communities to understand the reality of their specific worldview and needs (Sheikh, 2015).

It is then expected through these socio-theological interventions towards integration, these migrant church members would succeed to contextualise their faith and Christianity in their new homes in Britain. According to Shenk (1999),

> .... Contextualisation is a process whereby the gospel message encounters a particular culture, calling forth faith and leading to the formation of a faith community, which is culturally authentic and authentically Christian.

In other words, contextualisation would involve the processes through which the Christian message and church as an organisation is affected by the host community and in turn affects the host community, although the integrity of the message remains unaltered. From Shenk's definition there is first an internal process within a particular church or faith community that gives birth to an external engagement within the wider community. Further, the gospel message of a particular church or community carries nuances and a flavour, which distinguish it from others because of the church's cultural heritage as alluded to earlier above. It is the ensuing internal preparation and processes of integration, which involve the processes by which migrants settle into their communities; contextualisation, which is also the migrants' expression of faith that fits into their existential realities, and the quest to create the awareness of a transnational status that this book seeks to examine. This altogether is referred to as the socio-theological response to the communities that these churches serve. The internal preparation and processes shape the kind of engagement that is sought with the larger host community by the African migrant community. The internal preparation and processes that this book interrogates include: how these communities negotiate beliefs and practices; the extent to which the churches contextualise their beliefs and practices and the churches' programmes and initiatives to assist the members to integrate into the wider society; how the internal dynamics of the churches affect and are affected by the churches in the homeland; and their contributions to their larger host communities. Overall, this book provides an analysis from an African migrant perspective of the African religious presence in Britain and to what extent the churches assist their members to integrate into British society using a socio-theological approach.

Previous examination of how African churches are integrating and contextualising have focussed primarily on the 'mega' or large churches. To a large extent these churches do not paint a clear picture of African Christianity on Britain's religious canvas. For instance, the Ghanaian, Congolese, Malawian, Ugandan, South African, Zimbabwean churches which are predominantly nationals of these countries are growing in size and presence in London, but are not 'mega' in size in comparison to some of their Nigerian counterparts. Congolese, Malawian, Kenyan and South African Churches are growing in size and presence but are also not large in size compared to the Ghanaian, Congolese, Malawian, Kenyan or South African Churches churches. These churches have not received much attention from the scholarly community, unlike the African churches in Israel researched by Galia Sabar (2010); and those in Holland studied by Gerrie ter Haar (1998) and Rijk van Dijk (2002); and the United States by Afe Adogame (2013) for instance.

This book, therefore is complementary to other studies in Africa and the African diaspora (Adogame, 1999; Larbi 2001; Onyinah, 2002), considering eh intertwining religious and sociological space based on the realisation that much of the phenomena that modern people since the time of the European Enlightenment have called religion are related to other aspects of society, from economic and political factors to matters of social identity which is key in the quest to maintain their distinct identity while imbibing the new culture of their host community. It is from this perspective that the response of African churches and communities to the needs of these migrants takes a socio-theological turn, taking into consideration the cluster of actions and ideas relating to a notion of transcendence and of spiritual transformation that is affected by other aspects of public and private life. As a consequence, the communities and churches have taken the socio-theological task of recovering the internal logic of this perception of reality and placed it within its social milieu.

CHAPTER ONE

SOCIO-CULTURAL AND THEORETICAL MILIEU

Introduction

The combination of migrants' past experiences and their church leaders' beliefs and practices, with their present experience as African religious migrants places them in a peculiar position where their future is determined by an interconnection of the two. This inter-connectedness that is facilitated by the church then becomes the medium of reaching out to the host community. Often scholars tend to focus on the interaction of the church with the wider community with less attention given to the detailed internal processes of preparation towards integration with the wider host community, contextualisation and the creation of a transnational status and its associated challenges. This takes away from our understanding, the place of the church as an entity for facilitating integration. For these migrant churches the internal processes and preparation given by the churches subsequently shapes the kind of engagement it seeks with its larger host community. One cannot understand the responses of these Christian migrant communities to the wider host communities until one can understand the church as an organisation in itself and its contribution to the process.

The leadership, history, ethos and praxis of the churches shape the migrants themselves and subsequently determine the relationship they establish with the wider host community and place of origin to an extent. This approach is contrary to Schiller et al (2006), who propose non-ethnic pathways, which exclude the church as an ethnic community but rather an organisation of people who may share an ideology such as being 'born-again'. The concept of 'born-again' in Pentecostal understanding is a state of regeneration that starts with the process of belief in Christ as saviour, forgiver of one's sin and acceptance into a fellowship with God as His child and into the fellowship of other believers in Christ. The non-ethnic pathways towards integration into society do not work for migrants as many factors militate against them such as accessibility to funds and breaking into new social classes sometimes obtained through top job placements which they struggle to obtain. The church, which enforces ethnic connections either by default or consciously, therefore becomes the gateway for their integration into the larger host communities. Factors such as immobility through the social classes mentioned limit their ability to exert influence in their communities, but they are able to succeed through the church, as they are nurtured and given the necessary tools with which to pursue this agenda of integration to make it possible eventually albeit a longer process.

Somehow previous research by scholars such as Fumanti (2010), Krause (2008), Mazzucato (2008), have addressed issues relating to the transnational status of migrants focusing on the belongingness of individuals within the church community and its interconnectedness to the larger host community. In addition, Adogame (2003), Gerloff (2000), and Chike (2011) studies look at specific issues within the migrant churches in Europe without the focus on the church as an agency of integration into the larger society they find themselves. To be able to identify these efforts, the church has to be viewed as a collective representative of the people, and a shared entity of the people, and as such, emphasises religious identities and networks, such as that undertaken by Corten and Marshall-Fratani (2001) and Robbins (2004).

The African Church Communities

It is no coincidence that there is the conversion of cinema halls, discos, warehouses and other places of leisure into sacred spaces by African-led Churches especially of the Pentecostal strand in Europe which is considered the most vibrant among other strands of African Christianity, as this is in sharp contrast to the closing down and conversion of church buildings belonging to the mainline historic churches into pubs, residential homes and restaurants (Asamoah-Gyadu, 2004). These African-led churches have bought some of the sacred spaces belonging to the mainline historical churches. Some Pentecostals reckon that these are signs of the relative resurgence and vitality of African Christianity on the African continent, transported to Europe (Mkwaila, 2011). The trend has been that most of the conversions of public secular spaces into sacred places are being done by the African Pentecostal Christian community, whilst there is the conversion of sacred spaces belonging to mainline historical churches into secular public spaces. There have been suggestions from African Pentecostals to indicate that there is a resurgence of African Pentecostal Christianity and somewhat a decline of the mainline historic churches. It would be simplistic and a mere speculation to accept this perspective, as it is not solely the mainline churches that are in decline, some African-led Pentecostal churches have closed too, including the classical Pentecostal Aladura types. Some of the Classical Pentecostal churches and the Pentecostal Charismatic have shut down completely and some have seen their membership considerably reduced.

However, the transference of the resurgence and vitality of the African kind of Christianity to the west can on the one hand be seen as an active mission agenda, or on the other, simply as a consequence of the migration of its people either through political persecution, economic difficulties, academic pursuit and social revolts (Asamaoh-Gyadu, 2008). As Gerrie ter Haar (2001, p.2) puts it, 'human migration is something of all times and ages' and 'religion has always been a significant aspect' of it. As a result, African Christians who migrated to Britain have done so with their form of Christianity and have established places of worship in Britain. Whilst scholars like Asamoah-Gyadu claim that these African migrants have brought some vitality to their larger host communities in Europe, the problem is that most of these churches do not attract the indigenes of the host community due to a lack of a cross-cultural appeal. This means that their membership remains predominantly African (Adogame, 2005). An exception to this, however, is Pastor Sunday Adelaja's Embassy of the Blessed Kingdom of God in Kiev, Ukraine, which has as an immigrant pastor, yet the majority of the members of his congregation are the indigenes who are Ukrainians.

It is evident that African Christians experience difficulties in reaching out to their host community because a 'Christendom mind set' has developed in the churches. This kind of mind set according to Bosch (1991), is when the church in some way naturally begin to adjust the way it interpreted the Bible and organises itself due to the environmental pressures to reflect a new status quo. The African-led churches in Britain have developed a 'Christendom mind set' due to the economic and cultural pressures and challenges they face to fit into their new societies, thus readjusting themselves to issues within the churches themselves. An example is how the churches negotiate issues of community gospel outreaches and evangelism as part of its reverse mission agenda and co-habitation of male and females' church members living under the same roof as boyfriends and girlfriends, which most of these churches would have frown upon if it were happening in their homelands for instance. The Christendom mental framework of looking at their communities in relation to their own mission has resulted in the churches becoming inward looking other than trying to affect their host communities with their version of the gospel. According to Bosch, 'Christendom mind set' makes a dichotomy of ministry and mission, and churches are therefore not reaching out to those in their host communities who may be predominantly white (1991, pp. 467-474). As such, it can be argued that the churches have neglected mission although some believe the current posture of the African churches is mission organised in a different way to fit the new contexts. On the premise of this 'new' mission orientation of these churches, mission is considered as 'ministry by the whole people of God' as Bosch puts it. If that were to be the case, then the approaches of the church to mission is a response to the call for a specific mission strategy or a change in the mission strategy on the part of these African Christian communities to reach out to the 'white' host communities.

Juxtaposing this concept of Bosch onto the argument of reverse mission, would suggest that this should be a mission that targets all peoples irrespective of cultural or ethnic background: that is currently a limitation for most African Christian churches. However, an argument for the trend of having churches with a majority from a particular ethnic background is the question of the host community's acceptance of these churches on the whole (Kim Knibbe and Marten van der Meulen, 2009). Some from the host community have labelled them as being too noisy, aggressive and militant in their approaches to worship and belief practices, and have even to an extent branded them abusive, and portrayed their pastors as control freaks (Shukor, 2006). African migrant churches continue to provide their members with a safety net to help them to achieve a degree of security and inner strength, to counter the travail of a refugee, the pain of uprooted-ness, the alienation that comes with being a stranger and the 'experience of marginalisation in migration' (Ter Haar, 2001). These churches have resorted to setting up projects and linking up with other charitable organisations to help new entrants into Britain to integrate, to mitigate the problem Bosch describes as a 'Christendom mind set'. At the same time however, some leaders of a section of these churches claim that opening up the churches to the community destabilises and diminishes the commitment of their members to their churches and creates the grounds for competition among the churches (Knibbe, 2009) hence the inward looking focus. This view is equally shared by Glick Schiller, Caglar and Guldbransen (2006), who argue that the in some cases migrant churches are established as an outlet for international outreach to people from a particular part of the world in another land and that this probably explains why these churches bring in prophets and pastors from their homeland. Similarly, Boris Nieswand (2008, pp. 28-52) argues that these churches do not aim to integrate their members into the host society, as is suggested by much of the literature, but rather aim to incorporate Europeans back into Christianity and to a very large extent take care of 'their own' as migrants in the land of settlement. In practice, the focus of the churches is more on integrating members into their host community than it is on bringing the gospel to the host community (Krause, 2008). The idea of integration by the churches is on a micro level and that gives rise to internal initiatives considered as the socio-theological responses of the churches to the members' challenges to integration. It has to be said however, this is not an indication of lack of interest to reach out to the host communities but consider the integration as the first step towards that process. Within the framework of thought of these churches, incorporation of Europeans into these churches must be preceded by a unique process set in motion towards integration by contextualising their Christian message to reach out to the wider host communities.

Contextual Theoretical Framework

Due to the complex dynamism of migration, I use a migrations systems theory as the base for the theoretical framework. The migration systems theory whose proponents have included Mabogunje (1970), Portes and Borocz, (1989), Levit (1998) and Kritz et al (1992) has widely defined it as the relationship that exists between sets of places linked by the flows and reverse flows of the essentials of human existence, such as goods, services, information and people. Mabogunje's focus was on the rural-urban migration within Africa and Kritz took it further to include international migration. Castles and Miller summarise the parameters of the theory that:

Migration systems approach is part of a trend towards a more inclusive and interdisciplinary understanding, which is emerging as a new mainstream of migration theory – at least outside the domain of neo-classical orthodoxy. The basic principle is that any migratory movement can be seen as a result of interacting macro and microstructures. Macro structures refer to large-scale institutional factors, while microstructures embrace the networks, practices and beliefs of the migrants themselves. These two levels are linked by a number of intermediate mechanisms, which are often referred to as 'meso-structures (1993).

Considering the fact that the focus of this work is to analyse the internal integration strategies, this framework would assist in analysing the informal social networks developed by the migrants themselves.

To examine the internal preparation towards integration therefore, I use Clifford's theory, which lays emphasis on the locality and the host societies that the communities are embedded in as a guide (1994). And will draw on Robin's work, which does not consider that integration is a permanent stage but rather an on-going process and suggests that migration is in fact dynamic, with migrants constantly adapting to the changing legal framework of their host country (1996). These perspectives will capture the internal preparation and processes by which the immigrants integrate through the assistance provided by the churches, as their spirituality is central to sustaining their dignity and affirmation of life (Gerloff, 1999). Migrants' connection to a church that has links to their cultural background also affirms the ethnic pathway this research uses to establish how the church assists members to integrate, contrary to Gulbrandsen et al's (2006) view that this method is contradictory. It is not contradictory in the sense that most of the Christian migrants' lives are intertwined with the church and their self-definition. And it is at this point that the beliefs and practices of the migrants in relation to the church are essential as their self-definition intertwines with other political beliefs such as pan-african beliefs.

A derivative of the process of migrant integration is the transnational status as a response to the migration experience. Fumanti and Werbner (2010), study the migrants and their relationship with the state as part of the process of integration within the wider host community, without much attention given to the processes of preparation for integration into the wider community. Others such as Krause (2008), focus on the transnational status of the migrants and the residual benefits that accrue to these migrants, in spite of the distance from their homelands and the somewhat hostile conditions they face in these new communities. Along a similar line, Mazzucato provides an analysis of the informal insurance arrangements in the migrant's homeland as part of the reverse flow of benefits to migrants, ignoring the varied informal insurance arrangement within the migrant communities themselves (Nieswand, 2008). Mazzucato, Krause, Funmati and Werbner's tools for measuring the impact of the transnational status of the migrants have been somehow economic in their outlook as though the migrants have solely come to the new places of settlement for economic reasons. Aside from the established theories of migration, which focus on socio-economic reasons, there are also religious reasons or 'spiritual factors' to be taken into account. And examining the factors by which immigrants forge and sustain simultaneous multi-stranded social relations that link together their societies of origin and settlement.

Further to the development of the theories in this field, is the transnational theory. I include this as part of my chosen analytical framework for understanding international migration, as stimulated by the work of Glick-Schiller, Basch and Blanc-Szanton (2009). This theory examines the factors and conditions that necessitate the continuance of ties between the immigrant's present abode and place of origins. This includes issues of education, such as the development of the school curriculum to reflect the fact that the socialisation of many transmigrant children takes place in an interconnected social space encompassing both the immigrants' home country and their new home. They postulate that there are three main conjoining forces that give rise to transnational immigration, enumerated as:

(1) A global restructuring of capital based on changing forms of capital accumulation has led to deteriorating social and economic conditions in both labour sending and labour receiving countries with no location a secure terrain of settlement.

(2) Racism in both the U.S. and Europe contributes to the economic and political insecurity of the newcomers and their descendants; and

(3) The nation building projects of both home and host society build political loyalties among immigrants to each nation-state in which they maintain social ties.

The theory takes cognisance of contemporary migrants' or transmigrants' financial commitments to their families at the place of origin and their involvement in the social and political development of their home countries notwithstanding the steps they take towards incorporation. This theoretical framework rejects the idea that immigrants' having a settled status ruptures their ties with homelands and transforms them into a sentiment rather than an actual connection to their homeland. Rather it describes an emerging pattern among immigrants who, though they have a settled status, also maintain significant ties to the place they consider as their homeland.

Upon arrival in the land of settlement, immigrants seek economic, social, and political engagement. There are internal processes for preparing migrant church members for integration. These takes the form of programmes, orientation through sermons preached, publications, seminars and workshops, and informal arrangements set up by members of these congregations to mitigate the cost of economic, social and political adjustment in the host society. Both within and outside of these churches, there are also extensive support networks established to assist in the integration of migrants.

CHAPTER TWO

SITUATING THE SOCIO-THEOLOGICAL NEXUS

Introduction

The interconnectedness and long history of humans with religions has meant that different aspects of human lives has been examined under different disciplines. And so has religion been examined from different perspectives because of human impact on its expression and forms within those societies and on the other hand, religions impact on how different social groups operate within their spheres. Some of these interactions between humans and religions and the mythical or divine entities that embody the whole delivery of religion to the door step of those who seek it and subsequently identify with its tenets and practices is often what is captured in these studies.

In the development of religion as a subject of enquiry, Ninian Smart, in his book *Dimensions of the sacred: An Anatomy of the Worlds Beliefs* (1996) has established seven quantifiable elements that are somehow measurable and enable religion to be put through a methodical scrutiny at least from the sociological point of view. These elements are ritual; mythological; doctrinal; ethical; experiential; social and material. The execution and performance of these elements also involves an engagement of communities and the corresponding entities believed to be the objects of worship. And how these participation shapes communities.

It is from this perspective that Singleton, in his book Religion, Culture and Society (2014) situates the journey of the scientific study of religion citing an example of the leader of the Church of Christ, Scientist – Mary Baker Eddy. Mary slipped and injured herself and during convalescence with the encounter with a healing story in the bible. What followed was a founding of the church to share her thoughts and experience, formed into a set of beliefs expressed through rituals and consolidated into a set of doctrines. This gives such a movement an appearance of an organisational entity that can be subjected to a thorough scientific analysis to understand its people and changes that takes place in people and subsequently society at large. To wit, in the context of the subject of discussion in this book, individuals and social groups connection to religion could make a difference to how they perceive the happenings within society and their practical response to it. And in this case how African Christian migrant communities integrate into society.

Modernity, the Social Sciences and Christianity

Modernisation took place across western world, but with particular robustness in Britain and the United States. The latter part of the 19th century in the United States, in the aftermath of the civil war is known as the Gilded Age, and refers to the widespread industrialisation that took place. Modern life as we know it was well and truly underway. Modernity as known was more than a particular period in the west's recent history –it also refers to a process of social change. According to David Landes, in his highly regarded work the *Unbound Prometheus* (1972), industrialisation is at the centrality of the complex process known as modernisation. A 'combination of changes – in the mode of production and government, in the social and institutional order, in the corpus of knowledge and in the attitudes and values' (1972:6). These changes according to Landes (1972:6), entailed not just industrialisation and urbanisation, but also bureaucratisation, which is the highly organised administration of daily life by the government and other institution. And the implementation of state-sponsored universal education. Other commenters included social differentiation which is the development of the specific social institutions set up to undertake different tasks previously performed by organised religion, notably in education and healthcare, the rise of the scientific worldview (Singleton, 2014). This worldview introduces various terminologies within the social sciences in a way help us to understand the world in which we live from different sociological perspectives. One perspective states that, life can be explained in reference to natural and material causes, which forms the bedrock of rationalism. Rationalism is a rational explanation which can be adduced by reason for all phenomena. Another perspective is Individualism. Within this perspective, the individual is a recognised and valued unit in society; and also Pluralism, which is often seen as a multiplicity of ideas, conception of the world and institution (Wilson 1996; Tschannen 1991; Bruce, 2011).

Without doubt the infusion of these sort of conception of the world around us from the sociological point of view affected modern life and at the same time presented a challenge for orthodox Christianity, which had furnished society with the overriding worldview in pre-industrialised Europe and America (Chadwick 1975; McLeod, 2000; Taylor, 2007; Ustorf and McLeod, 2003). Pre-industrialised European and American societies were defined by what McLeod (2003:11) calls Christendom in which Christianity 'is the common language, shared, by the devout, lukewarm and the sceptical, through which a wide arrange of social needs could be met', and which provided generally accepted concepts and symbols. McLeod (2003:20) points to the Enlightenment, the French Revolution and the Industrial Revolution as all playing roles in the diminishing role of Christendom's central place in western society.

As part of the process of the diminishing presence of Christendom, there were vehement calls for the detachment of church and the state; advances in history and literature led to more progressive; non-literal readings of the Christian Bible where attention was paid to not just to the meaning of passages but the circumstances in which the text was produced therefore weakening the place of the bible as the absolute authority for spirituality, morality and instruction in society. More liberal variants of Christianity grew on the back of widespread contextualised interpretations of the bible which is advocated by many theologians church practitioners in different cultural settings in contemporary times around the world but this went further to challenge the notion of it being divinely inspired to be upheld as the word of God. The authority and teachings of the traditional churches were increasingly challenged by discoveries of science and rationalist thought. The development to this stage and era of Christianity is revealed through the work of Henry Sedgewick (1867); and Thomas Dixon who acknowledge the pervasiveness of the secularism and its consolidation in society after the published work of Charles Darwin, *On the Origins of the Species* in 1859. The churches diminished role and influence in society with its worldview exacerbated further by the many new religious movements who felt less bound by the institutional boundaries of traditional Christianity opening the door for many to seek alternatives to traditional religious orthodoxy. Nonetheless the church, continues to remain an entity of interest to social scientists as even with its diminished role in the western world, there is an injection of vitality which could push Christianity again to the fore led by the African Pentecostal strand of Christianity irrespective of the myriads of challenges they face. Thereby, creating room and a necessary platform for religion to be looked at with two lenses – sociologically and theologically.

Approaches to Socio-theological Study of Religious Communities

Modernism could be traced to the founding figures of social studies who also served paradoxically as progenitors and midwives in its delivery—most notably Emile Durkheim, Max Weber and Karl Marx.

Durkheim attempted to immerse himself in the thinking of tribal societies to understand the socio-religious significance of totemic symbols (Durkheim, 1915). He understood the social significance of religion and made it the subject of sociological analysis. His focus was on religion as an inherent social activity which in its process binds members of society together to make society more productive and maintain social order (Singleton, 2014).

Weber like Durkheim on the other hand, but not exclusively adopted a posture of verstehen in his social analysis that was sensitive to cultural values; and he integrated both theological ideas and social theory in his studies of the religions of India and China and in developing his understanding of the Protestant ethic. He among other things examined how religion was connected to social changes and precipitated the capitalism that drove the Industrial Revolution and wondered why protestant Christians were active in the rapid expansion of capitalist enterprise than Catholics, and concluded for instance that the values and beliefs of Protestants particularly associated with Calvinism were conducive to the conduct of business.

Karl Marx took seriously the relationship of ideological frameworks of thought to social structure, especially in his analysis of the role of religion and social change. He observed that society was stratified causing class divisions and this fed into the division between those who worked the land and those who owned the land (Marx and Engel, 1939). An observation made about Marx was often that of hostility towards religion as he believed that religion during the feudal times reinforced those ruling values and that religion continues to propagate ruling class values in the modern era. Marx's reflection on religion includes the often taken out of context and famous quote; 'Religion is the sigh of the oppressed creature, the heart of a heartless world and the soul of soulless conditions. It is the opium of the people (Marx 1970:131), which comes from his essay, A Contribution to the Critique of Hegel's 'Philosophy of right' (1884). Marx, by this statement was making the argument of the inevitability of religion as part of human existence, considering its practical role and function, drawing similarities with the function of opium to a sick and an injured person. Howbeit, also seeing religion as complicit in blinding people from the obvious problems created by the class structures and the oppression of the poor by the rich in society which it has contributed to create.

Within sociology, both Robert Bellah and Peter Berger have been hospitable to theological points of view with social thinkers such as Pierre Bourdieu and Antony Giddens accepting, albeit more reluctantly, the viewpoints from within religious traditions (Sheikh, 2015).

Anthropologists by disciplinary habit have been more disposed to take other people's perspectives seriously, and thus have accommodated more easily religious points of view. This has been true of such anthropologists as Clifford Geertz, Louis Dumont, Mary Douglas, Stanley Tambiah, Talal Asad, and Gananath Obeyesekere. According to Mona, within the fields of religious studies and the history of religion, religious perspectives are part of the objects of their studies, and some of the scholars who study religion have also been mindful of the social implications of religious ideas. These 'socially-minded scholars of religion have included many comparativists, including notably Ninian Smart and Wilfred Cantwell Smith' (2015, p.147).

Such diverse thinkers in European history as Adam Smith, widely regarded as the father of modern capitalist economic theory, and Charles Darwin, one of the fathers of evolutionary biology, began their intellectual careers studying theology. The same is true of many of the most influential scientists from the Islamic culture such as Ibn Sina (commonly known by his latinised name Avicenna), who is regarded as a father of modern medicine and creator of the concept of momentum in physics; Ibn Hayyan, known as the father of molecular chemistry; or Al-Khawarizmi and Al-Kindi, who invented algebra. A common element in their scientific approach was that they all studied, went into dialogue with, or drew on inspiration from the field of theology.

There is therefore a call to a socio-theological turn, which means incorporating into social analysis the insider-orientated attempt to understand the reality of a particular worldview. As a result, the social sciences need to recover an appreciation for a field long banished from the halls of secular academe: theology. The insider perspective on a religious worldview is, after all, what the field of theology has classically been about, long before the advent of the modern academic disciplines: attempts to structure the social, ethical, political and spiritual aspects of a culture's ideas and meanings into a coherent whole (Juergensmeyer and Sheikh, 2013).

Most of the sociological work on religion in the first half of the twentieth century, however, tended to be reductionist and unappreciative of the marked effect of religious ideas and imagery. Typically, social scientists have felt most comfortable by keeping theology far away enough, but the representatives of what we labelled a Socio-theological approach have provided exceptions. In some instances, the trend of combining a focus on faith with a focus on the social milieu has been a steady though often minority perspective within the disciplines.

Theology, encompasses the essential moral and spiritual connections in all aspects of life. The power of theology as an academic discipline in the early modern period was its comprehensiveness. It attempted to survey the whole range of human activity and belief. For this reason, theology was once regarded as the queen of the sciences. During the latter part of the modern era, theology fell into disrespect among social sciences partly due to the secularisation narrative that represented faith as the opposite to science, and theology became isolated as a field (Singleton, 2014). This was partly due to three limitations in the way that theology was increasingly practiced: it had only one religious tradition as its frame of reference, it asserted normative truth claims about its analyses, and its analysts often ignored the social context in which the ideas they study emerge and are cultivated. However, this may not be said to be the same in the last 50 years or so. Actually room has been made for the study of other disciplines together with theology and this is reflected by the curriculum of various universities across the world.

Socio-theology is based on the realisation that much of the phenomena that modern people since the time of the European Enlightenment have called religion are related to other aspects of society, from economic to matters of social identity. For this reason, socio-theological analysis is not often limited to a study of religion in the tapered consciousness, as if there were a separate cluster of actions and ideas relating to a notion of existence and of spiritual transformation that was unaffected by other aspects of communal and individual life.

To understand a perception of reality is to have an epistemic worldview which requires the socio-theological tasks of recovering the internal logic of this perception of reality and placing it within its social milieu. It also 'requires understanding the relation between those people who share a certain worldview and the social and power structures of the world around them' (Singleton, 2014, p.29-33). The task is similar to the hermeneutical approach to the interpretation of scriptural texts, an approach that has been employed in cultural sociology as well, in attempting to understand the range of ways that statements and social events have been perceived from various perspectives (Gee, 1992; Bergen and Harvey, 1992; Edwards and Potter, 1994).

Hence, epistemic worldviews are conceptual entities, but they are also tied to social realities. Others share these worldviews in a pattern of association that is usually contiguous with other social boundaries, such as a particular ethnic or religious community. This means there are concentric circles of social realities that coalesce with particular epistemic worldviews which has the potential to move boundaries and in the process drive social change.

Christianity as an Agent of Social Change

The rapid shift in societal norms and changes within the strata of society through modernism, secularisation, and the acceptances of the tools of social sciences in analysing various phenomena, religion still plays a major role in the organisation of people, leading them in a particular direction and also serves as an advocate through various plans of interventions in situations that adversely affect society. Christianity is going through a process of marginalisation in secular discourse, and in spite of that it is able to reorganise itself in ways to intervene in the effects of decisions made for society such as marginalisation of minorities to the fringes to remain relevant. This empowers the church as an organised embodiment of Christianity, to its place of influence within its walls although it's effaced and pressured to remain inconspicuous. That notwithstanding, it is able to lead small groups of marginalised individuals some of whom are migrants to remain significant through a process of integration using the church as a conduit for the realisation of the goals of integration.

The root of this nature and evolving Christianity was theorised by Weber, who believed the protestant ethics fertilised the ground for capitalism. He traces the churches involvement in this major shift by underscoring the fact that Calvinist for instance believed people could only attain salvation – eternal life in heaven rather than hell (Weber, 2005). And that those who were morally upright and professionally successful in this life were thought to be ones predestined for heaven. Making a strong case that one's eternal life involved commitment to hard work. As a consequence in Britain, Calvinist rose to prominence among the middle class and were instrumental in the development of the capitalist economy that drove industrialisation (Singleton, 2014). Therefore, in spite of the attempt to suppress Christianity during the age of secularisation, the church through its theology and teachings were able to maintain some level of influence in shaping society's perception or serve as an interventionist in the processes of social change.

Religion's nemesis in this process of social change has been rationalisation. Rationalisation by and large has had an adverse effect on the church through disenchantment which Weber (2005:322) predicted, but it's not far from the truth to also say that somehow society is also disenchanted by the extreme forms of capitalism which leaves a good section of society marginalised which is the opposite effect and the blind side of the observation of Marx in his capitalist theories. The balance created between rationalism and religion and for that matter Christianity within the context of this subject of enquiry over time, is how the migrant-African churches create cultural and social space for its members as an intervention to ameliorate the pain of uprootedness and can go further to assist them in their integration into British society. And this is where society is at the moment: disenchanted as an inevitable outcome of the modernity but contrary to what Weber predicted, the church has become very important in the lives of those marginalised individuals who find solace in the Christian faith and its values.

CHAPTER THREE

MIGRATION AND THE HISTORY OF AFRICAN CHURCHES IN BRITAIN

The integration of migrants with a socio-theological approach encompasses their migration to their current place of settlement, their perspective to integration, and the maintenance of ties to their homeland. A thorough discussion of factors that give rise to migration is therefore needed to set the stage for a meaningful examination of the socio-theological approach to the process of integration which leads to the kind of transnational status migrants assume as a consequence. The discussion in this chapter moves from the general to the particular in international migration and local migration. The focus will be on international migration in general and African migration to Britain in particular and it's interrelatedness to the churches that host these migrants. The churches selected are both 'migrant churches' with origination in Britain but led by migrants, and others as off-shoots of a mother church from their place of origin in Africa. The state may consider them migrants whilst the church consider them as agents of mission in these new places of settlement.

Analysis of Migration Theories and Factors Precipitating Migration

There is a growing unrest among academics on the on-going theoretical basis for understanding international migration. The dissatisfaction has risen from the fact that, the theories present are out of date with current reality of the surge in migration around the world, and the lack of a consistent theory that captures even the minority of people whose reasons for migration may be unconventional. Almost every developed nation on earth has in part become a multicultural and a multi-ethnic society with the influx of migrants from all over the world. Unfortunately, this pace is not matched with the development of a theory to understand the forces that drive migration, although various attempts have been made to put current migration trends in context. This observation is confirmed when Massey (1993, p.456) asserts that 'rather, the complexity of migration, its multifaceted nature requires a sophisticated theory that incorporates a variety of perspectives, levels, and assumptions'. It has to be noted however that, the development of a sophisticated theory as presented by Massey presents a herculean task as the dynamics of human existence keep changing and therefore what would precipitate a move by an individual to another geographical location could be fluid and even transient. There is the need for an incorporation of the current major theories of international migration for a better comprehension of the forces that drives it. The major current theories are; Neoclassical Economics, New Economics of Migration, Dual Labour market theory and World Systems Theory.

Theories proposed to explain the origins and persistence of international migration are fluid in nature due to the ever-changing circumstances of the human existence. Therefore, rather than adopting the narrow argument of theoretical exclusivity to any particular theory, I take up the broader position that causal processes applicable to international migration might operate on multiple levels concurrently, and which is why I highlight the emergence of another reason; the God factor described later as the religious factor which has so far not been adequately covered by existing theories. And that sorting out which of the explanations is useful is an empirical and not only a logical task due to its dependence on individuals, groups and trends (Massey, 1993).

Neoclassical Economic Theory of Migration

The neoclassical economic model returns a clear empirical prognosis that, in principle, should be readily confirmable: that the volume of international migration is directly and meaningfully related, over time and across countries, to the size of the international gap in wage rates. This theory has been divided into macro and micro theories. The macro theory that was originally developed by Lewis, Ranis and Fei (1961), and Harris and Todaro (1970), focussed on geographic differences of the supply of and demand for labor. Meaning that countries that have a high level labour availability tend to have a low wage rate and countries that have a low level labour availability have a high wage rate. There is also the micro theory also developed by Sjaastad (1962), Todaro (1969), and Todaro and Marusko (1987), this theory asserts that individuals make the decision to migrate due to a personal cost-benefit analysis of a potential change in geographical location with an expectation of a positive net return usually in monetary terms.

Subsequent modifications of the neoclassical model of both the macro and micro theory however, suggest that the relevant factor in migration decision-making is the expected earning's gap, not the outright real-wage differential. At any point in time, expected earnings are defined as real earnings in the country under consideration multiplied by the odds of employment there (Taylor et. al, 1993). Although it typically 'estimated as one minus the unemployment rate, the likelihood of employment is almost certainly more appropriately measured as one minus the underemployment rate', given the pervasiveness of irregular, part-time employment in low-skill jobs within developing regions. The key predictor of international migratory flows is thus an interaction term that cross-multiplies wages and employment probabilities (Todaro, 1969). On the level of the migrant, the Todaro model and its successors foresees that individual and household peculiarities that are positively connected to the rate of remuneration or the chances of employment in destination areas will increase the probability of migration by raising the expected returns to international movement. Hence, the prospect of emigration is forecasted to be credibly related to such standard human capital variables as age, experience, schooling, marital status, and skill (Massey et al, 1993). The predisposition for international migration is also estimated to vary with a household's access to income-generating resources at home, such as owning land or supporting a business enterprise, since these will affect the net return to movement, which is the case in most sub-Saharan Africa. Since human capital variables that affect rates of employment and remuneration in destination areas also tend to affect wage and employment rates in places of origin, a key empirical issue is where the effect of human capital is greater, at home or abroad.

Given the fact that international migration involves a change of language, culture, and economic system, human capital acquired at home generally transfers abroad imperfectly (Chiswick 1979, pp.357-399). According to Massey, in this case, international migrants may be negatively chosen with respect to variables such as education and job experience as it is the case in Britain, Australia and the United States. Taylor (1987), in his view notes that among rural Mexicans, for example, the economic returns to education have historically been bigger in urban areas of Mexico than in the United States. Whereas an undocumented migrant with a secondary education gets the same minimum-wage job in Los Angeles as one with no schooling at all, that education would qualify the same person for a clerical or white-collar job in Mexico City, thereby raising the likelihood of rural-urban migration and lowering the probability of international movement. This pattern of negative selectivity cannot be theorised universally, however, since selection on human capital variables depends on the transferability of the skill or ability under consideration, which itself is decided by social, economic, and historical milieu specific to the countries involved. In general, any social change that affects the market value of human capital in either society has the potential of altering the size and direction to the connection between particular predictor variables and the likelihood of international movement. In general, the only universal prediction that can be offered is that human capital should by some means be dependably related to the likelihood of international movement, but the force and bearing to the relationship are impracticable to know about the absence of historical information about the countries involved. Only after the historical events have been clearly specified, and their influence on the returns to specific forms of human capital clarified, can a critical test of the neoclassical microeconomic model be formulated. The only evidence that could conceivably cast serious doubt on the logic to the human capital theory of migration would be the impeccable absence of a relationship between human capital and migration (Massey, 1969).

The New Economics Theory of Migration

An antithesis to neoclassical economic theory, the new economics of migration concentrates on the household or family, rather than the individual, as the pertinent decision making unit; and it posits that migration is a response to income risk and to failures in a variety of markets, which together constrain local income prospects and hold back risk-spreading (Massey et al, 1993). Proponents of this position has been Stark and Bloom, Taylor, Katz and Levhari who add that the direct test of this theory would be to relate the presence or absence of such market deficiencies to households' propensities to take part in international migration (Stark and Bloom, 1985; Katz and Stark, 1986; Taylor, 1986; Stark and Levhari, 1982). If the new economics of migration is accurate, households faced by the greatest local market deficiencies should be most likely to adopt an international migration strategy, which also seems to be the case of some migrants spoken to. They are not much concerned about world trends but make decisions on the basis of their personal circumstances and how that affect their immediate families. One of the most differentiating contributions of the new economics of migration is its incorporation of migration decision making with migrants' remittance behaviour and households' remittance use—aspects of migration (Massey et al., 1993). If risks to income and a desire to overcome local constraints on production are the driving forces behind migration, then the outcomes of migration should reflect this fact. If risk diversification is the underlying motivation, then migrant remittances should be greatest in households most exposed to local income risks, and in times when this risk is most acute (Lucas and Stark, 1985). 'If a principal incentive of migration is to overcome risk and credit constraints on local production stemming from market shortcomings, then migration and remittances should positively influence local income-generating activities' (Lucas, 1987). Such discoveries would furnish verification in favour of the new economics of migration, because positive effects of migration on local production activities are ruled out by neoclassical economic theory, as are risk effects. Neoclassical theory concentrates on an individual's maximisation of anticipated income and assumes that markets are impeccable and well-functioning (Massey et al., 1993). The new economics of migration also places migration within a broader community context, specifically linking a household's migration decision to its position in the local income distribution. Therefore, a more unifying theory is sought through the Dual Labour Market theory.

Dual Labour Market Theory of Migration

In as much as dual labour market theory postulates a bifurcated occupational framework and a dual pattern of economic organisation for advanced industrial societies, 'in practice it has proven unmanageable to validate this segmented market structure empirically' (Cain, 1976). Rather than trying to validate the empirical framework of the labour market, therefore, a more effective strategy might be to concentrate on the theory's prognoses with regard to patterns of international movement, which are moderately precise and impartially testable (Massey et al., 1993). Piore and others argue that immigration is driven by conditions of labour demand rather than supply. Being demand-based, the dual labour market approach also forecasts that international flows of labour begin through conventional enrolment procedures rather than individual efforts (1979:118). Although world systems theory makes up an intricate and at times diffuses conceptual framework, it returns a number of comparatively straightforward and testable propositions, the first to which is that international flows of labour follow international flows of capital, only in the opposite direction (Massey et al., 1993). Emigrants are created by direct foreign investment in developing countries and the interruptions that such investment brings. Thus, we should observe that 'streams of foreign capital going into peripheral regions are played with by matching outflows of emigrants'. This basic migratory process should be enhanced by the existence of ideological and material ties created by prior colonisation as well as on-going processes of market penetration (Sassen, 1988).

World Systems Theory of Migration

If one were to specify a model of international migration flows to it would be world systems theory, therefore, one would want to include pointers of preceding colonial connections, the prevalence of common languages, the intensity of trade relations, the existence of transportation and communication links, and the relative frequency of communications and travel between the countries. This is a position of sociological theorists such as Portes, Walton, Petras, Castells and Morawska, which has been built on an earlier work by Wallerstein. This position states that the desire for higher profit and greater wealth, spur on owners and manager of capitalist firms enter poor countries on the peripheries of the world economy in search of the necessities for production and new consumer markets for their products (Portes, 1981; Petras, 1981; Morawska, 1990). World systems theory stipulates not only that international migration should flow from outer edge to crux along paths of capital investment, but also that it is pointed to specific "global cities" that channel and control foreign investment. Although the theory does not provide a precise criterion for defining a "global city," a set of operational standards might be developed from information about capital assets and corporate headquarters to global cities, in contrast to other places within the developed or developing world (Sassen, 1991). Finally, although the propositions, suppositions, and hypotheses derived from each perspective are not intrinsically inconsistent, they, nonetheless, carry very different implications. Depending on which model is advocated and under what circumstances, scholars and professionals in the field might recommend that policymakers attempt to regulate international migration by changing wages and employment conditions in destination countries; by promoting economic development in origin countries; by establishing programmes of social insurance in sending societies; by reducing income inequality in places of origin; by improving futures or capital markets in developing regions; or by some combination of these actions.

The Religious Factor of Migration

The theories of migration discussed eliminate to some extent, the probability that migration could occur for religious reasons, such as in the case of reverse mission, where people from the Southern Hemisphere are returning with the gospel to the people of the Northern Hemisphere who first brought the gospel to people of the south.

In other words, religious organisations within a noted sending country could send people to foreign lands to establish churches either for members who might have migrated for economic purposes, but these churches' intentions may not exclusively be economic. There could be economic intentions for these sending churches, because in some cases monies are sent in the form of remittances to support local projects of the churches in the homelands (Kalu, 2008). For example there are churches like the Trinity Baptist Church in London that has an orphanage in Accra, Ghana and funds are raised periodically to support this orphanage. In instances where migrants are sent for religious purposes, these become religious migrants, although upon entry into their receiving country, they are not immune from the other economic factors discussed throughout this section. The processes of would-be migrants knowing they are sent by God to migrate, involves visiting intermediaries which include 'men of God' and 'prophets' who sanction their quest to migrate from the beginning, with their visa applications (Obadare and Adebanwi, 2012). Besides the 'organised religious migration' through the churches and other religious agencies, there are also individuals who migrate because they feel 'led' by God to migrate as missionaries. Although these individuals' mission may not preclude making economic gains through secular work at their destination, they believe God has sent them. Others have also found the motive and a 'higher calling' of God for their migration upon arrival although their initial desire to travel was mainly economic.

Whatever the case, given the size and scale of present day migration flows, and given the potential for misapprehension and discord inherent in the appearance of diverse, multi-ethnic societies around the world, political decisions about international migration have often been deemed either sound or controversial and populist depending on the political climate at the time. An emerging understanding however is that there is a strong link between migration and globalisation.

Migration and Globalisation

Globalisation has led to the liberalisation of market economies and consequently, 'borders moving across people' (Bauman, 2004). The movement of 'borders across people' have also meant that people move across borders, and thus become the basis for world migration. It must be noted, however, that raw materials and goods generally flow with less hindrance in pursuit of 'globalisation', but the movements of people, whether groups or individuals, are more circumscribed (Bauman, 2004). The motive for migration may not be limited to the search for better standards of living but can also be influenced by numerous issues, which may or may not include economic factors. World migration is increasing, and its nature, as well as the factors that lead to migration, are constantly changing. 'The world's population of immigrants has increased at a rate surpassing world population growth and the potential for future growth in international migration is nothing less than astounding' (Massey and Taylor, 2004). For instance, migrants who have established family and community ties in receiving nations may choose to stay rather than return to countries of origin, in spite of the challenges they may be faced with (Sommerville, 2011). Others migrate because of famine and other natural disasters, civil unrest, war and disease. The cause of some of the conditions that create migration itself has been laid at the door of developed nations. According to Bauman, de Wet and Ward, much of the negative depiction by the western media and the imposition of their understanding of what constitutes negative and positive migration affect migrants in their receiving nations. Migration is constructed as positive when required by receiving nations for their own purposes, and as negative when it is not required or when refuge is being sought. Media stories position migrants as the cause of problems; however, the demands of capital lead not only to extremes of poverty and wealth but also to natural disasters of flood, famine and disease which can be attributed in part to nations of the western world meeting their own needs at the expense of others and refusing to admit their contribution to some forced migrations (Bauman, 2007; De Wet, 2006; Ward, 2010).

In addition, culture is an integral aspect of migration; migrants have their own-shared cultural understanding and practices, which are as valuable to them as the cultural understandings and practices of receiving nations are to their members (Cox, 2012). Cultural 'differences' and the obvious impossibility of belonging within more than one cultural region may be used to justify social disparities and exclusion in some cases. The consequence of the attitude of Western countries to migration discussed here is that much of what is considered international or transnational or labour migration today metamorphoses people of a wide variety of social rankings in the countries they migrate from, into labourers at the bottom social ranks of the countries they migrate to (Pajo, 2008). This demotion to the bottom of the social ranks in receiving countries contributes to peculiar problems, which non-governmental organisations, third sector organisations, the churches and the African Pentecostal churches seek to mitigate, through their initiatives, activities and sermons. Members of these African Pentecostal churches, as Black Africans in Britain, for instance, have a peculiar history that reflects their positioning within British society. There is the need to understand African migration to Britain in order to appropriately situate the African Pentecostal churches' history within the spectrum of the immigration policy debate.

African Migration to Britain and the Immigration Policy Debate

The presence of Africans in Britain can be dated back to antiquity; however, it was not until 1991 that their relevance to British society was recognised by the inclusion of 'Black African' as an ethnic category on the census forms (Daley, 1998). This categorisation has remained on equal opportunities monitoring forms to date, as part of the legislation to combat discrimination in employment. Migrants from Africa have come from potentially 53 different countries on their continent, although the number of migrants from each of these countries varies. The migration of Ghanaians does not follow the trend, for instance of Caribbean migration, whom the government allowed into the country to fill employment vacancies during the shortage of manpower in Britain after the Second World War. There are migrants from Africa who made their way to Britain for asylum purposes to seek refuge from political persecution, as well as for social reasons, further education, better standards of living and other purposes, which include religious intentions. After many years of the immigration debate as to the positive and negative effects of net migration into Britain, government policy introduced during the period in which Tony Blair was Prime Minster held that regular, large-scale legal immigration was necessary to the prolonged prosperity and international competitiveness of the UK economy. Indeed, David Blunkett, the cabinet minister who was responsible for immigration policy declared that he saw 'no obvious limit' to immigration (Coleman and Rowthorn, 2004). On the whole, the new communiqué found much favour among the liberal, and especially among the metropolitan elite, including industry interests and economic critics as well as left-liberal political groups. It enjoyed the general support from the broadcast media, notably the BBC and much of the high-end press, including the *Financial Times* and *The Economist*, as well as scores of pressure groups representing asylum, immigrant, and human rights concerns, the Commission for Racial Equality and other quangos, and the Christian church's opinion. This created a new and positive establishment 'orthodoxy' in favour of immigration (Coleman, 2004).

This was to be short-lived, however, as public opinion remained unconvinced, with the majority feeling that immigration is immoderate, out of control, and in need of further restriction. For example, opinion polls in Britain since 2003 showed that concern about immigration and asylum has risen to between third and first place among the most important current political issues reported by respondents, in sharp contrast to the comparatively inconsequential position that it occupied in most previous years. In a YouGov poll conducted in 2004, 82 per cent of respondents stated that immigration and asylum policies were "not tough enough", and even amongst ethnic minority respondents, 46 per cent agreed with this (Coleman, 2004). Opinion about the issues of immigration in Britain seems to be divided, even among the ethnic minorities. A significant percentage of ethnic minorities themselves seem to agree that immigration and its attendant problems need to be looked into. From a glance at the poll results from ethnic minority respondents, it could be speculated that a vast majority of these may be those who have their residency permit and may not have restrictions imposed on work and length of stay. In recent times, with the effects of the economic downturn being felt by many, there have been calls for a cap on immigration, which the Conservative-Liberal Democratic Coalition government under David Cameron introduced in 2010. The government announced a cap of 21,700 on the number of skilled workers from outside the European Economic Area allowed into the UK. The figure represented a reduction of 6,300 on the equivalent figure for 2009. It excluded employees transferred by companies from abroad - in the future they will be allowed to stay for up to five years if their salary exceeds £40,000 (BBC, 2010). From the immigrants' point of view this means that many who entered the country illegally or are unable to meet the residency requirements are relegated to take up 'undesirable jobs', which pay much less and may push them over the brink of despondency and destitution. The burden of caring for these migrants then falls on other civil-society organisations, including the church.

Statistics show that there were 1,088,640 Black Africans living in England in 2011, out of which 573,931 lived in London; 5,118 lived in Scotland; and 387 in Northern Ireland (BBC, 2012). The 2001 census counted 55,000 Ghanaians living in the UK, an increase of 72 per cent since the last count. Other sources such as MigHealth UK estimate there are about 96,900 Ghanaians in Britain for instance (MIGHEALTH, 2013). This figure is close to the actual figure of 93,846 published by the Office of National Statistics from the 2011 census (ONS, 2011). Orozco estimated that there might be as many as 300,000, largely based on money transfers. Taking Ghana as a sample of African countries, from pre-colonial times up to the late 1960s, Ghana enjoyed relative economic prosperity and was the destination of many migrants from neighbouring West African countries (Anarfi, 1982). During the period under consideration, international movement from Ghana involved a relatively small number of people, most of whom were students and professionals. Most of these movements were to the United Kingdom and other English-speaking countries due to colonial links (Anarfi and Awusabo-Asare, 2000). The initial emigration of Ghanaians started after 1965. From that period Ghana experienced an economic crisis of an unprecedented magnitude (Van Hear, 1998). This was manifested in a balance of payments deficit, growing unemployment and social malaise. The decline of the economy made Ghana unappealing to both foreigners and citizens. The percentage of foreigners in Ghana declined from 12.3 per cent in 1960 to 6.6 per cent in 1970. The migration was exacerbated by fading faith in Ghana's future due to bad administration by both the civilian and military regimes. Nonetheless, this most recent phase of the migration of Ghanaians is more importantly characterised by their 'diasporisation', which began in the middle of the 1980s. Van Hear categorizes Ghana as one of the ten countries caught up in advancing a 'new diaspora' in recent times. According to the UK Home Office, Ghana was among the top ten sending countries to the UK in 1996, and in the decade 1990–2001 about 21,485 Ghanaians entered the UK (Van Hear, 1998).

Migration and the African Churches

The above statistics of Black Africans in Britain are quite significant in the sense that among these migrants and their offspring are those who belong to African churches and congregate on particular days during the week to worship. With all the challenges presented by legislation and public policy, there is the effort on the part of the immigrants to adapt and integrate themselves into British society and maintain their ties with their country of origin. The statistics also give some credence to the numbers that congregate in Black Majority Pentecostal churches - the most conspicuous, around the country. There are some migrants who join these African churches because of their strong faith convictions, for others it is mainly because it is a gathering of their fellow countrymen and women with aim of maintaining a social network within the country. Another reason for joining these churches is because they are a place of refuge from the daily struggles of survival that are part of the immigrant lifestyle and thus, the grounds for building social capital. Others may also find these churches to be the place where they are inspired to hold on to their Christian faith and to the personal dreams and aspirations associated with their migration. These may be just a few of the reasons why these migrants assemble in the African churches, but more worthy of note is the fact that these churches meet the expectations of the people who come to them, maintaining their relevance to these communities of faith. In my view the more closely these churches are to meeting the needs of these migrants, the more they attract them. So there are those who belong to more than one church simply because of the factor of relevance.

It must be noted, however, that not all members of African-led churches are migrants; some may have been born in Britain and consider Britain their country of origin. Some of these Christians from the second and third generations within migrant families may never have been to their parents' countries of origin. In my view, these churches are significant because of the migrants; and the migrants are also significant because of these churches. The uniqueness of these churches can only be ascertained by finding their position on the radar of global Pentecostalism. As a derivative of these churches' positioning within global Pentecostalism the British context of Pentecostalism can not be ignored as in many ways it also has influence on Pentecostal churches elsewhere.

Ghanaian Pentecostal churches: A Microcosm of the African churches and Global Pentecostalism.

Pentecostalism in Ghana was not an American phenomenon, but rather part of a global move of God carried by the presence of the Holy Spirit whenever human hearts were open and ready for fro a new spiritual experience. Global Pentecostalism has widely been traced to events at the run down Episcopal Methodist Church on Azusa Street in 1906, an event that has come to be known as a revival, led by William Seymour. William Seymour led twelve-hour church session each day for about three and half years. The main occurrence at this revival was the baptism of the Holy Spirit, which according to them was accompanied by the initial evidence of speaking in tongues. This outpouring is what they believed was the restoration of the gift of tongues for the 'speedy and effective preaching of the gospel to the nations' (Anderson, 2005; 2013). Charles F. Parham developed this new idea of linking tongues speaking to the baptism of the Spirit further from the radical evangelical's position. At the time the leaders were persuaded that the 'experience of Spirit baptism was a fire that would spread to other nations of the world'. One of these individuals who later became very instrumental in the history of Pentecostal mission was John G. Lake (Anderson, 2005).

Building upon the belief that it was a revival that was meant to affect the world, Seymour launched a periodical that carried news and occurrences of the 'move of God' from the revival site, with the aim of spreading the fire. At the peak of its production and circulation the periodical, *The Apostolic Faith*, reached about 50,000 copies around the world in 1908 (Anderson, 2005). However it was another periodical named *The Sword of the Spirit* produced by Faith Tabernacle of Philadelphia in the United States headed by Pastor Clark. This was a splinter group from Alexander Dowie's Zion City, which influenced certain individuals who in turn became pioneers of Pentecostal missions in Africa. Notable amongst them around this time was Apostle Peter Anim the founding member of the Apostolic Church, from which the Church of Pentecost, Ghana's largest Pentecostal church evolved, and the present day Christ Apostolic Church in Ghana, is said to have been greatly influenced by the teachings of this periodical after reading it in 1917 (Wyllie, 1974). However the main influence in the beliefs and practices of Anim came from the Apostolic Church, Bradford after Anim and other affiliates from Nigeria seceded from the Faith Tabernacle in Philadelphia. This led to his association with

James McKeown, a missionary from Bradford (Larbi, 2001). The spread of Pentecostalism around the world has been assisted by the involvement of local evangelists and pastors who through contextualisation have helped establish it as a tradition. As such it has not been established solely through the efforts of western missionaries (Stanley, 2004). These gallant men and women some of whom have been voiceless and mere 'unsung Pentecostal labourers' need to be recognised and given their place in history recognising their contributions (Anderson, 2007).

Supporting Anderson's assertion that 'experience of Spirit baptism from Azusa Street was a fire that would spread to other nations of the world', within the first two years of the inception of the revival at Azusa Street, missionaries from the site had covered a whopping twenty-five nations which included nations such as Egypt, China, India, Japan, Liberia, Angola and South Africa (Faupel, 1996). This substantial spread of missionary activity was by no means the 'only connections' to the spread of the fire (Anderson, 2013). The history of the movement in Ghana begins a bit later with influences from sub-Saharan Africa, namely Wade Harris, and locals such as John Swatson, Samson Oppong and Grace Tani who had their own expression of Pentecostalism and are all considered a significant part of the emergence of the movement in Ghana (Larbi, 2001). This meant that Pentecostalism in Ghana as in other parts of Africa was not an American phenomenon, but rather part of a global move of God carried by the presence of the Holy Spirit wherever human hearts were open and ready for a new spiritual experience. There could have been Pentecostal revivals resulting in the establishment of Pentecostal churches in other parts of the world and even in Ghana before the events at Azusa Street in 1906. Anderson (2005), notes that there were a lot more Pentecostal centres such as Pyongyang in Korea, Pune in India, and Wakkerstroom in South Africa, among others that,

> Pyongyang, Korea, from which revival in 1907 Presbyterian
> minister Kim Ik Du and others spread out throughout the

country with a revivalist healing message; Pune, India, from Pandita Ramabai's Mukti Mission, where a Pentecostal revival beginning in 1905 resulted in scores of young women forming evangelistic teams; Wakkerstroom, South Africa -where the first African Spirit churches in South Africa under Daniel Nkonyane and others were formed; Lagos, Nigeria, from where the first Aladura (healing) movement began in the 1918 influenza epidemic; Valparaiso, Chile, where the revival in the Methodist church under Willis Hoover, beginning in 1909, was the start of the Methodist Pentecostal Church, the largest Protestant church in Chile; Belem, Brazil, where Swedish missionaries Vingren and Berg began the largest Pentecostal denomination in the world; Oslo, Norway, where Methodist pastor Thomas Barratt began Pentecostalism in Europe in 1907; and Sunderland, England, where Anglican vicar Alexander Boddy led the commencement of Pentecostalism. These were some among many other centres. Pentecostalism has many varieties very different from the North American 'classical Pentecostal' kind.

This serves to emphasise that Pentecostalism may not be a made-in-the USA product, suggesting that factors associated with the context of these movements outside of the USA, or the West in general, may have meant that they remained unknown to the global fraternity, unlike the Azusa Street events. It might be that the distortion of historical facts has been intentional on the part of some researchers who have sympathies towards the American version of events, running the risk of over-simplifying the history of the origins of the phenomenon. Considering the spread of the movement in Ghana, for instance, there were local factors and actors that aided this process of the emergence, spread and establishment of Pentecostalism. Many churches with similar beliefs and practices in Africa and Ghana at the time were considered 'sumsum sore' and it is therefore possible these churches were not looked into because they were new within their contexts.

Over the years, Pentecostalism has made great headway in the Pacific Rim, China, Latin America, Eastern Europe (particularly Romania) and

Ukraine, which has the biggest Pentecostal church in Europe. Significant to the recent Ukraine story is that a Nigerian migrant, who moved to the Eastern block for the purpose of education, leads this largest congregation. This in itself expresses the shared identity of the Pentecostal movement; the fact that a Nigerian Pentecostal can set up a Pentecostal church and attract predominantly the indigenes of the country. However this maybe an isolated success story when compared to many African-led churches that solely attract Africans. Pentecostal believers everywhere have a sense that they belong to an international community, although the local church may be known or unknown to them. It is an international community because there are shared values and tenets of faith as well as ethos. For instance, Zimbabwean Pentecostals have developed their own understanding of the prosperity message which helps them act as agents of rapid social change.

The same can be said of the Ghanaian context, where born-again believers seek to become 'autonomous through making a complete break with tradition by means of exorcism' as a means of accessing good fortune. Although it is on the same platform of tradition embedded in the indigenous religions that the churches have succeeded to reach out to their communities (Maxwell, 1998). In spite of the universal acceptance of the local Pentecostal churches to Pentecostal believers elsewhere, there are distinctive nuances and variations resulting from the locality of the church. The reason for this distinct identity is the influence of culture and indigenous cosmology. And even within the same locality or region, differences can be identified. At the regional level, Nigerian Pentecostal beliefs and practices, irrespective of their influence on Pentecostal formation and thought in the Ghanaian context through their video and media outlet, can never be the same as the beliefs and praxis within the Ghanaian context (Maxwell, 1998). Even within the same context there are differences, as in the case of Ghanaian Pentecostals holding differing views on certain practices, with a section of them holding onto practices which can be clearly identified as having been influenced by the Akan indigenous cosmology (Appiah, 2011). It is nonetheless important to acknowledge that in spite of the distinct identity that these Pentecostals bear within their context, they are to a large extent by praxis connected to the wider community of Pentecostals around the globe.

Pentecostalism, Ghanaian Indigenous Cosmologies and Communities

In this section I explore the indigenous cosmology that provided the impetus for the emergence and spread of Pentecostalism in Ghana. This examination of the Ghanaian context which resonates with many of the contexts elsewhere on the African continent, will form the basis for understanding why the African churches have the kind of ethos, structure, polity they have an agent and an agency. The theoretical framework for this subject of enquiry suggests that entities that have transnational statuses in a land of settlement maintain ties with their homelands and are affected by occurrences there and vice versa. The Ghanaian-led churches in Britain have been and are influenced by the indigenous cosmology of the country of origins of its leadership and the majority of its membership.

Pentecostalism and Ghanaian Indigenous Cosmologies

For the purposes of generalisation in examining Ghanaian indigenous communities and cosmologies it is fitting that the largest indigenous community be chosen for this purpose. The Akan form the largest ethnic group in Ghana. This group is made up of the Akyem, Asante, Akwamu, Akuapem, Brong, Assin, Denkyira, and Wasp, all of whom speak Twi as their language. It must be highlighted that there are differences in the accent of the Twi language spoken in these different areas. The centre of the religious ideas of the Akan can be applied to the various ethnic groups within Ghana and generally to the traditional African perception of reality as an integral whole (Larbi, 2001). The Akan worldview is that influential and powerful supernatural forces that have a jurisdiction that covers the earth realm inhabit the world and the spirit realm and can therefore affect their daily lives either for evil or for good. This interaction between the spirits of the spirit realm and the humans of the earthly realm gives room for the operation of mediums such as priests and priestesses known by the Akan as *akomfo* of the shrines; and of traditional healers also known as *adinsifo*. These play a mediatory role between the humans and the spirits. The *akomfo* and *adinsifo* are individuals appointed by the gods and approved by the leadership of the communities (Ekem, 1994).

They are believed to be endowed with special gifts, spiritual authority and powers, and have favour with the gods to represent individual members of the community and also the community as a corporate body, on varying issues that are of importance to everyday life from sanitation and health to governance and justice (Appiah, 2011). The area of speciality and focus of the *Odinsifo* is in diagnosing and providing cures through herbal prescriptions to the sick. The worldview of the Akan postulates that certain individuals of a particular standing before the gods and people of the communities can invoke the spirit forces and act as their spokespersons either for the good or bad of the communities they live in. It is because of this that the human intermediaries, the *Okomfo* and the *Adinsifo* offer sacrifices to these spirit forces to attract their blessing and also to inoculate members of the communities against such evil influences of other spirit forces that may seek to harm them. On the one hand this makes these intermediaries essential to the community of adherents, giving these individuals serving as intermediaries reverence and honour for their roles. This indigenous worldview also helps explain how pastors and leaders of the Pentecostal churches in Ghana have become very important personalities and are very influential within their communities. This show of reverence and honour to the pastors and leaders occurs because they are viewed with the same basic understanding as the *okomfo* or *odinsifo* in the community. Any individual looking at the phenomenon without a thorough understanding will draw the same conclusions as Gifford who referred to these leaders in Ghana as 'gospel superstars' (Gifford, 2004). The continuity or the discontinuity of the place and role of the Pentecostal pastors or leaders in the Ghanaian-led Pentecostal churches in Ghana will be critically examined in a later chapter. On the other hand, this makes the worldview of the Akan dualistic, that is 'interpenetrating and inseparable, yet with distinguishable parts (Okorocha, 1987). The Akan believe in the existence of two worlds that are in constant interaction with one another and occurrences in each affect the other and yet are distinct from each other (Appiah, 2011). The belief in a dualistic world gives rise to a plethora of performative rituals either to court favour from spirit forces for productive means or to inflict pain on one's enemies. The rituals are performed to ward off evil spirit forces that inflict evil and atrocities. The rituals are also meant to position an individual rightly in eyes of the spirit forces to receive good fortune. And they use charms and amulets provided by these *akomfo* and *adinsifo* to protect themselves from enemy forces, that they believe possess powers to create imbalances in an individual's life. There is significant evidence to show that Ghanaian Pentecostal churches still hold on to some 'ritualistic' practices that can be traced to the influence of the indigenous religious cosmologies (Appiah, 2011). In relation to the theoretical framework of this research, the full extent of 'ritualistic' practices within the Ghanaian-led Pentecostal churches in Britain will be examined in a later Chapter. The findings should enable one to argue the extent to which the churches in Britain have moved away from the influences of the churches in the homeland.

In spite of the dualistic worldview held by the Akan, and how their relationships with these worlds are expressed, the Akan believe in one Supreme Being who is *Onyankopɔn* but have gods known as the *abosom* and the ancestors, referred to as the *mpanyinfo,* through whom they send their petitions, with of course the *akomfo* and *adinsifi* being the mediums. This is contrary to the observations of the early missionaries, which suggested that the Akans believed in many gods (Parrinder, 1949). However, Idowu describes the concept of God among the African people as a 'diffused monotheism' "where we have a monotheism in which there exist other powers which derive from Deity, a being and authority that they can be treated, for practical purposes, almost as ends in themselves"

(Parrinder, 1949). The indigenous cosmology of the Akan often makes it very difficult to make a division between the sacred and the secular. They make the effort on a daily basis to maintain constant interaction with the spirit forces, as a result of the belief that every single aspect of their lives is affected by the influences of spirit forces that are much more powerful than humans.

This is an occurrence very similar to the dependence on the Spirit with Pentecostalism discussed earlier. In that section we see how in the beginnings of the Pentecostal movement missionaries could go to distant lands without any prior preparation such as learning the language of the locals or having enough financial support, believing that the Spirit will equip them and somehow make them successful. I argue that this understanding of dependency on the Spirit that formed the basis of spreading the fire as a way of life of the early missionaries fits into the Ghanaian indigenous context and in many ways assisted in its acceptance and spread. This also goes to confirm the assertion by Anderson that Pentecostalism was inherently flexible, responding creatively to different religio-cultural contexts (Anderson, 2005). Most Ghanaian Pentecostals believe in a world inhabited by strong spirit forces that have an influence on the daily lives of individuals. This is because these individuals are similar to those adherents of the indigenous religions who make contact with the spirit realm on a daily basis through prayer and other belief practices that seem to enable them to be in contact with the Holy Spirit, such as the use of tokens in 'prophetic ministration' including the olive oil which is discussed in detail in a later chapter. Therefore it is argued that the similarities in the worldviews provide the platform for the ease with which new Pentecostal believers can integrate into the Pentecostal Community of believers.

Pentecostalism and Ghanaian Indigenous Communities

To fully understand Ghanaian indigenous cosmologies as a context for the emergence and acceptance of Pentecostalism in Ghana and also for the transnational status of Ghanaian-led churches in Britain, the indigenous communities have to be explored. There are complex strands and levels of relationships that exist within the communities between people and their dependence on one another to bring about cosmic harmony. Due to the dualistic worldview the Akan hold, life is in disarray if the triangular relationship with one another in the community and the spirit forces is broken. The Akan see themselves first and foremost as an integral part of a community before giving any thought to his or her individuality within the community. This view is expressed in indigenous proverbs such as *'yen fa yensa benkum nkyire yen agyanom anaafo'*. Translated, this means 'we do not give directions to our father's house by using a finger on the left hand ', meaning 'we do not show disrespect to our kinsmen'. This sense of community is essential to the existence of Ghanaian traditional societies because it defines its shared humanity on the basis of communality (Appiah, 2011). The shared humanity and communality means that the individual participates in the beliefs, rituals and ceremonies that undergird the stability of that community. And for that matter a person who detaches himself or herself from his kinsmen is considered to have severed himself from his roots (Mbiti, 1969).

In order to maintain the cycle of harmony in the indigenous community it is essential to maintain a peaceful co-existence with fellow members of one's community and with the gods. The balance of this harmony is meant to be undisturbed and maintained to ensure that the community continues to receive the vital assistance of the spirit forces they believe influence their everyday lives. Pentecostal churches in Ghana have managed to maintain these indigenous values. The sense of community and communality in Pentecostal churches in Ghana can be identified in how the church celebrates the various rites of passage such as birth through outdooring ceremonies, marriage and death. Besides these rites of passages mentioned earlier some of the churches, have other activities such beauty contests, Ghanaian fashion shows, Chastity celebration for the youth as part of their yearly programme. That same sense of community is brought into the Ghanaian-led Pentecostal churches in Britain, to the effect that these churches consider those migrants who come to Britain from the homeland their kith and kin and thus have strategies in place to assist them to settle into British society. What this means is that, those who join irrespective of the local areas they come from in Ghana, are considered family in the churches. The strategies adopted by these churches are examined critically in a chapter designated for the subject. For any meaningful examination of the integration strategies of the Ghanaian-led Pentecostal churches in Britain to be done, their histories need to be looked into as this will situate the whole research in context.

Histories and Organisation of Selected Ghanaian-led Churches in Britain

The context of the significance of the histories of Ghanaian Pentecostal churches is to be able to do an objective analysis of these churches ethos. The choice of these churches represent the different precursors to their establishment whether it is accidental or deliberate mission initiative; and their supposedly differing operational outlook. The international Central Gospel Church and the Royalhouse Church International are off-shoot and satellites of existing mother churches in Ghana whilst the Domnion Centre and the Freedom Centre international are led by Ghanaian pastors but originated in Britain.

Background of the International Central Gospel Church, Ghana and London

The International Central Gospel Church (ICGC), Ghana is a Pentecostal-Charismatic Church, which was established by Mensa Otabil. Otabil is the General Overseer and founder of the International Central Gospel Church, Founder and Chancellor of Ghana's premier private university, The Central University College; the Chief Executive Officer and Consultant of Otabil and Associates, an executive and leadership growth consultancy. He also serves on several Boards and Trusts within Ghana and in other parts of the world (ICGC, 2014). The church had its first service on the 26th February 1984, in Accra. It was established out of a fellowship known as the Kanda Fellowship, so named after the suburb of Accra known as Kanda where it was first based. The first meeting of the church was held in a small classroom and had a membership of about twenty people. Within two years, from February 1984 to April 1986, those in regular Sunday attendance had increased to about one hundred and eighty. Premises the church rented to hold its churches services have included classrooms, a private residence, a public hall, a science laboratory, a mechanical workshop and a cinema theatre.

Around this same period in 1986, the church rented the Baden Powell Memorial Hall where they stayed for about ten years. The church saw an astronomical growth in its membership during this ten-year period with an adult membership of about 4,000 in regular attendance each Sunday. At this time most of the members of the church were students from secondary schools and the universities. This was so for a couple of reasons which included the fact that sermons preached were recorded onto cassette tapes and sold to members of the church who were encouraged to pass them on to their friends. Some claimed the leader; Mensa Otabil spoke with a refined accent as someone with an exposure to the western world; and the intellectual appeal of the sermons made it easy for these students to identify with them. The criticisms in his sermons of the inactivity and irrelevance to contemporary spiritual and social trends of the older main line churches and older Pentecostal churches that most of these young people were born into and raised in meant that these students had to leave their churches and join the ICGC. Otabil has since stated in an interview on a popular local radio station, that he regrets his criticism of the older main line and Pentecostal churches.

This increase in membership of the church gave rise to what they described then as aggressive missionary church planting activities, with local assemblies established in almost all the major towns and cities of Ghana.

Several other churches were also planted in cities in Europe and the United States. The first congregation, which was established in February 1984, now designated as the Christ Temple assembly, has directly planted about forty other churches out of the original congregation in the Accra - Tema metropolis of Ghana. Attendance at Sunday church services at Christ Temple exceeds 10,000. As part of its vision and social responsibilities, the church established a ministerial institute in 1998, to train a new generation of leaders to carry out its vision. This has since been developed into a university college and received the Presidential Charter as a full-fledged university in 2016. Again in 1988, the church set up Central Aid, an educational scholarship scheme to finance the education of selected needy students in pre-tertiary educational institutions.

History of the International Central Gospel Church, East London

This church started as a branch of the ICGC in Ghana on the 25th August 2001. It was registered as the Dreamgate Centre with the Charity Commission in England and Wales. The reason why it chose the name Dreamgate Centre was because the other branch of the church situated in South London had registered the name ICGC with the Charity Commission

and therefore could not be registered as such. It was also not possible to operate under the same charity as the South London branch because of some internal wrangling and misunderstanding between the two pastors leading the churches. Analysis at the end of this chapter will show that one of the problems these Ghanaian-led Pentecostal churches have is in-fighting among leaders at different levels of the churches structure. The church started in the front room of the residence of a couple, in Leytonstone. The pastor, is said to have used the ironing board of the couple as a pulpit from which he preached the first sermon to its 12-member congregation. The Pastor was an ICGC pastor from the Kumasi branch of the church in Ghana. He was sent by the organisation's general overseer to start this branch of the church in Britain. The first 12 members with whom the pastor began the church were all members of the ministry in Ghana prior to their migration to Britain. They were however in other churches prior to the commencement of the branch. This raises the question against reverse mission as the nucleus of this church had started without any evangelising at all. It was an assembling of people with previous affiliation to the mother church in Ghana, which has become a poignant characteristic of most the diasporean churches whose origins are from Africa.

Within a month of the church starting the number in attendance were approaching 20 and they therefore had to move into a bigger facility to accommodate the increase albeit a predominantly Ghanaian congregation. The church moved to one of the rooms of the Leytonstone Library, where in barely two months the church membership again increased to about sixty. As a result of this growth, in November 2012 the church relocated to the Warwick School for Boys in Walthamstow. The reason for the growth was due to the fact that there were members of the church in London living in the East and North of London who left their churches to join their 'mother church'. Another factor may have been the fact that the pastor was a long serving pastor with ICGC in Ghana and also well known by most of the people, who felt secure to be led by him. Also at the time ICGC Ghana had been in existence for close to 16 years as a popular Pentecostal church in Ghana with a leader who most people in Ghana admired and saw as a breath of fresh air to others before him. Consequently by March 2002 the membership of the church had doubled to about 120. The reason for this growth in the membership of the church in particular was because these people had once been members of this church in Ghana before travelling to live in Britain. As a result these members saw it as a 'home coming' experience for them to be part of the new branch in London. A detailed analysis of the reasons for the growth is made at the end of this chapter. In 2003, due to some internal administrative difficulties that resulted in the pastor of the church falling out with some of the church elders, and coupled with the pastor's difficulty in rectifying his immigration status to enable him to engage in ministry as a minister of religion, he had to move back to Ghana. He never returned to his post in Britain, but later on resigned from the ICGC and moved to the United States to begin his own ministry there. On the departure of the founding pastor, two ministers took over the pastoral duties of the church as caretaker pastors until the General Secretary, was sent in from Ghana to take over the church, with the strategy to start more branches of the ICGC in Britain and Europe. On his arrival, due to the previous challenges the Dreamgate Trust was closed down as a charity and its assets transferred to a new charity, Central Trust and the alias King's Temple was adopted to reflect his own vision and ideals for the ministry.

Organisation and Vision of the International Central Gospel Church, East London

The church has been predominantly a Ghanaian congregation with a handful of Zimbabweans who are also married to Ghanaians. The church is a branch of the ICGC in Ghana and therefore adopts its vision and ministry philosophy. The Mission Statement of the ICGC is: 'Raising leaders, shaping vision and influencing society through Christ'. They state that their purpose and desire is to constantly challenge the world through their life and conduct, and to live closer to God's ideal. As with the biblical narrative of the believer in Christ being the salt of the earth, they are committed to the preservation of Godliness; and as light of the world they believe they must transform society through the challenge of a Christ-centred life. They also have as their philosophy three main emphases: practical Christianity human dignity excellence. By practical Christianity, they claim that they believe Christianity is not a myth. God's word preached must bring truths that can produce results when applied to one's life. As a result they encourage their pastors to preach sermons that are easily applicable by the audience. Regarding human dignity, they believe every human being is created in the image and likeness of God and must be treated with respect and honour. As part of the philosophy they uphold the principle of excellence that everything the Christian or the human being will do must be done with excellence.

One outstanding feature of the church is their primary commitment to prepare the black person to be a channel of blessing to the world. International Central Gospel Church is committed to obedience to the great commission as set out by our Lord Jesus Christ and recorded in Matthew 28:18-20. In this biblical narrative Jesus urges his followers to preach the gospel to all peoples everywhere. They explain that the commitment to prepare the black person to be a channel of blessing to the world does not restrict the scope of the ministry open to the church to make the gospel of the Kingdom of God known to all people irrespective of race, colour, sex or age. They seem to align this part of their vision and reinforce it with a biblical example of the Apostle Paul whose ministry was primarily to the Gentiles. They believe that they have a special responsibility to the Black peoples of the world who in recent human history have been subjected to various de-humanizing forms of oppression through slavery, colonialism and apartheid. They believe that the occurrence of slavery, colonialism and apartheid for instance has made most black people develop a feeling of inferiority to other peoples of the earth and in the process has locked up their potential to be a blessing to humanity. This they claim has resulted in most black people becoming receivers, beggars and followers. This commitment they believe will be executed through the messages the sermons carry and also in demonstrating the ideals through self –funded facilities and projects to prove that black people are capable of responding to their own needs without hand outs from the western world. It is not clear what the actual limitations of their vision and philosophy leave them in the globalisation discourse, however it is clear that the church has a clearly defined focus of making people of black descent their target audience for their ministry. Ultimately, it is the conviction of the ICGC that the liberating truth of the gospel when properly contextualised to the immediate needs of black people would produce a free person who is equipped to give, lend and lead through serving. One important thing to take note of is the fact that, the London branch of the church derives its vision from the vision of its head church in Ghana. The vision of the church is written into a booklet that spells out the details (ICGC, 1995).

History of Royalhouse Chapel International, Ghana and London

Rev. Sam Korankye Ankrah founded Royalhouse Chapel International, after he claims to have had an encounter with the Lord Jesus Christ on 19 June 1991. The ministry began with 30 adults in November 1992 and has since gained a membership of over 5,000 at the headquarters alone (Ankrah, 2010). The reason for the church's exponential growth in membership was due to the use of the multi-media to get the message of the church out to the public. Churches which featured testimonies of people who claim to have been healed, or life having turned around as a result of them coming to the church was featured live on radio on Sundays. It also states it has one hundred Local Assemblies (branches) and seventeen International Missions eight in the United Kingdom and nine in the United States. It has 26 different Ministries (Groups) as well as all the other distinct organs incorporated under the umbrella name, Ahenfie.

History of the Royalhouse Chapel International, London

In 1998, prior to the commencement of the church in Britain, various consultations and discussions were held to ascertain the possibilities for establishing the church and developing the appropriate strategy to execute the plan. The implementation of the decision to start a church in Britain was undertaken in 1999, when Rev Sam Korankye-Ankrah, the General Overseer accompanied by Rev Derek Amanor, a senior Associate minister of the church in Ghana travelled to the United Kingdom and started a prayer fellowship on Tuesdays at 7:00pm in a couple's home. Part of the strategy of the church was to start a few more prayer fellowships around the city of London and its precincts. Therefore in May 2000 the fellowships were converted to branches of the Royalhouse Chapel International and were named Royalhouse Chapel North London Mission (the fellowship at Bounds Green) and Royalhouse Chapel South London Mission (the fellowship in Streatham Common).

Rev Benneh was initially appointed Pastor of the church after being sent from Ghana as a caretaker pastor. After a brief appointment with the church he was transferred to the Connecticut Mission, USA, as a temporary Resident Missionary. He returned from the Connecticut Mission after a year in 2005, to again take over as head pastor of the South London Mission. In May 2011, Rev Benneh was once again transferred after squabbles in the church, to start the Royalhouse International Missions Centre in Croydon, with some members from the South London Mission. These details of the changes and swapping of leadership for the church, indicates the fluidity and instability of the churches

Organisation and Vision of Royalhouse Chapel International

The Royalhouse Chapel International, has 'Touching our generation with the power of God' as its mission. The mission statement they claim was derived from a 'supernatural encounter' of the Rev Charles Benneh in 1991 whilst an immigrant in the Netherlands. They claim that during the encounter, God told him three things, which were to:

1. Bring people into the House of God through worship, praise and prayer.

2. Preach messages of hope that are relevant to the needs of the people.

3. Bring comfort to the people of God and providing a place in an atmosphere of love, caring, sharing and fellowship for them.

As a result of this encounter the Apostle General, as he is referred to, developed a vision for the ministry based on the instructions he claims to have been given during the supernatural encounter. The mission statement can be expounded as follows:

A. Bringing people into the House of God through Worship, Praise and Prayer.

B. Preaching Messages of Hope that are Relevant to the Needs of the People. In the preaching of the message of hope there are three things implied;

i. Full demonstration of miracle working power of God on the basis of God's word.

ii. Raising people to impact their world and to leaving a memoriam of their presence on earth for posterity.

iii. Growing in the ways of God through holiness sharing one's faith, and showing commitment to church activities.

C. Bringing comfort to the people of God and providing a place with an atmosphere of love and caring for one another. This point is also expressed in three areas, namely care, education and small groups

Care: They believe they must take care of the aged, the needy, the vulnerable and the like in society.

Education: They intend to promote education through offering scholarships, free extra tuition, discipleship and leadership training.

Small Groups: They believe that every worshipper must actively participate in a ministry group within the church to be wholly integrated in the vision of RCI and through that enhance their spiritual and social development.

The effect of this vision on migrants' experience is that it gives them a collective sense of hope. Once the church starts working towards this vision there is a diminishing of the sense of hopelessness where individual struggling migrants suddenly believe they can achieve something more significant with their lives. For some, although they are predominantly

Ghanaian, it gives them an outlet for engagement with the wider community.

From the broader vision of 'touching our generation with the power of God', The Royalhouse Chapel has a more operational vision that was developed from the broader vision called Vision 2018. Their quest is to 'touch'; and by this they mean continuing and aspiring to build Royalhouse Chapel into a ministry where those experiencing the pain of rejection, non-achievements and hurt, over the years can find solutions to transform their lives. They expect that people who come through their doors, irrespective of their social status, position and significance will find a sense of belonging, purpose and vision to pursue with their lives. As part of the strategy to touch their generation they intend to build a multimedia platform including internet presence, TV ministry and audio-visual and reading resources to bring the church experience and the power of God to people in a life-changing way.

Their goal is also partly to raise a mega church of over five thousand people touched by the power of God and making significant impact in their world. It is their expectation that more than fifty per cent of the expected five thousand church family will be fully active members pursuing the Royalhouse vision. It has to be said that this vision statement calls for questions into the feasibility of building such a large church considering the number of Ghanaians who live in London, and this is also applicable to other African-led churches that make ambitious vision statements for their churches. An analysis of the vision of the churches is discussed at the end of the chapter. Aside from the intention of opening the mega church their plan is to establish Community Branch Fellowships (House Group Ministry) in every suburb and municipality of London where their members reside, for the purpose of extending the Gospel of Jesus. It is the vision of the leadership to grow potential Community Branch Fellowships into city churches which will become self-reliant and in turn pursue the vision of growing more Community Branch Fellowships which shall also mature into churches until the knowledge of Jesus Christ covers the city of London and beyond.

It is the vision of the church to engage the communities into which the Lord sends them by using the resources available to them to enhance the lives of the members of those communities and in that way they make Royalhouse Chapel relevant to the communities. To achieve this they aspire to build a modern 2000 capacity multi-function ministry building with enough function rooms for offices, children, teens and youth church services, prayer and counselling rooms, a Foundation School block, internet café, library, restaurants, performing arts rooms, studios, gym, barber and beauty shop, day nursery and the like. It has to be said that the above plans remain an aspiration, as there are no signs of building the structures itemised above. However it gives you an insight into the mind-set of these churches that in spite of being a minority and somehow classified as marginalised they try to prove they are able to positively affect not only the migrants who come to the church but society at large. They like to believe that they are able to replicate the success that they believe God has given them at their head branch in Ghana, which is very much involved with the communities where they are located.

History of the Freedom Centre International, London

Freedom Centre International (FCI), formerly South London Temple (SLT), was birthed in 1997 out of Universal Prayer Group (UPG) Ministries. Samson Kwaku Boafo, who came to Britain as a law student, founded the UPG Ministries in the 1960s. He left in the 1970s to practice law in Ghana and upon his departure, the church collapsed. However he returned in 1986 to seek political asylum from persecution by the Provisional National Defence Council (PNDC) government, the military junta in Ghana. He brought back together the scattered members of the church and re-started the UPG with a few remnants of the ministry who were at this time worshipping in other churches. With these people he began

Sunday services at a location at Chalk Farm. By 1990, the membership of the church had grown and therefore had to move to Edmonton in North London where the church assumed the name Edmonton Temple. Around this time, with talk of Ghana returning to constitutional rule, Samson Kwaku Boafo moved back to Ghana as one of the founding members of the largest opposition party in Ghana to contest the elections in 1992. Subsequently, the party won the election in 2000 and he became a cabinet minister, until they were voted out of power in 2008. However he still remains an MP.

Later in the church's development, a branch of the church was established in Birmingham and called the Birmingham City Temple. In line with the church's aim to move to other regions and locations across Britain, a decision was made in 1997 to start a branch of the church in South London to make it more convenient for commuters from South London to the church in Edmonton in North London. Shadrach Ofosuware was then asked to take over as pastor of the church. The branch in South London assumed the name South London Temple and was later changed to Freedom Centre International when the church moved the majority of its members to its present place in Welling in Kent. It must be highlighted that all churches that were established out of the UPG Ministries are autonomous and independent. Thus FCI is independent from any other branch of the churches in its operations and administration. Apart from its history there is nothing else to show the link to the UPG Ministries.

The first meeting place of South London Temple was at the Euro Business Centre in Brixton with a membership of about 25 people. Under the leadership of Pastor Shadrach Ofosuware normally referred to as Pastor Shadrach, within four months South London Temple moved location to Peckham where its membership grew to over 500 within five years. To accommodate the expansion of the church, the church relocated out of the South London area to Welling in Kent, and was renamed Freedom Centre International in 2009. The church went further to establish branches in various areas around Britain and was able to launch the first FCI assembly in Luton. Other branches have since been established by the initiative of FCI London in Luton, Telford (England), Edinburgh (Scotland) Dallas (USA) and Accra (Ghana).

Organisation and Vision of Freedom Centre International

FCI's name reflects the pastor's passion for the liberty of God's people, to see people set free from demonic oppression and to pursue their God-given purpose in life. Also Pastor Shadrach's vision is that the downtrodden in society would be lifted and given room to express their God-given talent and abilities. His desire as he notes is to see overcomers raised and God's people prosper. The church claims that its aims in ministry are two-fold: first, to provide support to help create social stability within the local communities in which their churches are based and within the whole of British society; and secondly to positively affect other communities around the world where they establish churches. By social stability they mean helping individuals to recognise diversity within British society and creating equal opportunities for all, especially those of ethnic minority.

They believe in practical Christian living and by that they mean doing the will of God in reaching out to the communities and the nation at large. They state that their desire and endeavour is to make 'disciplined disciples' of Jesus Christ where their lifestyles exemplify Christ in all areas of thought, conversation and conduct. Their desire is that members would grow in Christ, and in the grace of God and in the understanding of the Holy Scriptures. They are currently working on establishing churches in each of the nationalities represented in FCI such as Ghana, Ivory Coast, Kenya, Uganda, France, Nigeria and Malawi.

History of Dominion Centre, London

Dominion Centre traces its founding to Samson Kwaku Boafo, who came to Britain to study law at the University of London, founded Universal

Prayer Group (UPG) Ministries in the 1960's in Britain. It is from this same group that the Freedom Centre International came out of as discussed above. Whilst Sampson was away in Ghana after his education and few years of practice, the church was run by other leaders including Sam Ohene-Apraku, a young man who had just come to Britain to pursue theological education; and Shadrach Ofosuware, who had also come to live in Britain for his studies from the communist state of Yugoslavia. A decision was later made in consultation with Samson Kwaku Boafo for Shadrach Ofosuware to move to South London to start a new branch of the church, with autonomy and independence though sharing the same charity status. There he initially called the church South London Temple and it is now known as Freedom Centre International.

Sam Ohene-Apraku remained with the Edmonton Temple as head pastor until the church acquired a property in 2004 on the high street in Wood Green, North London. In moving to this £3m facility the name was again changed to Dominion Centre to reflect the personal vision of the head Pastor, Rev Sam Ohene-Apraku. They have since refurbished the derelict building they bought into a state of the art complex with a restaurant, bookshop, meeting rooms and a banqueting hall. The church has grown with over a thousand people in attendance every Sunday for worship. The Dominion Centre is independent and autonomous just like the Freedom Centre International although they can be traced to one founder.

Analysing the Churches: The People and the Vision

The People who make up the Churches

It is realised that the churches used in this research as case studies are all predominantly Ghanaian, although I received a rebuff of that fact from all the leaders of the churches. They believe that their countries of origin do not necessarily reflect the people they attract, although it is currently the case. The leaders believe that in the course of time their white majority host communities will soon buy into their vision as a church and would come along. One of the leaders I interviewed stated that in spite of the fact that the predominant membership of the church is currently Ghanaian, they consider themselves a multicultural church, citing as an instance that there are members whose parents were originally Ghanaian, but were born in Britain with British citizenship and therefore cannot be described as Ghanaian. Some of these people have never been to Ghana before although they trace their ancestry to Ghana.

There are also those who have gained citizenship from other European countries such as Germany, France, and Holland and have moved to Britain to settle and therefore cannot be fully described as Ghanaians due to their current citizenship. In spite of these explanations, one thing that is common beyond mere nationality is that the members share one ancestry and interestingly after the close of service one can hear a number of the Ghanaian languages being used among the members in conversations. From the observation and interacting with some of the lay leaders of the churches it looks as though the reason for the use of the Ghanaian languages is that most of the migrants that arrived from Germany, Holland and France are a bit elderly and not as highly educated as those who they come to meet in Britain. Some Ghanaian migrants who come to Britain from the non-English speaking European countries have not mastered the national languages formally used in those countries. They could only speak what is normally used in the street and for that matter found it difficult to support their growing kids with school homework and had to relocate to Britain. Also because Ghana is a former British colony and since that is home to them, the English language could be useful in case any of their children had to return to their ancestral home in future. Unfortunately, most of them were also not highly educated in Ghana prior to their migration to those European destinations; they do not have competence in the usage of the English language. The implication of this lack of competence at the time of entering Britain is that some of them tend to rely on benefits or do menial jobs that do not require much interaction with others. This in my estimation would lead any individual migrating to Britain from Ghana or even any of these European countries such as Germany, France and Holland to find a Ghanaian-led or a predominantly Ghanaian church as a form of social security and building social capital. The result of this movement into Britain either from Ghana or from Europe is the growth of the membership of these churches. On the other hand, the role of the church in assisting in integration may prevent some migrants from exploring other perspectives and opportunities for a much effective way of integrating into British society, thus diminishing the social capital.

There are two consequences I observed from this phenomenon. The first is the sense of security that these migrants seek; resulting in them building a close knit church community. The expression of love and concern for one another is strongly evident in their interactions with one another; something that can be explained as a continuation of the communal type of living that exists in most cultures in Africa. The closeness gives them a sense of identity through a shared vision which most of the church leaders confirm is the driving force of the churches. My view would rather be that the vision is cast to take advantage of the community they have other than the vision being shared. In other words they gather together before they have a sense of accomplishing a vision, rather than the vision of the churches being the point of attraction or gathering. This is evident in the leadership of the churches knowing that these migrants seek some form of social security; through the networks they have in the churches. Their commitment to those networks will keep them in the church and whatever vision is cast; they would have their support, as they otherwise risk losing their identity as members of that church community. The second consequence is that the members of the churches often rally around their leaders and are somehow dependent on them for leadership and as God's spokespersons.

The Vision of the churches as they Imagine

All the churches used as case studies in this research have elaborate and clearly stated vision statements that they claim are the driving force of their ministries. Details of the visions of these churches as stated by the leaders of the churches and also on their websites are pragmatically questionable to the researcher. Are some of the infrastructural bits of the vision possible? For instance RCI wants to build a five thousand capacity auditorium and looking at the demography of the church as predominantly Ghanaian and the number of Ghanaians who live in London, the question is: is it entirely as simple as that or even at all possible? Notwithstanding the fact that there are hundreds of other Ghanaian churches in London competing for the same group of people. Of course they claim their intention is to attract not only Ghanaians but also people from other ethnicities and races. However as I raised this question of the feasibility of the vision to build a five thousand capacity auditorium with the pastor of the church he clearly stated that it is God's work and that if God gives a vision he is able to make it happen. He also stated that there is an example in the city, referring to Matthew Ashimolowo's Kingsway International Christian Centre, which is said to have about ten thousand members attending services each week and has acquired a tract of land in Rainham in Essex, near London to build a church facility. The scheduled time to commence building have delayed due to some planning permission issues and have since acquired property in Kent for its use.

However, it is without doubt that the vision of the churches gives the members a collective sense of identity in spite of their micro-ethnic lineages within the Ghanaian community. This sense of identity as ethnic minorities also spurs them on to achieve great things to prove to their host communities not only have they come to seek greener pastures but have something to offer to their communities. In one such instance during the opening of the FCI Building at Welling, political leaders were invited as though to bring them in to see what they have been able to achieve as an ethnic minority. The whole organisation seems to have been done in a way to make this statement; 'who said we couldn't do it, we have come of age'. In an intriguing turn of events that the choir of the church sung a song written and composed by Labi Siffre titled 'something inside so strong'. This is a song that Labi is thought to have written after watching a TV documentary on apartheid South Africa about their liberation struggle. It also became a song that resonated with a lot of black people around the world in their struggle against racial discrimination, and their determination to break down the racial barriers to personal and collective achievements in society.

Inasmuch as most of the members of these churches may struggle to have their voices heard, collectively they believe that by pooling resources together to accomplish those collective visions they will be noticed for their efforts. In so doing, FCI, DC, with the exception of ICGC still in the process of purchasing a building, have acquired huge properties in London to house their churches. RCI still uses a rented school premises. One of the three however is in negotiations to refurbish it for use. The cost of the refurbishment is estimated to be £1.2m and has been contracted to Richmond, a firm owned by an Irish Christian family that specialises in building and refurbishment of churches and halls. A bank in Britain part-finances the purchase; however the refurbishment of the property is partly funded by a CEO of a private bank who is a member of the parent church in Ghana. This goes to show the transnational status of these Pentecostal churches, not only do funds flow out to their places of origin as many people may assume but funds also flow in to advance the course of these churches in Britain, as this example shows. In the expression of identity and recognition through their visions, they make the statement from the colonial era during the struggle for self-rule, from which most of the leaders have grown that 'they are able to manage their own affairs and ready to take responsibility of others too'.

Narrative of Leadership in the Churches

As discussed earlier, it is the leaders of the church that normally cast the vision; takes advantage of the shared and collective identity of the people within the established networks of the churches. It is not just because the vision gives them something to rally around. I observed that there were people in the churches who could not properly articulate the vision of the church but had so much to say about the atmosphere of togetherness in the church and the excellent leader they have. Several issues came to my attention about the leadership of the churches that in my view help maintain the transnational status of the churches.

The constant changes in the leadership of the RCI in London during the first few years of its establishment, those pastors who come in from Ghana to pastor the churches assume that because the members are predominantly Ghanaian, they may only have dealings with Ghanaians and are most of the time not prepared for the cultural shock. Unfortunately the people they come to pastor are in the process of integrating into British society and may have inculcated some aspects of the British culture, which makes them different from the pastors, who are familiar with culture in Ghana. For example in Ghana, a pastor of an average sized church could have a lot of the young members in the church give the pastor's family a helping hand with household chores because of their position as their 'spiritual parents' and also as those who rely on them for 'akwankyere' – direction in life. The discontinuity of this aspect for these migrant pastors is because, apart from the fact that it is only the affluents that have that kind of support in British society, most of the migrant members do shift based jobs. Some of their members even commit to more than one job at a time and would therefore have no time to spare at the pastor's house to help out with household chores. And so very soon some of these pastors realise that their 'religious superstar status' does not fit into the culture in Britain, although they are celebrated to some extent. To some of these pastors this is a cultural shock.

Summary and Discussion

Migration involves people moving from one part of the world to another. This movement is either on a short term or long term basis. The duration of stay of these migrants in their new places of abode is normally determined by the factors that give rise to their migration. There is an ensuing debate on the subject of migration in nations across the world. This debate involves sending and receiving nations. It has been assumed over time for instance that people move from poorer nations to richer nations. For the poorer nations that these migrants move from, the argument is more of brain drain and its effects on economic and social development but has in more recent times shifted to brain-gain concentrating on the benefits to the receiving countries. But at the same time there is enough evidence to suggest that in some sending countries of the world such as Ghana, remittances from migrants across the world form a substantial part of their budget and for that matter their Gross Domestic Product (GDP). As at 2002, remittances formed about eight per cent of Ghana's Gross Domestic Product. From the perspective of the receiving nations these immigrants increase their populations and therefore put pressure on social amenities, such as health care, housing and schools within the communities where they reside. There have been instances where there are claims that the presence of migrants puts pressure on jobs, thus prompting the slogan 'British jobs for British people' in some communities since the economic recession began in 2008 until the present day (Brown, 2014). There are calls for a tougher immigration policy for Britain for instance, as the statistics from the 2011 shows that fifty-five per cent of the 3.7 million increase in the population from the census in 2001 is caused by immigration (ONS, 2011). It is also evident that some of these migrants take the lower end jobs that most citizens would look down on and reject.

Various theories have been propounded as to the factors that give rise to migration. Among these theories discussed are the neo-classical economic theory, the new economic theory, dual labour theory, world systems theory, migration systems theory and transnational theory. These theories are somehow linked to the economic circumstances of the migrants and the prevailing circumstances in the receiving nations. However this raises a lot of practical questions such as why in the last decade alone a lot of British people have moved to much sunnier portions of Europe, such as Spain. It is estimated that about 400,000 British people live and own property in Spain (Guardian, 2012). In spite of the fact that most of these migrants to Spain are pensioners and those who move to establish their own businesses, the motivation according to some is the weather conditions and the house prices. This factor is normally not captured by the economic theories put forward to explain the migration phenomenon. Other factors such as education and religion can also be reasons for migration. For instance, people may believe God has sent them with an assignment to evangelise a nation. I met some from the churches used as case studies for this research that believe that this place is their promised land. They cite the biblical patriarch Abraham's example, as having been told by God to leave his parents' house for a place He (God) has prepared for him. They continue that although the road was not easy for Abraham, as he fought some wars along the way, he finally got there. For some migrants, these biblical narratives have become the inspiration to be strong in their struggles of integrating into British society and also the hope of a better future for them and their families in Britain. This is besides the fact that they are also sent as bearers of the good news for the revitalisation of Christianity in the northern hemisphere of the world. In some instances such as the International Central Gospel Church and the Royalhouse Chapel International a deliberate strategy was laid out to send ministers of the gospel to migrate to Britain with the purpose of evangelising and starting branches of their churches. However, Dominion Centre and Freedom Centre International were established to provide an avenue for migrant students and their families to worship with their 'kith and kin', and as a fraternity for social networking among others. It is also clear that these churches might have altered or moved on from the motivation for their establishment towards other reasons for their continuous existence.

It must be noted however that some Ghanaian-led churches other than the ones used as case studies in this research are established in foreign lands as an indicator of success or purely for social prestige. They normally display their foreign branches on the websites of the home churches. This is done in a bid to increase the international prestige of the church as an organisation. This is the case because the average Ghanaian still associates success and ingenuity with the western world and reaching out to the western world is an indicator of the success of a ministry. If the 'white man' accepts the Ghanaian churches ministry in the 'white man's' country then the ministry is considered very significant. It can be clearly seen that the host communities negotiate the identity of the churches on the basis of the acceptance of the migrant churches. Also, although not once mentioned by the leaders or members of the churches, some of these churches began as projects at home with the view to improve the lives of the citizenry at their countries of origin. Others have also got plans to establish projects with the same purpose. From the perspective of a critical observer, one could state that part of the reason for establishing churches in Britain by these churches from the homelands are partly to raise economic capital to help their countries of origin. This is a point that could possibly be met with a vehement rebuttal or denial from both members and leaders of the churches. And also apart from the fact that the churches have invested into infrastructure as earlier discussed in this chapter.

There is generally a strong case made for the link between migration and globalisation; and globalisation and Pentecostalism are working hand in hand to bring about the current influx of African-led churches and specifically Ghanaian-led churches in Britain. Because of globalisation, Pentecostals in other parts of the world have discovered the affinities they share with others around the world, such as their values, praxis, beliefs and tenets of faith. However there are nuances that Ghanaian-led Pentecostal churches carry, that are unique to them because of the influence of the indigenous cosmology from the places of their origin. Transnational migration has to do with migrants maintaining ties with their countries of origin whilst in the foreign land. These ties could be political, social, economic and also religious as demonstrated in this chapter. It is likely that this uniqueness expressed by the Ghanaian-led Pentecostal churches due to the influences of the indigenous cosmology of their places of origin is in itself is a factor in defining the churches' transnational status. This is the case in the sense that the history, organisation and vision, and beliefs and praxis are constantly influenced by the spiritual formation and the current state of affairs in the country of origin. The churches profiled in this chapter all have a transnational status in this sense, and to an extent their membership growth is also linked to the state of affairs in the home country. This is because certain prevailing factors prompt people to move from their home countries and since people take their religious beliefs and affiliations with them, the Pentecostals among them will worship in these Pentecostal churches. This creates opportunities for increases in the membership of the churches. The opportunity for growth in these churches brought about by new migrants joining also places a responsibility on the churches to help these migrants to integrate into their new society.

Certainly, when these migrants become part of these Ghanaian-led churches, deliberate and non-deliberate integration strategies are put in place to settle them in the churches and the communities in which they live. The integration strategies that these churches have in place, or intend to develop, to help their members are discussed and analysed in the next chapter.

CHAPTER FOUR

THE SOCIO-THEOLOGICAL APPROACH TOWARDS INTEGRATION

Introduction

The merging of national markets and economies and the breaking down of geographical borders have led to the movement of goods and services, and even of people and cultures. Nations and states have criteria for admitting people through their borders on the basis of their likelihood to fit into their societies. Britain started welcoming migrants in large numbers soon after 1945. Migrants came from the Caribbean in the 1950s; the 1960s saw migrants arriving from the Indian subcontinent; expelled Ugandan Asians arrived in the 1970s; and there were sizable inflows from Eastern Europe and sub-Saharan Africa in the 1990s (Manning and Georgiadis, 2012; Algan and Bisin, 2012). Various immigration strategies have been developed over the years to bring in people with the requisite or desired skills to contribute to building a healthier British economy and society. Special criteria were drawn up to outline the skills shortage area where vacancies were to be filled by migrants (UKBA, 2016). Once these migrants have been admitted into the country, the concern of the government and the host society as a whole is how to integrate them successfully into society. The reason that integrating them becomes necessary is because most of the migration routes into the UK provide pathways that lead to permanent residence and citizenship. These migrants come from different parts of the world with different cultures and so in order to build social cohesion, integrating these migrants into British society becomes paramount.

There has been much research on the various aspects of migrants' lives. Some of this research has examined migrants' economic and social circumstances and how these differ from those of the white majority population.

Some scholars have measured earning and employment (Chiswick, 1980). Others have researched the diversity of the ethnic minority experience (Blackaby et al., 2002; Clark et al, 2007). The differences between first and second-generation immigrants have also been explored, as have the role of migrants' religion as opposed to their ethnicity (Lindley, 2002; Blackaby et al, 2002; O'Leary et al, 2005). And rates of integration by migrants (Bell, 1997; Clark and Lindley, 2006). Since many ethnic minority populations in Britain are of relatively recent origin, until very recently there has been little research into how migrants integrate into society and what they consider as integration, to assist in policy drafting by the government. Schiller et al. introduce another conceptual term in an attempt to define integration in a more practical way. They use the word incorporation from a transnational perspective instead of integration and define it as the processes of building or maintaining networks of social relations through which an individual or an organized group of individuals becomes linked to an institution recognized by one or more nation states (Schiller et al, 2006). In this book, I use the word integration may be used to refer to the processes of maintaining networks of social relations with recognition from one or more nation states, but also to individuals or groups immersing themselves in a society so as to feel a part of the society, being law abiding and accordingly benefiting from the privileges of association and residence. Therefore the word integration is used as a more encompassing term in this book.

On Integration, Society and the Church

Within the broad framework of Schiller et al.'s understanding of integration, churches are one such institution that has recognition in both Britain and in Ghana, as institutions of biblical instruction, spirituality and culture. They are also social groups that provide a platform for networking for the advancement of the individual within the group. However, migrants prefer the use of the term integration in the way I have explained above. Unfortunately, the role of churches in the process of integration has not been critically examined to ascertain the practical ways by which they assist their migrant members to integrate. In this chapter, I focus on the internal strategies and programmes the Ghanaian-led Pentecostal churches adopt in integrating their members into wider society. The churches not only provide a community for belonging, but they also embark on wider social, economic and religious programmes to assist in the integration of their migrant members. These programs and initiatives not only mitigate the pain of being 'removed' but they also assist with integration in the place of settlement. This enables migrants to have a transnational status, maintaining ties between the place of origin and settlement (Funmati, 2010).

Most of the churches' initiatives to assist their members to integrate are internally organised. These initiatives have included: welfare assistance to migrants in the form of financial hand-outs; holding immigration and nationality forums to inform members about how to regularise their stay and avoid falling foul of the law; organising personal development and leadership training for members to give them the necessary tools for personal development and effectiveness in leadership and to increase their confidence, which they consider key to success in every area of endeavour; and financial empowerment and business workshops. The churches have also used external training agencies to bring information and skill training to the members. To facilitate these programmes, the churches have used both local speakers and international speakers with strong ties to their communities, and have employed mass media including TV and radio. The churches have assigned themselves the task of charting and appropriating religious space both within and outside the immediate cultural contexts from which they emerged in order to legitimize their place within British society (Adogame, 2003). The extent to which they integrate will determine how strong their ties with their places of origin will be, and thus how stable their transnational status is, as the stories of the migrants suggest.

The importance of churches as agents of integration comes to the fore in filling in the gaps of state-funded initiatives where the rhetoric and practice do not match. Migrants as minorities can feel swallowed up by the culture of the host society and sometimes feel left out. Attempts to correct this have emphasised examining the conditions required to achieve a just society where both citizens and migrants feel catered for (Mason, 2010). This has been the position of governments of the host society and is evidenced in a speech delivered by the former Prime Minister Tony Blair in December 2006 (Blair, 2006). In that speech he maintained that migrants in Britain had to find a way to integrate into British society. The Prime Minister and many others who shared his view at the time were proposing that migrants who are part of ethnic minorities should make the effort to be absorbed into the culture of the larger host society. Many considered this to be not far removed from the assimilationist policy directives and strategies that existed before the acceptance of the integration idea. The lack of a definite definition of integration at the time led to a distinction being drawn between integration and assimilation. Instead of having a working definition of the subject that had the potential of shaping public policy and directives, it was assumed that integration in practice was a straightforward issue, which it was not. Long before the Blair era, Home Secretary Roy Jenkins gave a speech shortly after assuming office in 1966, in which he confirmed this confusion about defining integration.

Integration is perhaps a rather loose word. I do not regard it as meaning the loss, by immigrants, of their own national characteristics and culture. I do not think that we need in this country a 'melting pot', which will turn everybody out in a common mould, as one of a series of carbon copies of someone's misplaced vision of the stereotyped Englishman........I define integration therefore, not as a flattening process of assimilation but as equal opportunity accompanied by cultural diversity in an atmosphere of mutual tolerance. This is the goal (Jenkins, 1967).

In his definition Jenkins gives us an account of what assimilation is rather than defining integration. He seems to point out that the process of assimilation is when ethnic minorities are made to abandon the values and practices which give them their peculiar identities in favour of the predominant culture and way of life of the majority in society. The meaning carried by Jenkins seems to have changed a little since. In 2004, when launching the *Strength in Diversity* consultation document, the then Home Secretary David Blunkett reiterated that 'in Britain integration is not about assimilation into a common culture so that original identities are lost' (Home Office, 2012). This statement recognised the confusion around the subject of integration of migrants by policy makers, politicians and leaders of civil groups, acknowledging that previous approaches to integration had in practice been more assimilationist than had been intended. Trevor Phillips, Chair of the Commission for Racial Equality, argued that the existing policies and strategies were merely treating 'integration' as an alternative word for 'assimilation': practically, nothing had changed because the definition of integration still required some form of uniformity in the way 'we speak, look, dress and act' (Home Office, 2012). However, from the discussions above, one thing that emerges from attempts to distinguish integration from assimilation is that the policy of assimilation strongly persuades members of ethnic minority groups to transform their identity to become more like the majority. Although there could be some overlapping between these policies, the idea of integration is about persuading not only the minority but all groups in society 'to change and adapt to some or all of their values, practices or behaviour so that the lives of members of different groups become intertwined – in effect so that they can live their lives together' (Mason, 2010). This is where the differences in opinions of migrants and policy makers are clear, as most migrants are not much concerned about the adaptation of the values and culture of the host community because they believe the process of cultural adaptation is natural. They are more interested in integration that recognises them as who they are and being able to access the opportunities, privileges and benefits for all who are resident in the state. It is this perspective that underpins the policy that promotes the learning of English and the British way of life through the 'Life in the UK Test' as a requirement for permanent residence and of naturalisation to British citizenship, for example.

Many migrants regard 'Life in the UK Test' as a way for the establishment to make money from them. The authorities are seen to have taken advantage of their inability to present an organised front to present their grievances. Sections of African migrants are of the view that, the consultations the government undertook prior to setting out some of these policy initiatives do not go deep and wide enough to involve the very people who are affected by the policies. From the perspective of the policy makers, there is some sense that these and similar policies have assimilationist tendencies, but these assimilationist policies are inevitable in facilitating the process of the integration of the migrants themselves. Policy makers argue that 'Life in the UK Test' which was introduced in 2007 would enable migrants to feel at home when they become British citizens due to their mastery of the English language and their basic knowledge of British life. (Mason, 2010). This approach they believe would make migrants feel a sense of belonging based on their knowledge of the culture, values, politics, economics and social life in Britain. In spite of the motive for this approach to integration, one cannot ignore the subtle assimilation strategy embedded in this policy, which produces a tendency towards greater uniformity in society. However, this same example of the 'Life in the UK Test' can also be a basis for integration, because the content of the test seems to provide information on accessing opportunities, privileges and benefits that are important to migrants (.gov.uk website).

Considering the policy initiatives highlighted from the 1960s to the present in Britain, various definitions and distinctions have been made about policies of assimilation and integration. In the end one thing that is clear is that the perspective of the migrant differs considerably from that of the policy makers; although it is fair to say that each want to achieve the same goal of providing the basis for social cohesion whilst still enabling the identity of groups to be celebrated. There is evidence, there are both similarities and differences in the way that policy makers, politicians, and migrants, understand integration and make policy approaches to it. Whereas the policy makers and politicians approach integration with what I refer to as a 'top-down' approach, the migrant community approaches integration with a 'bottom-up' approach. The 'top-down' approach is where the policy makers persuade members of both the minority and majority communities to adapt to each other's values and practices so that their lives are intertwined through 'macro' level policies. Policy makers consider this to be an effective way of promoting integration in society through social cohesion.

However it is obvious that social cohesion as a vehicle for integration does not happen only through the adaptation of values; in addition, the individual's wellbeing and social status influence their confidence in being accepted by the cultural majority. For someone from an ethnic minority background, accepting their way of life without facilitating their involvement in community-building (such as their representation on teams, committees and boards that actually matter in shaping policy or delivering initiatives of conspicuous value to the community) will still fall short of the ideals advocated by the policy makers and politicians.

Migrant groups and the African church communities through their interventionist programmes to help migrants to integrate, use the 'bottom-up approach', although they do not refer to it as such. The bottom-up approach involves migrants being given the necessary recognition, acceptance, skills, and opportunities to fulfil their potential and make use of their creative abilities, at the same time as contributing to building society and realising their personal goals. In this way these migrants gradually find their place in society and build up their confidence to network within their communities through the people they meet in the process of pursuing their aspirations. This networking then provides them with a platform to positively affect others in their communities and can also be better understood from the perspective of their culture. This paves the way for a natural form of integration to take place at the 'micro' cultural level of society. All the approaches used by the minority communities are guided by the philosophy of being successful and using success to gain recognition. Recognition leads to networking and the networking becomes the platform to integrate. The migrants wants to be seen as a part of their new society, and not to have their presence perceived as being detrimental to the host society. The only way to prove their recognition and acceptance is through involvement in community building (Wickes et al, 2003).

There is a different response to the issue of integration from the perspective of the ethnic minority. There is a general sense that more can be done if the approach of policy makers and politicians became more pragmatic, taking into consideration the perspectives of ethnic minorities (Sturgis, 2013). It is at this point that the responses from the migrant community become important, particularly in relation to their 'bottom-up' approach to integration, in contrast to the 'top-down' approach of the policy makers. This reflects the way in which these migrants gradually find their place in society and build up their confidence to network within their communities through the people they come across in the process of pursuing their aspirations. This networking provides them with a platform to positively affect others in the communities and can also be better understood from the perspective of their culture. This paves the way for a natural form of integration to take place at the 'micro' cultural level of society. All the approaches used by the minorities are guided by the philosophy of being successful and using the success to gain the recognition, recognition leads to networking and the networking becomes the platform to integrate (Liew and Scott, 2012). A specific biblical narrative that is often given as a guiding philosophy of the churches and migrants, although not many would acknowledge that as a deliberate philosophy developed by any one person, seeing it rather as a result of the collective wisdom of people in their search for a solution to their marginalisation by society. The biblical narrative is from Luke 11:33; 'No one, when he has lit a lamp, puts it in a secret place or under a basket, but on a lampstand, that those who come in may see the light'. From the perspective of the 'elitist' leadership of these African church communities, is that the only way by which society would find need for the ethnic minorities and actually make room for them is when people within the ethnic minority shows signs of success and excellence in what they do. And this [point of view is further buttressed with another verse from the Bible, Proverbs 18:16: 'A man's gift makes room for him, and brings him before great men'. From the collective perspective held, both individuals and the ethnic minority community as a whole can gain recognition through the expression of their gifts and abilities and in contributing to the various communities where they find themselves (Middleton, 2005). This they believe will attract the attention of the wider community, and they will in turn seek the source of the success, beginning a process of integration through the networking that may result from that initial enquiry by individuals into the success story. In effect the process of integration begins from their theological perspective, a union with God as the basis of integration into the church through its norms and practices and the church as an agent assist with the process of integration into the larger body of society. Thereby, giving a sociological problem a theological interpretation with solutions which may be deemed problematic considering their misplaced theological root.

The concentration of some of the churches concentrate on developing members in being successful at what they do as a way of assisting them to integrate into their communities through gaining recognition and acceptance, which is a component of social cohesion. This is a trend some scholars, such as Gifford, wrongfully refer to as the Americanisation of the Pentecostal churches in Britain, because of the prosperity dimension to it. In my view the churches do what they do as a response to the socio-cultural and economic milieu. In converse, the African churches' focus on emphasising success in their churches is not unique to the church in Britain but can be traced to their countries of origin in Africa, although the circumstances scholars attribute to causing the phenomenon may be different through their own unique standpoint.

The emphasis on success and prosperity in Pentecostal churches in Britain and Ghana and for that matter countries on the African continent, once again reinforces the transnational links of these churches and their members to the country of origin. In Ghana, the religious cosmology, economic deprivations and poverty in general could be cited as contributing to the appeal of the success and prosperity message in Pentecostal denominations (Appiah, 2011). Through training, the churches provide members with an environment and socio-economic tools with which to develop themselves. And to an extent the African Pentecostal churches have attempted to become micro communities where these tools are tested. As a consequence, the 'bottom-up' approach to dealing with integration becomes inward looking in focus. The churches focus on integration within their own community first before seeking integration with the wider community. This is done as part of the quest of the church to fulfil part of its mandate to bring back the gospel to the northern hemisphere, within the context of reverse mission (Wahrisch-Oblau, 2000). A migrant's association with a support network such as the church is crucial for the individual and the whole community's recognition within the wider society. From the perspective of the church and the ethnic minority as a whole one cannot achieve the social cohesion that policy makers and politicians deem vital to integration if individuals are not empowered to fulfil their potential and use their gifts and talents. It is an observation that these churches were preoccupied with making their mark within their communities through ambitious projects. The churches don't assume the 'top-down' approach of the policy makers and politicians is ineffective but they think their approach can go further in bringing about integration.

Below I analyse the various integration strategies adopted by the churches to help migrants and ethnic minority members integrate into society, with specific references to initiatives and people involved in executing the initiatives.

Social Welfare Intervention Programs to Mitigate 'Uprootedness'

Many European countries, including Britain, have in recent years experienced an influx of migrants from sub-Saharan Africa. Most European states have had to rely on the third sector in responding to social welfare needs within their countries (Gocmen, 2013; Abrahamson, 1999; Hardill and Wilson, 2011; Bode, 2006). In more recent times, studies have focused on social policy and how the roles of the private and voluntary social welfare providers have changed with time (Bode, 2006; Daly, 2003). Historically, the church has worked together with state agencies in facilitating social welfare schemes to support the needy in society, although that has not been the case in other European countries, such as France (Bode, 2006). The point of departure from this historical reference is, Pentecostal churches provide social welfare intervention programmes with very little and in most cases no link at all to state agencies and they do not solicit support from the state for their initiatives. It is an internal initiative aimed at supporting members to integrate. Not much research has examined how Faith Based Organisations (FBOs) that fall under the third sector have provided social welfare to their members and what has been the motive. Interactions with these entities reveal that the social welfare interventions initiated by FBOs and African churches in particular are to assist members to integrate their members into society.

In most Western European countries, as in Britain, there are different generations of migrants depending on which part of the world those groups of migrants have come from.

> The six largest ethnic minority groups in Britain today and in descending population size order are: Indian, Pakistani, Black Caribbean, Black African, Bangladeshi, and Chinese. These groups differ in the timing of their arrival. While the majority of immigrants from the Caribbean arrived in the period between 1955 and 1964, the main time of arrival of Black African, Indian and Pakistani first generation groups was between 1965 and 1974 (Peach, 1996).

The 2011 census records few changes in the ethnic minority composition as shown by Peach in the 2001 Census above. The largest ethnic minority groups according to the 2011 Census are as follows, in descending order: Indian, Pakistani, Black African, Black Caribbean, Bangladeshi and Chinese. This excludes ethnic minorities of European descent such as Polish (ONS, 2013). Comparing the findings of the 2001 and 2011 censuses, on the composition of the ethnic minority groups' shows that Black Africans, defined as those who consider their origins from Africa with African parentage moved to third position, overtaking the Black Caribbean population. There is however no indication of whether this increase is as a result of the increase in the birth rate in the last 10 years of those who already reside in the UK or whether it is due to the increase in the arrival of new migrants. However, unsubstantiated claims suggest this is the result of the intermarriage of Black Caribbean males to white women whose 'mixed race' children tend to be integrated physically and culturally into the white population (ONS, 2011).

To this end, the growth of the Black African minority group is quite because it is linked with the influx of migrants into the African churches.

It has to be noted that these migrant groups are predominantly made up of those seeking asylum, students, those seeking better standard of living and also the professionals (Conoly and White, 2013). In seeking to understand the interventions provided by churches to their immigrant congregation members, the intergenerational mobility of migrants and the integration of migrants into their communities need to be examined on a case-by-case basis. This is because in certain instances these migrants who patronize and accept support through these church-based welfare interventions are from a mixture of first, second and in some cases third generation migrant groups. The first generation migrants refer to migrants who are the first from their families to travel to the UK without having a relative already resident in the UK. Second generation migrants here refer to migrants who are the offspring or very close relatives of migrants already resident in the UK, such as children, nephews, nieces, aunts and uncles. In some instances these second generation migrants have come to the UK through some other relative and were once dependent on the relative who served as their host. The third generation is made up of those who are third in line in the family through birth; children of those born in Britain. It is also worth noting that the typical Ghanaian cultural definition of an 'acquaintance', ranges from a biological relation or just someone who hails from the same village or town. This has to be understood from a sociological perspective as most societies in sub-Saharan Africa live communally, and there is a sense of 'sisterhood and brotherhood' when they meet outside their villages and towns of origin. This has given rise to hometown associations, former secondary schools and year groups associations for instance, but these will not be discussed any further because they are loosely formed associations.

As mentioned earlier, migrants who accept support through the social interventions established by the churches can be found across the generational divide (Warnes and Williams, 2006). One would have thought, examining the composition of the generational divide, that only those of the later generations would seek this kind of support. One might presume that those migrants who have been here longer should be settled enough to be self-supporting. Among these first generation migrants, there are those who have done odd jobs, even to pay agents to bring their relatives to the UK, and as yet they have been unable to access the opportunities within society for a better life. The issue of paying agents to bring relatives over to Britain is almost a tradition in some families where resources are pooled together to get an individual to travel abroad and that individual in turn within a specified time has to pay an agent to bring another hardworking family member over to Britain.

As a result these illegal, migrants cannot look for work on the open job market. Although some would argue that there is still help outside of the church for those in these kinds of situations they often would not approach charities for fear of being deported. There is generally no trust for white-led initiatives of support for African migrants among these migrants. Some of these migrants who are parents have had to maintain two or three jobs in order to make ends meet making them absent from home to be able provide support to their children's school work. The result is that often they do badly at school and are unable to continue their education beyond the GCSEs and so are unable to hold down any meaningful job.

There is an examination of some of the programmes of action the churches have embarked on or plan to embark on, to assist their migrant congregations to integrate into British society. Each of the churches have their own programmes depending on their composition and some of these programmes have been discontinued due to peculiar difficulties associated with running them. These programmes include Immigration and Nationality Fora; Financial Empowerment and Business Workshops (Social Enterprises); and Personal Development and Leadership Training.

Organising Immigration and Nationality Forum
There are strong indications of the sense of urgency that leads to the organisation of the Immigration and Nationality forum among the

churches. Though the word immigration features prominently in how these churches identify their initiatives on providing information to members on immigration, each of them have called them different names for example 'Eat the good of the land', 'Tread upon it, possess it'. In some cases subsequent programmes with the same focus have had their names changed or altered to disguise them to the outside world. The idea of changing the names of the fora is also to make the members comfortable to attend these initiatives without making them feel that sense of giving away their immigration status at such meetings. These meetings strongly feature on the agenda of the churches as part of their responsibility to help stabilise their members and assist them in their integration into British society. The leadership of the churches believe that the future of their churches depends on stable members who can freely move around without fear and can access the opportunities that society presents to them. In so doing they can financially contribute to building the church and fulfilling the churches' visions.

It is worth noting that the consciousness of the immigration status of congregations is not the concern of African churches alone; due to the increase in the number of migrants that come to Britain each year, several churches which are predominantly white but have become home to some of these migrants have also adapted some of these measures to integrate their members into British society. A survey conducted by Gladys Glaniel from the Irish School of Ecumenics, Trinity College Dublin, reveals that;

> 55% of clergy and faith leaders say that they have preached or taught on immigration, diversity or welcoming strangers in the last 12 months. 44% of clergy, pastors, ministers, and faith leaders have never done anything to accommodate minority-ethnic people. 19% said that the languages of minority-ethnic people had been used in services during the last 12 months. This was more common under the heading 'Other Christians' which may well include migrant-led churches (Glaniel, 2013).

This is more an acknowledgement of how pluralistic and diverse congregations in Ireland have become and of the need to hold on to these ethnic minorities in the churches as a means of maintaining high levels of membership than a real effort to integrate them. The Irish situation bears some resemblance to the British situation and the findings of that research resonate with views often expressed in the British-migrant religious discourse. Predominantly white churches that do not do anything special to accommodate ethnic minorities are not necessarily rejecting their membership but – either the church leaders, or the organisations themselves – have not as yet recognised themselves as agents of integration. On the part of the white majority churches one may argue that this adaptation is quite significant to their growth and sustenance over time due to the fact that some of these white majority mainline historical churches are closing down. It will take the ethnic minority and migrants to revitalise these churches. In congruence, the experiences of the participants seem to follow a trend that suffering and discrimination deepens their religious convictions as migrants. The religious migrants will always congregate where their needs are recognised (McAndrew and Voas, 2014).

Provision of Personal Development and Leadership Training

As part of the churches' strategy to empower their members and also to position members to ensure their capability to finance the church, its programmes and projects, most of these African Churches hold meetings, run workshops and training. The content of these workshops and training differs from one church to the other but with the same focus and delivered by different speakers. This training was also career oriented, to support those who are already working to improve their personal effectiveness, and for those not working they were challenged to find jobs or create employment for themselves through the use of their gifts and talents (Brimrose and McNair, 2011). These training initiatives offered by the churches are often more instructional and drawn from the leaders of the churches understanding of the needs of the members to be effective in their lives, in and out of the church. The intention at these training seminars and workshops is to give participants a set of knowledge and skills that can help them to act appropriately in different circumstances they may be presented with (Stogdill, 1974). This form of motivation for training people into leadership and encouraging them to act as leaders is a departure from the historical underpinnings of motivation in such contexts, which was normally built on fear but in this case for their own benefit (Daft, 2001). Because the members are trained not only to serve in these churches alone but everywhere they find themselves it is not a cynical move on the part of church leaders to create a control system, although it is acknowledged that the churches in the end also benefit (Ryan and Oestreich, 1991).

There are few speakers from abroad and in Britain who have been invited in their individual roles as pastors and consultants as trainers and speakers to these Personal Development and Leadership Training Seminars and workshops. These pastors and speakers have been regulars on the Christian speaking circuit in most of these churches in Britain, and most of them are regular speakers in Pentecostal churches in the countries of origin of these migrants in Africa too; their involvement with churches in Britain therefore seems to be a transnational occurrence. The speakers include: John Maxwell, the late Myles Munroe (Bahamian), Mensa Otabil, Bill Winston, Celia Appiagyei-Collins and Michael Hutton-Wood. An observation of their teachings on personal development and leadership leads one to generally conclude that although these speakers are coming from different continents and from different racial backgrounds they share a similar background of economic and social deprivation at some point in their lives. For their audiences who seek comfort, direction and a way of out of their personal socio-economic difficulties, which are accentuated by their current migrant status, these speakers and what they have to teach them are considered very relevant.

The Churches, the Speakers and Training Syllabi

The speakers profiled above are not the only speakers who regularly speak in these African churches but these are the ones well known and noted for speaking on personal development and leadership. It is worth noting that apart from Celia Appiagyei-Collins and Michael Hutton-Wood who are migrants from Ghana and have a settled immigration status in Britain, Mensa Otabil is a Ghanaian and resident in Accra. It seems obvious that both Celia and Michael are well aware and familiar with the struggles of the migrant and therefore could relate to their predominantly migrant audiences in these churches. Myles Munroe was from the Bahamas whilst Bill Winston and John Maxwell are from the United States. Another observation was that it seems as though the relationships of the pastors were dependent on the size of their churches re-echoing the same observation made by Marx religion helping in creating class systems. In the end, these churches operate to some extent as learning organisations where a pattern of thinking is nurtured, collective aspiration is set free, and people are given the necessary tools to achieve their clearly articulated organisational vision, nurturing people who can move from the bottom of social class as migrants to significance in their immediate community and beyond (Senge, 1990).

Regarding the speakers, there are a few observations that one can make about what has made them regulars in these churches and their affiliates in London. All of these speakers share a bond that makes them relevant to their audience and those pastors keep bringing them over to speak. They share a similar background of deprivation and poverty earlier on in their lives. Mensa Otabil once made a remark at a conference where he spoke alongside Myles Munroe that as he sat down with him talking about how they began life, they discovered they had a similar background and experiences although they come from different continents. And for many of these migrant members of the churches they could identify themselves with the struggles of the speakers. Many of the migrants moved because they dared to relocate, experiencing with it all the attendant challenges and some regrettable experiences. Some even risked their lives to come to Britain for a new life traveling through deserts, and some hidden in trucks; others even sell family properties to fund their journey. Similar stories from these speakers who have suffered deprivation or have had to go through difficulties in their childhood, resonate with the migrant's own situation and mean that they take the information given seriously, because they look at the lives that these men have now and they tell themselves they can make it too. It seems to bring them a lot of encouragement and strengthen their hopes of a better future, irrespective of their age.

Again the style of speaking and illustrations used shows an eagerness on their part to share their stories and their passion to let others know how they used to be where these migrants are today and therefore they too can become better people with a better standard of living. These speakers sometimes make mention of assets they acquired or how they now live to inspire people. At the 2006 Dominion Summit, Myles Munroe – before he encouraged people to give to pay for the organisation of the conference – stated that he came to Britain and to that conference to speak because of his passion to help people like those in the audience to become successful people. He stated that if he had flown to London in his own private jet that would have cost him twenty thousand pounds but he travelled on a commercial plane so as not to burden the conference host. However this was certainly not economy class but first class which most of their audience in their churches cannot afford. The buying of private aeroplanes has become a power symbol to 'separate the men from the boys', in other words to differentiate between those pastors who are successful and those who are not, at least from their perspective. One would have thought that he could have made a contribution himself to offset the cost of hosting the conference, rather than asking these same migrants who are looking for ways of succeeding in their lives' endeavours to fund the conference. This seems to be a bit contradictory, but one thing that is common with such encouragement to give is that people are made to understand that that's the way to prosper and to make money. In this sense the pain and the pressure to give is minimised and people give with the expectation that they will also be blessed because the speakers themselves are testimonies of the principles these speakers espouse. In effect both churches, members and speakers become links and connectors to the transnational organisational stage as global actors.

Further, the speakers are characteristically well dressed. They normally put on smart suits except in the case of Mensa Otabil, who wears a smart African print and tailored clothing. This smart dressing can be considered to have a psychological effect on the audience in that it proves the speaker's level of prosperity and success in their field of endeavours, and therefore their audience can aspire to be like them. It is used to make the statement 'I used to be down there like you but now look at me, I'm up there'. Mensa Otabil once remarked during the 2009 Dominion Summit whilst preaching a sermon titled 'Growing your capacity', that he was for the first time speaking in a predominantly white church, with the pastor originally from Trinidad and Tobago, in the United States. He recounted that after he was introduced he mounted the stage with his flowing African print called 'boubou'. According to him, everyone looked at him with bewilderment and it was as though they were asking in their minds 'what is this bushman with this strange clothing doing with a computer? However when he had finished speaking the members came to him to congratulate him for an excellent sermon and he was invited again at a later date'.

Appearance, and the kind of apparel African Pentecostal preachers wear, is very important to them unlike their counterparts in the mainline historic churches. The reason for this is that they intend to inspire their audience about how God can prosper them to raise them up from their misery. There is nothing more appealing to a struggling migrant who has lost all hope of their initial vision of travelling to Britain, than assuring the person in word and in a practical demonstration of what you wear, drive and live. This feature also enforces the 'big man rule' and mentality where these few speakers enjoy the authority and legitimacy for what they do because of the social gap between the speakers and the audience (Mccauley, 2013). It is possible that this largely contributes to the reason why these speakers are brought in year after year by these Ghanaian-led Pentecostal churches. For the migrants the hope of where they want to be is epitomised in the stories of and lives these speakers live and they consider them their heroes. This gives the migrant some form of stability, as some of at the various points of sojourn want to just pack their baggage and go back home when they can take the associated hardships anymore. Others come to a point where they want to go back to their countries of origin but can't afford it. There was a time when the British government offered assistance to illegal migrants who wanted to leave the country on their own accord on the Assisted Voluntary Return (AVR) scheme established in 1999, but some migrants felt too embarrassed to go forward to the authorities (Black et al, 2011). To that end some of these conferences provide them with the encouragement to stay on and see the positive side of their struggles until such a time that they believe God blesses them in the land. From the perspectives of the migrants premised on such biblical narrative such as Abraham's, if God picks people from nowhere and blesses them then why not them?

Another important observation about these speakers is that they reference their source of success to their relationship with God, expressed in the love of God for them, their commitment to apply principles in God's word, which is often how they describe the scriptures, and hope of a better future based on the prophetic declarations in the scriptures. So in doing that not only are they inspiring their audience through their own stories of success, which they demonstrate in what they wear, drive or where they live, but also with the promises of God in the scriptures. The result of this is that these migrant members want to stay in their churches and also maintain their faith in the God of prosperity they are presented, to see through their own 'breakthrough', a term used by most of these African Christians to embody the process of overcoming difficulties and becoming successful. The two ends of this from a sociological perspective is: firstly, it assists the churches in their quantitative organising as they need that within the context of power and influence in the communities and other end is the 'connection to the promise of signs and wonders to a global modernity and its material rewards' to migrants (Nieswand, 2009).

An important issue in the organisation of these leadership and personal development events is the information that members receive. The information given as its the case through Nieswand's (2004) ethnographic investigation in Germany, it's deliberately put together in all cases, 'what might appear on first examination to be ethnic, particular, linguistically bounded practices and identities to contain pathways of incorporation that confront standard notions of membership and belonging within the boundaries of a single nation-state'.

The leadership and personal development initiatives take the form of conferences, workshops, retreats, and training sessions. In one such training Celia spoke on 'Discovering your Mission in life'. She gave out handouts of the outline she wanted to teach with scriptural backing to the issues she raised at the session. The meeting was held on a Saturday and lasted for 2 hours, with the last hour of the session reserved for questions and answers. At the session Celia stressed the importance of having a mission in life because God never did anything without a purpose. She quoted a scripture from Ecclesiastes 3:1; 'To everything there is a season, a time for every purpose under heaven'. Elaborating on the fact that God never made anything simply for the sake of making it, she said that everyone has an assignment and this assignment makes an individual unique and very important in the eyes of God. This is a popular scripture often taken by these speakers as the starting point for anything they decide to teach. Bill Winston, Mensa Otabil, Michael Hutton Wood and John Maxwell have always made this the starting point of their teachings in their conferences in these churches. Thus it has become the foundation upon which most of the principles that are taught by these speakers are based.

These popular Pentecostal literature which becomes an embodiment of inspiration for coping, have the intention to inspire the reader to change course in their personal lives to maximize their opportunities for personal achievement. Fundamentally they stress the fact that everyone can be someone very important in life if they discover their place in the plans of God (Munroe, 1992). The pastors and leaders of these African churches rely heavily on some of these materials. It is understandable that teachings on the basis of these literature such as this, can have a phenomenal impact on the lives of migrants who may be disillusioned with life in Britain, and are seeking ways to make their lives count, on the backdrop of their disappointments and unforeseen struggles upon arrival in Britain. The teaching and information based on scripture also helps the migrants to sustain their hope of a better future and ameliorate the pain of their struggles. So the message of purpose that becomes the starting point for any discourse of personal development and leadership has a transnational appeal.

The subject of leadership development resonates very well with the migrants whose sense of worth and pathway to becoming significant is impaired by their struggles and pain. Receiving the recognition that they have something to offer to humanity, and being given the opportunity to be taught about leadership, is uplifting to them. The effect of this is that the churches build an army of optimists who dare to put their history and circumstances aside to pursue higher objectives beyond their present circumstances.

Again, advantage to the churches is that when the church presents a project to be accomplished they see it as a way of stretching beyond their limitations to accomplish something that will epitomise their collective efforts and enhance their image as migrants. Thus on the strength of that collective accomplishment they make a statement that they have the capacity to make a contribution to British society. This in itself is a psychological boost to step out in pursuit of their own dreams, which in some ways becomes the starting point for integrating into wider British Society. To these migrants the process of integrating begins with proving that one has something to offer that is unique and that leads to acceptance by the populace, and enabling them to access the opportunities that are available for everyone. This position of the migrants provides evidence to suggest that the socio-economic reasons underlying most of the migration theories discussed in chapter two are valid as the claims of religious reasons for migration. Besides the religious empowerment, these church organisations provide migrants with economic empowerment too.

Financial Empowerment and Business Workshop

One of the main challenges for the migrant is getting access to a regular and substantial source of income. Money and a better standard is a major reason why most people migrate to Britain. Migrants come to Britain in search of a better life for themselves and their families. In response to these challenges they tend to look for housing in areas where they can afford it, in order to save and also take care of family members in their countries of origin. The search for affordable housing brings about a concentration of these people in particular areas of the town or cities where they dwell. Besides this challenge and many others that migrants face, the churches where they worship are also affected by the lack of access to funds. Churches are concerned about the financial need of their members, not only because of the burden of supporting those affected, but also because of these individuals' limited ability to respond to calls for monetary contributions for the running of the churches and projects the churches embark upon. There are three main ways through which financial empowerment and business start-ups are approached. The first is the pastors of the churches themselves teaching, and the second is inviting other guest pastors and Christian experts who are considered qualified to teach, using biblical narratives to explain the principles and information they give to their audiences. The third is the use of existing companies who have the expertise to inform, train and assist members to take pragmatic steps to actualise what the two earlier approaches have established. These approaches are done in succession over a period of time with natural progression. The process in the churches is that after the first two approaches have been exhausted the third is done almost immediately before members lose the sense of urgency to act.

Leadership's Teaching on the 'Tithe'

In the African Pentecostal churches where 'tithing is taught as a biblical principle for every Christian, the jobs people do and consequently the income of the members has a direct correlation to the incomes of the churches. Having heard exhortations on tithing and offering, most of the time before tithes or offerings are taken, individuals are told that paying a tenth of their incomes to God through the churches will invite God to intervene in their financial difficulties. In most of these churches a scripture that is often quoted is Malachi 3:8-10;

> Will a man rob God? Yet you have robbed Me! But you say, 'In what way have we robbed You?' In tithes and offerings. You are cursed with a curse, For you have robbed Me, Even this whole nation. Bring all the tithes into the storehouse, that there may be food in My house, And try Me now in this, Says the Lord of hosts, If I will not open for you the windows of heaven And pour out for you such blessing That there will not be room enough to receive it.

The churches are dependent on the command of tithing of which they normally quote from the scriptures. In contemporary Judaism tithing is of little significance although there is ample evidence that members of the early church gave from their means to support the church and the needy (Leach, 1960). Churches then and churches in the present day predominantly depend on the giving of their members to finance their audacious projects and run the churches' activities. It seems that regardless of the arguments for or against tithing, it has become the main source of finance for most Pentecostal churches, without which most churches would struggle financially. Individuals' giving in the churches is considered a participation in the sacred (Mundely et al, 2011). And not only that but a participation in the body of beliefs upheld by a community of believers whose social circumstances are interlinked through migration and the desire to fully integrate into the wider society. In as much as the decision should be left to the individual's own level of commitment, the leaders of these churches seek ways to make it more of a compulsory element of the worship than an act that reflects the individual's own understanding of the espoused biblical principles and commitment to the sacred. The churches have taken an approach to ensure that their sources of income are protected at the same time as they claim to empower their members to have a better life through the act of tithing. Various methods have been used to raise money to finance the local church which include Jewish tithing as discussed above from the Old Testament, as well as more complex methods by today's African Pentecostal churches (Leach, 1960). Thus the church has an unwavering interest in members' financial dealings, as for most of the church leaders, the life of the church is heavily intertwined with the lives of the members that attend. In as much as the churches visited exhibited a great deal of organisation in all respects, there is also the sense that the state of the church at any time reflects the state of the members' lives in spiritual and material terms (Leach, 1960).

Although it may seem somehow an egotistical move on the part of the churches to financially empower members from whom they will eventually benefit, the individual has the opportunity to harness their abilities and talents for financial gain. Although this in itself is not wrong, it may be viewed by those who look at issues through a political lens as a way to gain influence in the community, in spite of the clear message of the churches and the invited trainers and speakers which focuses on the migrant member.

Expert Advice on Start-Ups

The churches' financial empowerment and business start-ups initiatives have been organised in different ways. There have been conferences with the emphasis on wealth creation, workshops and training sessions as ways of empowering the members of the churches. The church and religious groups as a whole are known to influence community and individual well being through various strategic pathways which include some of the initiatives of the church mentioned in the previous sections of the chapter (Maton and Wells, 1995). In one of such event, Mensa Otabil spoke at a 3 day conference on wealth creation at Freedom Centre International; his sermon was entitled 'Borrowed Vessels'. The scripture for his teaching was 2 Kings 4:1-7. The main thrust of the sermon was that anything an individual possesses, be it a gift, a talent, an ability as simple as cooking, talking, arguing or anything that is used for your domestic advantage or profit can be commercialised and turned into a source of living. He charged his audience to look beyond being employed to being industrious and entrepreneurial.

Whilst he spoke he made references to the fact that the Ghanaians for instance have not standardised cooking their traditional meals; if this were done, African restaurants could be opened could even be exported to other parts of the world. To prove the possibility of this he cited as an example the way in which people of all colours and races go to Chinese restaurants to patronise Chinese foods. Some of the migrants see themselves as limited by their circumstances either in terms of education or resident permits, and – linking to the title of the talk – he stated that even under such circumstances you can borrow 'vessels', including expertise, knowledge, wisdom, money and others things, from those who have what you need in order to accomplish your objectives or fulfil a dream. The reason this perspective of Mensa Otabil is important is because later training and conferences organised in these churches have followed similar lines of challenging these migrant members to make use of their abilities and develop their own businesses. This is done with the mantra, 'if you have your own business you manage your own time and can make room to be present at church for services and other events organised by the church'.

As part of the conference style of informing and training the members, Freedom Centre International brought an expert from the HSBC bank in an unofficial role to talk on how to benefit from the financial services that banks provide and also dealt with issues of mortgages and how to buy your first property in Britain. A range of issues was dealt with at the conference including how to use a credit card for your benefit without getting into debt. The Dominion Centre ran a similar conference and also had an expert in financial products offered by the banks. In both cases at the end of the conferences, members were given opportunity to make a personal appointment to seek the services of these experts. The benefits to the church apart from what has previously been discussed is that the churches do not have to pay these experts to be present because they get business at the end of the sessions, whilst at the same time individuals receive the necessary assistance for investments. In the end these seminars and workshops are supposed to empower the migrant member for the acquisition of wealth, which has become an attraction to many migrants who join the churches (Spinks, 2003).

At the International Central Gospel Church, 2010 was a significant year in terms of the wealth creation theme: they held two major events in the space of six months. The first was an investment forum for the whole church to educate members of the church about the investment opportunities in Ghana. At this event, personnel from First Capital Plus Bank in Accra, Ghana were invited to come over to speak to the members. The owner and CEO of the Bank at the time, Mr Ato Essien was who is also a member of the International Central Gospel Church in Ghana was in attendance. After the general presentation of the investment climate in Ghana, another person took over to talk about the investment opportunities with the bank that they were representing. It is assumed this vested interest in an investment in the country of origin would further establish and strengthen the pathway to maintaining transnational ties to the place of origin. In a sense widening the global social field of these Christian modernists (Nieswand, 2004).

The encouragement to have members invest in Ghana reveals the transnational status of the individuals and the churches themselves, since the churches organised these investment workshops to deepen the ties these individuals may already have with their places of origin. And this is certainly the case due to the constant on-going liberalisation of the local markets, which leads to increased visibility of consumer goods in the places of origin.

Should these investments prove worthwhile then there is a possibility they could eventually draw these members to go back and settle in their land of origin and even in some instances where landed properties are built or bought for letting, an income can be generated from country of origin, which some of these migrants could rely on. The reason there is the potential for improving one's financial stability in Britain through letting property in Ghana is that most of the homes let in very good neighbourhoods in the capital are paid for in US dollars (USD). Therefore the investor and their dependents (some of who may have never visited Ghana) would benefit from transnational financial gains. Some of these funds could be accumulated over time and transferred over as a deposit for a mortgage in their host country.

Workshops by 'Secular' Training Companies

Besides the conference style of training and motivating people to start their own business, a workshop style of training is also organised using other established companies to accomplish these purposes. This is probably because they present a pragmatic approach to empowerment and have personnel with diverse expertise to advise and guide the members of the churches.

Nexgen Initiatives Limited

A reputable and popular company among black majority churches in London is Nexgen Initiatives Limited. Many African churches, particularly in London, have depended on the company for informing and training people in the churches in business start-ups. The company also targets churches, informing them of possible regeneration opportunities within the communities and about how to access funding to embark on regeneration. They say this of themselves on their website:

> ... We aim to stimulate new, entrepreneurial ways to tackle social problems more effectively and more efficiently through connecting people in various communities, bringing together those from voluntary and not-for-profit organisations, especially those who have a background of being from disadvantaged communities, with the public and private sectors. This enables the sharing of ideas and practical experience, and encourages innovation (NEXGEN, 2008)

This company's managing director is a Nigerian with a passion to see people of African descent, and individuals and churches, as a whole get recognition by their communities as major players in development and not as scroungers, as migrants are depicted in some sections of the media. From the company's perspective, the only way by which the majority in the host country will see the minority as important is when they make a contribution to society through finding ways of solving some of the problems within the various localities where the individuals reside and churches are located.

With this strategy of reaching out, Nexgen has been able to extend their work from their base in London to churches, organisations and individuals in Leeds, Leicester, Nottingham, Birmingham, Wolverhampton, Manchester, Cardiff, Southampton, Liverpool, Plymouth and Newcastle. The relationships established with these African pastors and leaders of churches means that the company organises the training for as many of the churches in that particular city as would attend.

One such workshop was organised in collaboration with PMP and Helping Hands, another charity in London, which trains people in Prince 2 Project Management (Introductory Level and Foundation), without cost to the attendees. For this workshop, PMP provided the professional teaching, Helping Hands organized the catering, and Nexgen was responsible for the invitations distributed, and for general oversight. At the end of the 3 day workshop those who wanted to open their own businesses in order to work as contractors were given further information and assisted in completing company registration forms. Nexgen received lottery funding for this purpose. Prince 2 was chosen because apparently there had been a shortage of Project managers and more were needed in anticipation of London hosting the 2012 Olympics at the time.

Nexgen also held other workshops for the churches, informing them about where money is available from the government and from donors for community projects, and how to access these funds. The workshops normally cover the whole process from giving information on the need for the churches to engage their communities, through to discussing the difficulties to expect, funding opportunities, how to complete the funding forms and actually being assisted by the personnel of the Nexgen to complete the forms.

These collaborative efforts of these entities acting as social agents and agencies, is a way of assisting the African communities to integrate into British society because by doing so they are joining the debate and thus making their voices heard and getting their contributions noted. This may include identifying areas of concern to governments, such as assisting marginalized groups and regenerating communities, whether it is organizing after school clubs, setting up social enterprises to train people to attain employability skills, helping the aged in society through home visitation and care, or even assisting the homeless with food and shelter. These projects are not only for ethnic minorities, although some of the initiatives are targeted to the ethnic minorities who are normally categorised as the marginalised. Nevertheless, in undertaking them, the whole community gets involved and a bond is built through mutual respect and learning from one another.

Stewardship Services (UKET) Limited

This is a company established in 1906 in England. It has a predominantly white management team and facilitators but with the rise of black majority churches and their efforts to integrate into British society Stewardship's services have become useful to these churches. The company claims they have a core evangelical Christian ethos upon which all their values are based. They state their values by which they seek to conduct and measure themselves as generosity, relationship, integrity, quality and improvement. They describe their mission as being to release Christians to live and give generously to resource God's Kingdom and also to equip the Church to develop excellence in legal and financial governance. Though the company has gone through different phases over the years the main thrust of dealings has been with churches rather than individuals.

Stewardship organises information dissemination and training events and invites churches to take part in these training programmes. In one of their informational events at a conference centre in Hemel Hempstead, the focus was to educate the churches on new regulations for charities regarding the responsibilities of a charity trustee and the new guidelines for trustees who receive remuneration for their services. The second part of the informational seminar style event was on how to develop a community development project and how to get the necessary funding to execute it. Aside the general informational seminars and workshop the company organizes, there are specific seminars organised sometimes to clarify statutory regulations that affect churches. One such seminar was organised for churches to clarify changes to the gift aid applications and claims. The presenter in relations to donations, noted that there is the need to train people on how to have a household budget. He quoted a statistic to back up his claims that households rarely have budgets for their money. And therefore for people to have some money left over in order to give to their church, the church must share in the responsibility to help their members' budget well.

The creation of a new 'African-British' identity through Mass Media

The social welfare programmes embarked upon by the churches to mitigate 'uprootedness' among the migrant church members both internally and externally have involved the use of media tools. In most of the forums and functions a projector screen is used, with video clips from platforms such as YouTube being shown to disseminate information to the participants. Some of these churches stream their services live each Sunday for their online members around the world (Chiluwa, 2012). The churches also professionally produce their Sunday services on DVDs for sale in their bookstands and shops. In some cases services are streamed live via the Internet to allow non-members of the church to be part of the service as well as individuals who are abroad and who want to stay in touch with their mother churches or ministries (Helland, 2007). For instance during

the thirtieth anniversary of one of these churches, the Sunday celebration service held at the Sports stadium and was streamed live so the members in London could be part of the service that particular Sunday morning. Some of these productions are done wholly in-house whilst in some cases production is outsourced to reputable media companies around the country. These African churches are well represented on social media sites such as Facebook, Twitter, Instagram among others, and use these as a platform to reach out to the public in ways that were totally non-existent a couple of decades ago. The churches use these social media tools to establish their identity, presence and reputation, as will be discussed in the sub-sections below (Kietzmann, 2011). As such, through the live Internet streaming, these churches have a local presence they also have a global presence and participate in the globalisation of Pentecostalism and religion in general. As well as registered local members of the churches they have 'informal members' who follow them at random and take part in their activities through these media platforms (Garton and Wellman, 1995). The challenge with these virtual members is that they endanger religious authority and there is no control over the application of content by the virtual audience (Campbell, 2007).

In spite of the challenges, these churches use mass media to advertise the God they worship, the church as an organization, and as a way of making a statement to the world about who they are. Lehikoinen (2003), assert that the media use by these churches reflects the 'media theology of the institution'. As an addition to Lehikoinen, I posit that the media production of these churches actually reflects their practical theology and enforces their cosmology among their community of believers; a cosmology which is influenced by ties to their countries of origin. Their socio- cultural and philosophical lineages of the African churches are in many cases revealed through these productions. They also become the avenue through which the leaders of these churches carve an image for themselves on the black majority churches' religious landscape in Britain. Not only do they use the media to do this, but also to make a statement to the world around those to secure their share of the religious market share (Asamoah Gyadu, 2004). These modern media outreach tools that the churches employ can help us understand the religio-cultural values of these migrants within the context of transnational migration (Asamoah Gyadu, 2007). Due to the fact that the Ghanaian-led Pentecostal churches are transnational in nature, their use of the media is at times reflective of their past, their present and the future. These productions and their content reveal their past origins and the belief systems they held, as well as their present, and how they intend to be in the future, having made strides towards integration through creating a new identity for themselves. Within the media however, there is very little to show in terms of a deliberate effort and strategy for assisting the migrant members of these churches to integrate into British society as you find in these churches. However, the effort put into these productions gives a certain image of these migrant dominated churches, which affects the self-worth of the migrants, and could go a long way to assist them in their integration efforts. It must be noted that these are all internal programs put together to assist the migrant members and not something of a global appeal, as some of these forums are held privately.

As we found out from the previous section these social welfare interventions are organised in such a way that people do not have to necessarily know the immigration status of individual participants. These strategies are further epitomised in the kind of personal development and motivational sermons that are preached, and which are normally found on their DVDs, making these integration efforts an internal activity rather than external. Ironically, although these churches have the intention to train and educate their predominantly migrant members through the mass media, with the ultimate aim of creating a new identity for the members through integration, cannot be ascertained. The initiatives through the mass media rather seem to promote the pastors, the organisation and God, and the migrant members by inference but not directly. Alternatively the churches can adopted both approaches to reaching out as well. Therefore, I posit that the use of the mass media by the churches is for the promotion of the leaders/ pastors, the churches and God and migrant members by inference, rather than about action or about the direct promotion of migrants and could have been for both motives. That is not to say that they do not intend to use this platform to educate, train and help migrant members, but in practice what is actually happening is contrary to their initiatives as may have been intended.

Promoting the Pastors through Media Initiatives

However, the African churches are able to use the media to their advantage. This is because of the contexts and their main target audiences are accustomed to the churches' use of the media in their places of origin. The use of the media according to Maxwell has become part of the Church's 'Pentecostal self-definition' (Maxwell, 1998). To some extent some of the churches and the pastors use the media, broadly expressing their breaking away from the past where the media has been left in the hands of the devil to accomplish his own plans (Asamoah Gyadu, 2005). And although there is some divisive programming shown on TV, for instance from most of the prophet-led Pentecostal churches featuring deliverance sessions, generally most of the migrants view the use of the media as positive because it gives them a presence in the virtual religious space. The churches claim to use the media to educate and train the migrants towards integration and have maintained this as their motivation for its use. However, as the churches make efforts to carry out their intentions of educating their members and training them towards integrating into British society, the media has also become the grounds for contesting for religious space by the pastors and leaders of these of churches in Britain (Appiah, 2011).

Over time, this has become an issue one cannot ignore. A little over a decade ago on the Sky TV platform one could only mention God TV, Wonderful TV, TBN, EWTN, and Revelation TV as the only Christian TV stations with completely Christian programming. Out of these stations the only station owned by an African was Wonderful TV, which went into liquidation in the last few years. Currently, these are the Christian TV stations using the Sky Media platform for their broadcasting aside from those already mentioned: Open Heavens TV, Daystar, UCB TV, Loveworld TV, Inspiration Network International, Gospel Channel Europe, Eternal Word TV Network, The Word Network, KICC TV, Believe TV, Faith World TV, Olive TV and SonLife Broadcasting Network. These stations also broadcast programmes from other churches that pay for their programmes to be aired. The TV stations which are mainly owned by African churches and predominantly broadcast programmes of the churches with African orientation are: Open Heavens TV, which is owned by the Redeemed Christian Church of God, led by Enoch Adeboye; KICC TV, which is owned by Kingsway International Christian Centre, led by Matthew Ashimolowo; Believe TV, which is owned by the Victorious Pentecostal Assembly, led by Alex Omokodu; Olive TV, which is owned by Gilbert Deya Ministries, led by Gilbert Deya; Faith World TV, which is owned by World Evangelism Bible Church led by Samson Ayorinde; and Loveworld

TV which is owned by Christ Embassy Church led by Chris Oyakhilome. The other Ghanaian TV stations on the Sky TV platform such as Klear TV and ABN, are not designated Christian stations as such but also play host to a number of Ghanaian-led churches.

The influx of these TV stations has also led to a surge in the number of churches and leaders who present programmes on these stations. It is on this stage that most of these pastors promote themselves and also jostle for members from the Christian marketplace to increase their 'market share' and the number of members for their churches (Marleen, 2003). As most of these churches are transnational in nature the rush to be on TV is something that is still happening in the various countries where these churches and pastors originally come from and hold ties. The situation in Britain is a continuation of the phenomenon that exists in the countries of origin and due to the transnational ties the practice and quest to be on TV is carried over to Britain, their current place of settlement (Mitchel, 2005).

Besides the transnational nature of the pursuit and development of a media presence by these churches, it has to be understood that a particular stand of African Christianity, the Pentecostal and neo-Pentecostal by their organisational arrangements 'have remained autochthonous founder-led congregations and the personal charisma and psychology of the leader shapes their orientation' (Asamoah Gyadu, 2004). As a result of the structures that exist in most of these churches, members and the other lay leaders tend to promote the pastor and seek in every possible way to build an image for him or her befitting an individual designated as the face of the church in the media. The image-building quest has particularly been part of African Pentecostalism, and encompasses what pastors wear, eat, drive, where they live, and other accessories available to them as a sign of 'blessing from the Lord' (Meyer, 2002).

As a result, the quest to promote these pastors besides what happens in the media, have in some cases created underground rules not taught or verbalised such as lay leaders and other pastors not driving the same car or similar cars of the same value as that of their senior pastors. In most of these churches, not only are the pastors' seats visibly different from those of the rest of the congregation, but also the senior pastors seats are different. Again, as an indication of the status of these men and women who are perceived with so much reverence and honour as leaders of the churches. In some cases, pastors often join the congregation for worship after the service is well advanced with an usher or appointed chaperone carrying their Bibles, Tablets and personal effects into the service; also an indication of the higher status they enjoy among their members. A transnational perspective helps explain this phenomenon. In most Ghanaian societies during durbar of chiefs or during festivals the chief is the last to appear on the durbar grounds as all those present stand for them to take their seat before everyone else sits. In spite of this transnational twist to this phenomenon there is a similar occurrence in other churches other than black majority Churches where pastors and the top hierarchy of leaders walk into the service late. Therefore this practice of honouring leadership in this particular way could be concluded to be something akin to the Pentecostal and neo-Pentecostal churches, rather than just a cultural influence. However, the cultural transfer element, which is traced as a transnational occurrence, cannot be ruled out completely. It has to be noted that most of the churches use the TV broadcasting and the social media sites more than the newspaper and radio stations which are comparatively expensive to the previously mentioned media platforms.

As part of the promotional endeavour of members and churches of their leaders and pastors, these churches resort to the use of TV broadcasting to showcase their pastors to bring in more people into the churches. There is also the issue of packaging the broadcast and creating an impression of the pastor being a super star who has attained the heights most of the audience are striving to attain, thereby creating an incentive to find out what else they as individuals can do to emulate such attainments.

There is a philosophy that these churches operate by and it is that once your leader gets there you get there too. In some cases being on TV or radio is used as a status symbol. Hiebert notes that:

> The mass media bestow prestige and enhance authority of individuals and groups by legitimizing their status. Recognition by the press or radio or magazines or news reels testifies that one has arrived, that one is important enough to have been singled out from the large anonymous masses, that one's behaviour and opinions are significant enough to require public notice (Hiebert et al, 1985).

There is some credence to what Hiebert et al claim to be the effect of the mass media on the populace regarding the impression it creates amongst them. In order not to create the impression that these media houses are in search of these churches and their leaders to feature them on their platforms it has to be understood that most of the time these media solicitations are strategised and paid for by the churches themselves, and not a free-to-air gesture from the media houses. This action and the sense of urgency of the church is informed by the millennialist beliefs that they are agents for God's end time plan of reaching out to as many people as possible (Hackett, 1998). It is also a deliberate action by the churches themselves to be on those platforms to create that impression on the minds of the populace, as well as to create the impression that yes, that the African-led churches have come of age. But often members of the churches are left to foot the bill for the cost of these broadcasts, thereby increasing the financial burdens on the members of the churches in addition to their usual offerings and tithes. In effect more money is needed to fund the multiple airtime slots.

The content of the broadcasts of these churches can be heard and seen in other churches that are not on TV, so why the rush to get on TV? The TV broadcasts become the grounds for espousing the theology of the churches and how that theology metamorphoses into the practical life of the pastor. In doing so they project the pastor as the object of authentication of the message they hold and preach in the churches, emphasising that 'the appropriation and use of modern media technologies facilitates the dissemination of the Word to the masses' (Hackett, 1998). This disposition to broadcasting and the image building that goes with it has been borrowed from the American TV evangelists such as Oral Roberts and Kenneth Hagin whose broadcasts were on TV in some sub-Saharan African countries such as Ghana and Nigeria in the 1970s. Programming of these broadcasts is done carefully to promote the pastors who speak in them as having something special to give to society. However, as to the direct influence on migrants seeking integration into British society, there is currently no evidence to suggest a direct influence of the broadcast on the integration of migrants.

The pastors are most of the time depicted as having been highly anointed by God and also as being very down to earth in their relationship with the congregations, to prove they are in touch with current social, economic, religious, technological and political trends. Although there have been attempts to 'suggest their participation in the globalisation process is not merely an attempt to adapt to modern trends in keeping with change and progress' (Asamoah Gyadu, 2004). There is no doubt that these pastors divide opinion on their mode of operations within their churches but these operations also become the vehicle to enforce the African traditional worldview that answers to life's sometimes complex problems can be obtained supernaturally through those whom the gods and ancestors have appointed. Therefore the portrayal of the pastors in the media as successful 'former migrants' is intended so that the migrant members or audience can look at the pastors' lives now and aspire to attain the same life and even better lives than they have through their prescribed mode of integration.

This seems to justify their portrayal in the mass media avenues that they use for this purpose.

Promoting the Church and its International Connections

Besides the promotion of the pastors as the faces of the churches, the second element for promotion on these mass media avenues are the churches themselves as ministries or organisations of repute. A critical look at the websites, social media sites, internally published newsletters, magazines and programmes broadcasted by these churches gives one the impression that the images placed on these sites are carefully designed to align with other elements of the church in its promotion endeavour. On the churches' websites there are pictures of cross sections of their congregations taken from very good photographic angles; their church buildings; smartly dressed staff; and groups who are smartly dressed and organised, to complete the story of success. There are pictures featuring other activities and programmes of the church such 'Day in the Park' and summer picnics; games; community initiatives and many more. The audio-visual depictions of the churches in the mass media are deliberately done to create the impression that the churches are in tune with current social trends. However, these images they create of themselves also depict the churches as projects of modernity from the perspective of consumption. There are instances that those presentations in the mass media are targeted towards the upwardly mobile youth in the communities who many of these churches consider as the next generation of leaders, in all sectors of the nation. The depictions of the churches through the images used in these media productions are of very successful people enjoying the high life and if anyone associates with the church they are more likely to be among them. According to Meyer, 'conversion to Christianity also was a conversion to modernity, and Christians formed the new elites in colonial society' (Meyer, 2002). If that was the case then there would be no need to embark on initiatives to assist migrant members, some of whom are grappling with basic issues of daily survival, and for whom 'modernity' might have eluded though they seek it earnestly. In reality it is not as the images would suggest, although each of these churches have members who are well placed in society and fit the depictions in the mass media campaigns.

The other reason why the churches have these representations in the media is to give them a global appeal, creating the impression that they have arrived on the international scene as major players in the religious arena, with answers to the problems that confront humanity (Meyer, 2002). The connection to this internationalisation phenomenon is embedded in the idea that their message is universal to other problems confronting humanity beyond their local context. To further enhance their international pedigree as churches, they tend to introduce speakers from other parts of the world in their churches that they usually advertise on their mass media platforms. One cannot fathom the importance of this for these churches except that it is placed within the context of being a 'blessing of God' for their efforts (Asamoah Gyadu, 2004).

This situation can be set within the context of the theories of migration where migrants believe that their migration is not only prompted by socio-economic or political factors but also by religious factors, where the migrants believe God sends them. Within the theological understanding of these churches having friends in high places that they could potentially rely on at any point is a blessing, something they refer to as 'divine connections'. This sometimes features in their prayer meetings where they pray that God brings them into contact with people who can be sources of help to them. However, this psyche is actually not a recent phenomenon: the mainline churches in certain countries in Africa similarly invited rich prominent men of a high social standing to chair 'harvest' celebrations, yearly fundraising initiatives of the churches to support major church projects. There is always a yearning to look to their connections elsewhere for some form of support or affirmation. Studies into the expectations of relatives of migrants abroad have shown that relatives wait on their support and remittances for poor family members in the countries of origin, because it is assumed that migrants are in the land of endless economic opportunities: there is little or no awareness of their struggles as migrants (Arhinful, 2002).

The issue of remittances from migrants for instance has made prayer prophesies for visas a significant part of these churches' requests of their members in the countries of origin as well as in the host countries (Van Dijk, 1997). The reason for these kinds of prayer is because of the apparent difficulties in obtaining visas to countries in Europe and the Americas, in spite of the fact that the embassies and High Commissions in these African countries claim the applications are each processed on their own merit. Notably, the African Presidents who attract most direct foreign investment are those who have connections abroad and therefore from a socio-political point of view these churches are only mimicking on a micro scale what happens on a macro scale within their countries of origin. This development from their religio-cultural roots as African churches undermines assertions that this phenomenon is an imitation of a largely 'American phenomenon' because of the perception that North America's superior technology and material abundance represents the kind of modernity that these churches seek to portray through their mass media platforms (Rogers, 1995).

These churches seem to use mass media to advertise the church as a solution centre for human problems. The sermons preached and captions of happy people either singing or enthusiastically responding to the sermons being preached with shouts of affirmation and approval sends the message to the viewers that one can be happy in church. This is a significant striking feature in these African churches in the sense that, contrasting this with the mainline white British churches, it is easy to map out a unique identity for these churches by the show of enthusiasm and vibrancy exhibited by the members. Also one of the driving forces behind all that is done is their ambition to use their mass media platforms to draw members to their churches. These platforms provide information on how one can become a member of the church and be a part of the success story. This becomes the eventual expectation of the churches for every minor detail they put into their mass media campaigns. If these did not culminate into gaining an increase in their membership, these churches would be unlikely to pump in the huge sums of money that go into these mass media campaigns. However, not all of them get the desired increase in membership as other factors may have an influence, such as the packaging of these productions. Though they may not admit that the inconsistencies on the paid media platforms are a result of the packaging and money problems, these hold the clue to inconsistencies in representations on the various media platforms.

It is possible that these African churches may fall short in using their media platforms to directly educate and train their migrant members to integrate into British society and also in helping them to create a unique African-British identity. The Christian dimensions of these Africans' participation in global affairs cannot be overlooked since they are making significant contributions in the process of globalisation of African Christianity in general (Bediako, 2000).

Promoting God

An additional motive in these churches' use of mass media is their promotion of God, and since God from a particular perspective can be considered as a globalised commodity in the religious market place, it places the churches within a certain sphere of acceptance of those who patronise 'the God commodity' who is inclusive and accepting in all social, political, economic and cultural market places and therefore epitomises the integration agenda. The churches that present themselves on the mass media platforms, especially on television, are very much aware that their audience is varied and does not just include Christians. For instance, the audience may include those who consider themselves spiritual but does not necessarily reflect in their church attendance as their spirituality is premised on a sense of awareness, of a suprareality or a state of being related to a divine, order of reality (Wuthnow, 2001). With society increasingly being said to be secularising the churches use these platforms to advertise the God they serve as being a relevant part of everyday life. There is awareness that the mass media is open to all and there is seen to be a contest of spiritual power and authority over the airwaves, so the church has no choice but to step to the mark by asserting the power of God (Asamoah Gyadu, 2005). This fact is encapsulated in Viney's description of the nature of the audience of these broadcasts:

> A closer examination of the audience shows that religious programmes are still watched by the majority of the adult population. And although viewers over 55 are well represented in the audience for many programmes, the audience for religious television is in reality more diverse than public and broadcasting industry perceptions would suggest (Viney, 1999).

Therefore other than the broadcast of Christian stations intended exclusively for the migrant church members or Christians in general, there is a sense that 'non-church-goers' or non-Christians are equally a target audience for these churches. It has to be said however that Viney's assertion refers to public television stations and makes references to BBC and ITV and their religious programmes. However, there is some similarity with other independent private stations where most of these religious programmes are aired. This initiative seems to fulfil their reverse mission agenda of bringing back African Christianity with all its fervour to the Western world. It has to be noted that there are no signs that these media campaigns advertising God have attracted any people from the predominantly white communities, who represent the majority of the population; most of these churches have very small numbers of white members. There was no indication as to whether these white members are married to blacks or were there simply as worshippers. In most of these African churches in Europe, the vast majority of their white members become members because their black spouses attend those churches. The wider reason to capture this occurrence is the Ghanaian cultural influence on the practice and organisation of the church service, which is a transnational influence. The focus of these broadcasts by the migrant churches has largely been targeted to the migrant community. Advertising this God as the source of strength in dealing with the everyday struggles of the impoverished migrant makes them relevant to their target audience.

There is a constant reminder on these media platforms by the churches of the fact that the pastors who present these sermons are God's men and the churches are God's houses. God's men or Men of God as they are often referred to, go on to show how God is brought to the fore in the achievements and attainments of those who present these programmes for the churches. The audience are given the impression that God is responsible for all that happens and all they see in those productions. This applies to the actual production props and the testimonies of God's activities in the lives of people from all kinds of life situations. Once again, some of the things they attribute to God are debatable although there is no suggestion to limit the involvement of God in any individual's life. Most of the time accounts are subjective but some of the issues are quite trivial to attract a non-believer to this God. For instance in one of the clips was a testimony of someone who claimed to have been looking for a job for months, until the pastor called her out and prayed for her against a spirit that prevented her from obtaining a job. About a week later, she was called by a company she had applied to a couple of months previously but had received no response from, except an acknowledgement letter of receipt of the application. She said that they called her unexpectedly and asked her to start work without having to attend an interview. These testimonies are not verifiable on their own, and can be problematic.

The whole idea is about personalising God to their audiences, creating an image of God as a being interested in the everyday mundane affairs of those who seek him (Meyer, 2010). The theological problem is the extent of God's involvement in an individual's life, a perspective that could be traced to the African holistic worldview which states that everything physical has a corresponding spiritual cause which is 'interpenetrating and inseparable, yet with distinguishable parts' (Okorocha, 1987). Africans 'believe in the existence of two worlds which are in constant interaction with one another and occurrences in each affect the other and yet are distinct from each other' (Appiah, 2017). The interwoven nature of African traditional beliefs is a significant point in the transnational discourse in that though they are physically removed from their countries of origin these African migrant Christians seem to be hugely influenced by the belief systems of their countries of origin. Considering the example of the churches' television productions, these churches are in this case affecting the nature and development of Christianity in the western nations and also providing an alternative to the kind of Christianity that the western nations have been used to as expressed in the mainline churches. That aside, the programming is meant to teach migrants and assist them to deal with issues that confront them using the scriptures.

The audience are also given the impression that these churches are the houses of God; God leads and rules in those houses and blesses those who belong to those houses. The message is that everything you see in the production is as a result of the involvement of God who is the solution to the peculiar problem of migrant's settlement and integration. Critical analysis of these television programmes reveal that a large chunk of the emphasis of sermons and the entire production reflect the mission of the churches. In these broadcasts of the African churches, suffering is

attributed to the devil, which is also an issue of a cosmological leaning. The God they serve is the God of the here and now and not much of the eschatological views of the church universal is discussed on these television programmes. Therefore the focus of the message resonates with the migrant in their efforts to integrate into the host society. Gyekye sums up this point of view as he notes that,

...Traditional African religions do not appear to be concerned about the kind of life that will be led by the immortal soul. They present no elaborate doctrines about what are referred to in other religions as 'the last things' (in Western Theology, 'eschatology')... in contrast to the silence on matters relating to the destiny of the soul in afterlife, the emphasis on the pursuit and attainment of human well-being in this world is unrelenting (Gyekye, 1998).

It should therefore not come as a surprise, given observations about the focus of these Pentecostal churches in Britain on the existential realities of their members, that their broadcasts do not get into theological debates about the 'last things'. It is however that most of these pastors also do not engage in these eschatological debates because most of them have had no extensive theological education prior to their appointment to lead their churches. To these pastors promoting God is promoting the source of help for the migrant and the myriad of challenges they face in their efforts to integrate into society. From my perspective, some of the teachings are populist in nature; with an emphasis on scriptural truths discovered by others, rather than on teachings derived from deep personal theological convictions and leanings. This in itself creates a unique religious identity for the churches, which I would refer to as 'African-British' identity. This is an identity that hinges largely on religion as the focal point for social networks and expression; and therefore the transformation of the churches through the socio-cultural influence of British society creates a situation in which the churches are mimicking both the past heritage and present social context. It is the combination of the factors of nurture and nature that determine the identity of the churches.

The 'Nature and Nurture' Combination Determining African-British Religious Identity

In spite of the influence of African traditional cosmology on the practice and theological outlook of the African Pentecostal churches there is an attempt to create a religious identity that can be traced to both Africa and

Britain as a pathway to integration. The churches have assigned themselves the task of charting and appropriating religious space outside the cultural contexts from which they emerged in order to legitimize their place within British society (Adogame, 2003). Some specific features become apparent when one takes a critical look at the churches.

Mass media presentations of the churches on TV and elsewhere give these churches a unique identity. Anyone familiar with such broadcasts would realise that these broadcasts are not the same aesthetically, theologically and professionally as those from the USA. Despite the fact that these churches sometimes copy aspects of their presentation from their 'older American brothers' who have years of broadcasting experience, broadcasts produced in Britain have an element of British cultural values to them. This is partly because they are produced in Britain and the footage is cut to the taste of the wider British audience who are somewhat conservative in expression compared to the sometimes 'over the top' presentation of their transatlantic neighbours, the Americans. In as much as aspects of the broadcast can even be copied from elsewhere, these presentations define the identity of the presenters. In other words, the content of the broadcasts is an expression of the identity of the individuals and the churches they lead, as most of the time the leader's ideological values influence the formation of the ideological values of the followers. In relation to this, Fiske (1987) asserts that 'characters on television are not just representations of individual people but are encodings of ideology, 'embodiments of ideological values'. In addition, the distinguishing factor of this identity discourse lies in 'their commitment to a "full gospel", highly evangelistic, Bible-centred, not forcibly, but leaning toward, literalist, religious orientation'. This would set these pastors and their churches apart from each other whether it's the mainline historic churches or Pentecostals from both black and white communities (Hackett, 1998). This is an identity forged from the cultural heritage of the churches and their leaders as Hackett's assertion referred to an observation on the African religious scene.

Again, looking at these African churches they come across as very well organised, with formalised organisational hierarchies and administrative structures; but a closer look within reveals that they are less formalized than they appear and lack functional structures. Power is concentrated in the hands of the senior pastor who is involved in all day-to-day administrative management of the church. Most of the churches have a very lean paid staff and volunteers are usually relied upon in the running of the church services, other than management. The interaction between the nature and nurture aspect of their religious identity can be drawn from the fact that most churches in Britain, and the Charity Commission regulates all churches. This requires that certain administrative and management policies be put in place to ensure the smooth management of the churches, which are required by law to register as Charities. The Charity Commission for England and Wales declares itself to be 'a non-Ministerial Government Department, part of the Civil Service' and to be 'completely independent of Ministerial influence and also independent from the sector it regulates', with 'a number of quasi-judicial functions where it uses powers similar to those of the High Court'.

Once registered, there are certain administrative and management requirements such as the submission of annual report and accounts to the Commission, which detail among other things the financial standing of the church and the focus and forecasts of its activities in the previous year and year ahead. This is purely a British institutional initiative, which churches must comply with if the Charity Commission registers them as a Charity. These issues of compliance with Charity Commission regulations are environmental factors, which I refer to as nurture, since the state of the churches is determined by external factors, which are imposed by the social cultural context within which they are established. This attempt by the churches to comply with the Charity Commission regulations gives them a unique identity akin to the British mode of institutional organisation, compared to the administrative and organisational structures these churches might have adopted from their countries of origin. In most countries of

Africa until recently in Rwanda where government has specific guidelines for' religious enterprises', there are currently no regulatory body that deals directly with churches as the Charity Commission in Britain does to ensure that certain administrative, hierarchical and management procedures are in place to curb excesses and to assist the churches in accomplishing their goals. Notwithstanding the seamless interaction of nature and nurture that gives the churches a unique African-British identity, the African churches are still largely practically and functionally loose; they are less formal in their administrative structures and management as control is often in the hands of the senior pastor.

A factor that contributes to this is that the Charities Commission's regulations allow the pastors of the churches to act as trustees of the charity and therefore the church. Charity trustees are the people who form the governing body or 'board' of a charity. 'They may be called trustees, directors, board members, governors or committee members, but they are the people with ultimate responsibility for directing the business of the charity'. This permission to allow pastors of the churches to act as trustees concentrates too much power and control in the hands of the senior pastor and so churches still mimic the African church structures, although not entirely.

The African churches organise themselves in such a way as to 'validate their sense of ethnic and religious identity', through their established networks with other churches and in some cases with other organisations interested in diaspora matters (Adogame, 2003). This kind of network with other organisations is not limited to churches alone but also to other religious groups such as the African traditional religions. In 2011 a series of meetings were organized by the Donipa Foundation International in Amsrerdam, Holland, which invited Nana Kwaku Bonsam a popular Indigenous Religious Priest based in Ghana to visit and divine for interested Ghanaians and other Africans who needed spiritual help (Appiah, 2011).

The networking seems to be within the African communities which appears to continue to advance their African identity but it is also a unique identity in their current context in that there is a development of ideological values that are intended to mediate the difficulties associated with their migration, such as their denigration and demonization within sections of the media, and to further enhance their status within British society (Gerloff, 2000). One emerging aspect of this networking endeavour is the pastors preaching in each other's churches with introductions such as 'an honorary member of this church...', 'a brother and friend of this church....' inter alia. These introductions usually state how long these pastors have been in Britain, their accomplishments and their significance as a friend of the church and in the community of migrants. These kinds of pulpit exchanges and introductions are intended to breakdown every barrier that may exist in the minds of people about the differences between the pastors and their churches about their differences. These pulpit exchanges help to cure the unhealthy competition among these churches and their pastors, which sometimes tend to create a huge gap between some of them with respect to the extent of their influence in their communities. It is worth noting that there is some who are much accepted and respected by the wider host community and as a result seem to see themselves above the others. Besides, the networking happens on different levels such as 'between churches; across language divisions (mainly French and English); and between African communities' (Gerloff, 2000). These levels of networking often also serve as points of divisions too. Therefore the exchanges of pulpits and the celebratory introductions are used as means of bridging any potential gaps that may exist and as a way of showing acceptance. In doing this they validate their religious and ethnic identity.

The Multi-cultural Pendulum: Oscillations of Religious and Social Convictions to establish African-British Identity.

The nature of transnationalism means that migrants bring their socio-cultural and religious orientation with them into every aspect of their lives in their new settled environment, which gives them their unique identity. The migrant's socio-cultural and religious orientation provides the basis for networking within and outside of their community as a means of validating their identity and consequently use it as leverage. Through the expression of this socio-cultural and religious orientation most migrants are caught between what has been imbibed and practiced over time and what they are exposed to in their places of settlement. They are left to make decisions on a daily basis between their religious convictions and the prevailing societal norms. There are instances where these societal norms of their settled community challenge their religious convictions and therefore are left to belong to one side of the oscillation of the pendulum of multiculturalism. An example is on the issue of co-habitation, which would be discussed in detail later in the chapter. There are also times when the exposure to the culture causes some of these migrants to close up to the culture of their host society, especially if their experiences challenge them to shift their paradigm, such as kissing, engaging in sexual activity whilst dating among others. However in most cases, there is a hybrid culture, which is a fusion of some of the desirable aspects of the hosts' culture, and the migrants' imbibed culture: this inevitably aids in the process of integration. This development takes place with regard to the relative relationships between people of similar ethnicity, their places of origin and settlement, and it is evidenced by alterations and adjustments in the people's lifestyle (Panayi, 2010).

The African migrants were seen in this study to have developed a new form of identity that is neither wholly British nor wholly African: it is African-British. The term African-British refers to individuals and groups of people who first identifies themselves with their ethnic African origins but at the same time considers themselves as part of their new society. Historically, the emergence of the concept of dual identity can be associated with the level of hostility which post-war migrant groups have faced over time: migrants were forced to pledge their loyalty to Britain, while their ethnic origins and even in some cases ties to their countries of origin were emphasised (Panayi, 2010). However, this does not eliminate the dilemma of choices the migrants face each day between their religious convictions and the cultural norms in their place of settlement. Having an African-British identity means having an altered lifestyle which enables an individual to integrate successfully into society without necessarily abandoning their religious convictions altogether. Therefore, although one may consider some aspects of the culture to violate the religious convictions they hold, over time they soften their stance to accept it as the prevalent norm but not necessarily as the right thing to do. For instance a couple may decide to have a child together whilst unmarried which maybe tolerated by British culture, but there could be a counterforce of guilt against them because, it is against the religious position that African Pentecostals may fundamentally hold. There are also instances where migrants abandon their own religious convictions to enable them fit in as part of the process of integrating.

Co-habitation and the Marriages of Convenience

Marriages and weddings in Africa are spiritual, economic and social affairs that involve the coming together of two independent lives, two distinct families and even two communities. The fundamentals of nation building have always involved marriage, as the wellbeing of individuals affects families and families make up the population. The soundness of an individual influences significantly and collectively the soundness of a community and of the nation as a whole. Marriage is a rite of passage that is very much cherished and celebrated because it is considered to bring new life and hope into the family and community. It is often characterised by a series of celebrations notably marked by eating drinking and making merry. An extended family system, which normally encompasses the entire community, is important in a marriage in most parts of Africa, as they are often involved in sharing responsibilities of rites to mark the occasion. In instances where a woman is unable to have her own biological children, her role as a mother is often accepted. This role of motherhood for women without children may not be the same in every community as in some cases the individual's social status determines the kind of treatment she receives as a woman without children. It is without question that in most instances the whole community considers that it has a collective responsibility in contracting marriages and even bringing up the offspring. The popular Akan adage *'baakofo ntiti abofra'* means that an individual does not do the bringing up of children.

There is always a cultural shock regarding how British society regards marriage in general. In spite of the fact that there are so many similarities with the African system of marriage where a man and a woman living together in a sexual relationship, are expected to have performed the necessary rites and duly recognised by society as husband and wife. One has to be a conservative British person to hold on to the kind of ideals that most Africans hold about marriage. Migrants are sometimes completely put off by their exposure to this cultural difference, but like all other elements of the British culture that seems opposed to the religious beliefs and cultural orientation, in the course of time they accept it and become participants in the culture. In most British communities it is acceptable for a man and woman to live together and even have children without having to be formally married. Some of these couples eventually get married but it is not an issue to be frowned upon by many people. It should be noted that people do sometimes live together as a couple without being formally married in parts of Africa but there are cultural penalties to it that deters people. For instance in the Akan culture when a woman dies whilst living with a man who has not as yet performed the marriage rites, although parents and families of the couple may be aware and approve of their living together, the man is made to perform the marriage rites of the dead woman, becoming the husband of the dead woman. After these marriage rites have been performed, since the man has now become the husband of the dead woman, he is also made to go through the widower-hood rites and consequently made to shoulder the cost of the funeral, as any husband would organise the funeral of a spouse. This is one reason that sometimes makes people think it is much simpler to rather get properly married before living together and having children because in the event of this eventuality, the cost is sometimes too high to bear.

On one hand, whilst one may think that cultural values should inform the choices people make concerning their decisions to live with another person, some migrants practice co-habitation because of the lack of penalties in their current context. In an informal conversation with certain young people in the churches, some of them were living with people they were not married to. There was an acknowledgement that this carries it's on own penalties: should there be a pregnancy whilst unmarried and one of the couple has a visible role to play in church then the rules of the church to suspend an individual may apply. This is one thing that seems to depict the churches as hypocritical in their application of the rules of morality. It is also a difficult situation for the churches to deal with without supportive legislation, in a country of rule of law where individuals have many rights. The church only falls on its moral authority to affirm and in some cases enforce these spiritual-moral rules. For instance, 'marriage is compounded by the social culture of the 'baby-mama' syndrome. This according to some experts is a manifestation of immaturity and lack of moral responsibility'. In the past, the reason why young couples had children was to help them on to the social housing ladder, as it was much easier for the council to give an expecting single mother a flat than to provide the same for a married couple. The Conservative government led by David Cameron sought to change this state of affairs because of the economic burden they create, not necessarily because of the spiritual implications. However, unlike the position of the politicians, the stance of these African churches to discourage people from cohabiting is from a spiritual perspective. They teach abstinence from sex until marriage often quoting Hebrews 13:4 'Marriage *is* honourable among all, and the bed undefiled; but fornicators and adulterers God will judge'. However, this has not deterred migrants from getting themselves involved in such relationships. It is more of a cultural change that those involved look at the economic or social benefits rather than the spiritual aspects. Migrants in spite of their spiritual convictions may be prone to cohabit for socio-economic reasons due to the difficulties they face, even though churches provide assistance as discussed.

Another dimension to this is that there are instances where, for the convenience of obtaining the necessary resident permit to stay in Britain legally, migrants cohabit or marry British citizens to afford them the opportunity to live in the country. The churches not necessarily condone this practice except they choose not to talk openly about it as it could make people feel condemned and eventually leave the church. What they have chosen to do is to introduce them to the opportunities available through the immigration forums organized by the churches. It is important to note however that not everyone lives with a partner for the purposes of getting onto the social housing ladder or obtaining a resident permit (Dunt, 2013). There are those who are genuinely in love but cannot afford a wedding: because of the kind of wedding they dream of is expensive and they have to live together and wait until they have saved enough. In some African societies like Ghana, weddings can be equally as elaborate, involving feasting and dancing for days within a community. They can be very simple, or they can even be performed in huge marriage ceremonies involving many different couples. But one fundamental issue regarding weddings is that, since people live communally, some family members who have some responsibility for the couple who are getting married take up the cost of these elaborate weddings. In more conservative traditional areas, a couple living together without performing the rites is an abomination. As a result, the entire society takes responsibility for the marriage: women who are ready for marriage are given tutorials on how to have successful and happy marriages. People take a collective responsibility for the marriages and that normally includes cost.

The adoption of the Ghanaian-Akan culture in the practice of marriage of Ghanaians in the churches for instance is a confirmation of the strong transnational ties these churches share. The link between the practices of the churches to the practice in Ghana is found in the traditional marriage celebration normally referred to as 'engagement', and the follow-up of the church wedding, which sometimes takes place sometimes hours apart from each other. Also, this leads to the examination of the extent to which these churches have contextualised their beliefs and practices as discussed. The practice of cohabitation by these African Christian migrants does not only violate the law of God as the conservatives would claim but it also points to the loosing of the grip of cultural ties of the place of origin on these members of these new societies. In spite of how cohabitation and marriage is generally considered and viewed in the Pentecostal community, these oscillations of religious and social convictions which sometimes polarise communities because of their differing views and perceptions is a sign of the exposure to a new culture. The attempt of the individuals caught up in oscillations at the different ends of the multicultural pendulum have to find a way to adapt in order to integrate into the community. The decisions that are made by the individual may on their part be the way to negotiate the terms of their stay in Britain as migrants, independent of what others judge them to be, either from a religious or socio-political perspective. It is not suggested that it is an easy process, as some may have to abandon their religious beliefs or cultural orientation in order to enable them integrate through sharing vital affinities with other members of the British society.

Church Worship and Liturgy

One of the distinctive features of the African Pentecostal churches and their counterparts of the mainline historic churches is their unique form of expressional worship, characterised by singing of loud songs, shouts of praise by the congregation, drumming and vigorous dancing and speaking in tongues in congregational prayer. The other characteristic is also the duration of their church services. Most African churches have a relatively shorter service than their mother churches in Africa, however compared to the predominantly white mainline churches, the time these

African churches spend in church for their services are still much longer. The average duration of services in these Pentecostal churches is about three to four hours, not including the time people spend on the premises socialising after the service is over. Time for socialising is even much longer in churches who have other quasi-commercial activity because they have a catering facility selling snacks on their premises and people spend more time with friends as they eat. This can be argued to be the culture of most of these African churches, and a definitive characteristic of the some of the African churches in Britain.

When these African churches set up branches or their leaders set up branches, cultural context in which they operate differ. Work patterns and times at which people go to work influence the time and duration of services. There were instances during the services where people came in late from work in their work uniforms whilst others left to go to work before the service officially ended. Awareness of this trend would make the leadership make adjustments to their services as most of the migrant members do a rotational shift and Sundays happen to be a day of work for some of them. In a few Ghanaian-led Pentecostal churches examned, there is a conscious effort to attract non-Ghanaian and non-African members, although they have not as yet succeeded with that objective. This is partly because the services are organised in a way that reflect the current cultural context.

A preliminary conclusion may be that the personal outlook of the pastors of these churches – itself influenced by their cultural exposure – plays a major role in developing of the culture of these churches. The other conclusion is that strong ties to mother churches in Africa influence the culture in these churches and ultimately these affect the speed with which these churches integrate into British society by adapting to the British way of doing things. In both cases, churches are quite different, although they have varying degrees of likeness to the Pentecostal church culture in Britain. The churches seem to have an identity that is an amalgamation of cultural values from both Britain and the African countries where they originate. This new identity is not limited to the church culture but is also reflected in their messages.

Personal Giving and Money Management as a Tool of Integration

One issue with a multi-cultural dimension that helps in defining identity is migrants' culture of parting with money and how they manage their money in general. Most African societies are communal in nature which means that what belongs to one belongs to the community. Children born into the community are children for everyone. Any adult at all in the community can ask any young person at all to run an errand for them, in return this person can be invited to eat in the home of that particular adult or even be given a gift. People serve one another in the community they also share in their responsibility for one another. Even with economic and technological advancement and the cultural influences of individualism from the west, not much has changed. During times of rites of passage such as naming ceremonies at a birth popularly known as outdooring, marriage ceremonies such as weddings and engagements which is normally the traditional marriage ceremonies, funerals for the dead, most people celebrate with giving of gifts and providing other forms of support. Giving to one another is fundamental to the collective cultural value that people hold and also holds them together as one people. Giving is seen as a way of showing responsibility as well as being a social insurance scheme where those who support others in times of need will themselves be supported when in need (Funmati, 2010). It is this network of support for one another within the African communities, and the subsequent social capital built on the back of this economic capital through the churches become a duct for integration from an integration point of view of the churches.

Some of the Pentecostal churches in Africa are self-financing. Being self-financing means that they have no links with churches abroad that give them aid in financing their activities and projects and they do not accept any form of assistance from foreign churches and para-church organisations. Pastors and the church leadership encourage members using scriptural texts to give towards projects and to the leadership of the churches. At a point in the development of the Pentecostal charismatic movement, there was an emergence of a pan-Africanist wave which was led by Mensa Otabil the founder of ICGC Ghana, who encouraged not only his members but also other pastors under his sphere of influence to reject foreign donations from richer and bigger Pentecostal churches abroad and to take the destiny of their churches into the their own hands and into the hands of God. He taught that accepting foreign aid was a new form of colonisation by western religious powers. In a related issue in 1995 shortly after which he passed away, Lester Sumrall was in Ghana with aid to distribute to the communities and his local anchors to coordinate the distribution of the aid were the Bishop Nicholas Duncan Williams of Action Chapel and Apostle Yaw Adu of House Prayer Church International in Koforidua, Ghana.

Sumrall was an influential American Evangelist who was considered as one of the pioneers of Christian television. Towards the latter part of his life he was engaged in organising food aid to parts of Africa. On their arrival most Pastors and leaders of the Pentecostal charismatic fraternity were there but notably absent was Mensa Otabil. Otabil's absence at the meeting was attributed to the aid that was brought by these foreign donors. So strong was this view that in 1998 when Central University College obtained accreditation to operate as a university college in Ghana, a popular Pentecostal church in the United States intended to make a donation of about 50 computers to the school's computer laboratory but their gesture was rejected. Instead around that same time, Matthew Ashimolowo, the Nigerian Pastor and founder of KICC in London made a donation of 80 computers that was accepted and announced in the church in Accra and at the school. It was a gesture that was accepted because it came from an African source. Another recent occurrence was when Mensa

Otabil went to speak at the newly built Perez Chapel of the Word Miracle Church International led by Bishop Charles Agyin-Asare. Mensa Otabil made a comment to congratulate the church for their contributions to building the house of God and said that the edifice they have built would have taken years by the Government of Ghana to build even with aid from abroad. This comment was received with much cheers and shouts from the congregation. The pan-Africanist views notwithstanding, most African countries including Ghana, in particular run their economies virtually on aid from foreign donors and there are churches that accept foreign aid either directly or indirectly from rich church in Europe and the United States (Whiltfield, 2010). Most of the Ghanaian-led Pentecostal churches are self-financed and self-managed apart from a few whose branches receive support from their headquarters in Accra because a percentage of their income goes to their mother churches in their places of origin in Africa.

Apart from this example, African churches raise all the monies needed for projects within the church from the members of the church. Due to the fact that most of their members are predominantly African, their support for church community from their country of origin is meant to have an influence on their giving in support of the churches. Then there comes the situation in Britain, where some pastors and leaders claim people do not give: this is not just in reference to members of the church but also in reference to the general public. This is a subjective analysis of the situation depending on who you are and where you find yourself. Some have recounted their experience with giving at their places of work where during special celebratory occasions by colleagues at the office, managers and other staff members asked other staff to donate, and to their amazement, it was all coins. The result was that the amount collected at the office did not exceed £50, so for them the British do not have the same level support for community projects. An often referenced incident is the issue of the financial malfeasance charges that were levelled against Matthew Ashimolowo where he was asked to repay the amount of money the church used to buy him a car among other gifts on his birthday. Contrary to what this informant claims, an article in April 2009 carried by the Guardian newspaper states from its own research that:

> Charity Commission investigators of financial irregularities; Ashimolowo was ordered to repay £200,000 after it emerged he used church assets to buy a £13,000 Florida timeshare and given £120,000 on his birthday celebrations, including £80,000 on a car (Guardian, 2009).

To some, the further changes and amendments introduced by the charity commission in allowing charity trustees to be those who also serve as pastors of the church attests to the acknowledgment of the African way of life regarding giving. However, some don't seem to know that Ashimolowo was asked to step down from the board of trustees and a new board elected to run the Trust, suggested by the Guardian newspaper. As to whether this was an admittance of guilt it is not known. Giving in the churches is high as the Guardian's research on the church showed. They state in comparative terms to the Church of England that:

> …church's wealth stems largely from the donations it encourages from its 8,000-strong largely African and Caribbean congregation. They gave £9.5m in tithes and offerings in the 18 months to April 2008, dwarfing the £33,000 that the average Church of England congregation gave over the same period (Guardian, 2009).

The statistics is staggering in comparing giving in a typical African Pentecostal church to a predominantly white church, however the Church of England has black members too. Those of the Anglican Communion in other parts of the world including Africa continue to worship in Church of England churches in Britain. Not all African Pentecostal Churches are so rich and have such generous members, because giving can also be related to the kind of jobs the members do for instance. A member of

KICC interviewed by the Guardian said that;

> People give because of how they have been blessed by what they
> receive from the church the teaching, the prayer and the church
> community," said Soji Otudeko, Director of finance. "People
> give voluntarily and because of their love of the work of God
> (Guardian, 2009).

This statement shifts the focus of giving in the churches by the members
from a transnational perspective to a giving that is merely based on the
understanding of spiritual principles as taught by the pastors and leaders
from the scriptures. It is a generalisation and there is not always evidence
to suggest that the situation with regards to giving in one church can be
generalised to all African churches.

Summary and Discussion

In Britain various policies, laws and rules are established to make
sure that the qualified migrants are allowed into the country to make a
contribution to building its society. As a result, specific strategies are put
in place to help these migrants integrate into British society. It is reckoned
that until migrants have fully integrated they would not be able to make
their contribution to their host communities. However, further studies and
understanding of the life of the migrant and the processes of integration
brought about various changes in the rhetoric of integration using the
term assimilation. Ultimately in spite of the struggle to find appropriate
terms to describe this process of integration, by examining policies and
rules migrants were encouraged to take personal responsibility in the
process of integration. The Home Office together with United Kingdom
Border Agency established 'Life in the UK Test' for instance, which every
migrant applying for settlement in Britain must pass in order to proceed
with his or her application. From the point of view of politicians, this is
with the intention of assisting migrants to integrate but it is perceived by

the migrant as nothing but a money making scheme by the government from those who make a decision to remain in Britain.

Over time it became evident, that most of the regulations and policies were initiatives derived from the perspective of the politicians and policy makers but do not necessarily take into account how the migrants themselves see as the process of integration. A gap therefore emerged which other civil society groups and non-governmental organisations stepped up to fill. The African churches, which have a considerable amount of migrants, see and experience first hand the challenges migrants face as they make their efforts to integrate into British society. As a result they set up their own initiatives to assist their migrant members. Most of the initiatives to assist their members to integrate are internal in nature. These initiatives have included: welfare assistance to migrants in the form of financial hand-outs; holding immigration and nationality forums to inform members of how to regularise their stay and prevent falling foul of the law; organising personal development and leadership training for members to give them tools for personal effectiveness and to increase their confidence, which is considered the key to success in every area of endeavour; and financial empowerment and business workshops. The churches have also used external training agencies to bring information and skill development to the members. As part of this the churches have used both local speakers and international speakers with strong ties to their communities.

In delivering the training, and disseminating information to the migrant members, the churches use various media platforms to train and disseminate information to their migrant members. These initiatives have included selling video productions of church services and buying airtime on the various Christian Television Networks on the Sky platform. The proliferation of Christian TV networks has somehow served as an impetus for these churches in their quest to train and educate members. However a critical examination of their dependence on the media reveals that, instead of the migrants being beneficiaries of the programmes, they are also the funders of the productions: it is the pastors that get promoted, it is God that is advertised, and the church that is out-doored to the world as part of the motives for their media broadcasts. It is not being suggested that these three main areas of focus by the churches were intended but in this does seem to be what can be observed.

Eventually the intention of the churches is that these media initiatives will assist their members to integrate into British society and in the process develop a Ghanaian-British identity. Transnationalism holds that the migrant is supposed to maintain ties, including a cultural tie, and creating a Ghanaian-British identity has to do with taking on some aspects of the British culture and fusing it with Ghanaian culture. Therefore the migrants develop an identity that is neither wholly Ghanaian nor wholly British. It is evident that the process of developing this identity is not always easy as there are times migrants are caught between their religious convictions from their transnational ties and the culture of their host community. There are contrasts between the practices in the churches of their places of origin and the church culture in Britain. For instance there may be issues around co-habitation and marriages of convenience; there is also the issue of personal giving set against money management and its appropriation in the culture of origin and the culture of settlement. In spite of the fact that most of these migrants seem to be caught up this cultural dilemma, others choose to integrate by taking on some aspects of the culture, creating a unique identity.

CHAPTER FIVE

SOCIO-CULTURAL INTERFACE OF INDIGENOUS AFRICAN BELIEFS AND PRAXES IN SETTLED COMMUNITIES

Introduction

The theory of transnationalism states that immigrants forge and sustain simultaneous and multi-stranded social relations that link together their societies of origin and settlement (Szanton et al, 1995). As a consequence, African churches in Britain that are led by these migrant pastors and also host these migrants are partly shaped in their outlook by the beliefs and practices of churches from their countries of origin. Therefore an insight into the beliefs and practices of the churches in their countries of origin would provide a basis to explore similarities and differences with the beliefs and praxis of the African churches in Britain. Except that the approach and agency in the respective countries may differ due to the different socio-cultural milieu within which these churches are situated. At the same time, it is important to note that the beliefs and practices of the churches in the countries of origin have somehow been influenced by their socio-cultural milieu. The starting point of this journey is to identify the specific elements of beliefs and practices within the churches that have been influenced by the beliefs and practices of the indigenous religions in the countries of origin. Churches in Africa and therefore the African churches in Britain carry within their ecclesiastical framework and understanding, elements that are uniquely African because of the African indigenous religious influence. At the same time the African Pentecostal churches have introduced elements that are also uniquely British. The influence from the culture of both the places of origin and of settlement reveals the uniqueness of these Pentecostal churches.

These churches can neither be described as wholly African nor wholly British. In this chapter, there is both the narrative and an analysis of specific elements of continuity of Ghanaian-led Pentecostal church practices in Ghanaian-led Pentecostal churches in Britain. The analysis has been done by establishing the link between the practices of indigenous religions, Pentecostal churches in Ghana and Ghanaian-led Pentecostal churches in Britain. The indigenous religion examined is that of the Akan of Ghana. The Akan are the largest ethnic group in Ghana and have been chosen for this analysis because their core religious ideas are similar to other ethnic groups in Ghana and to traditional African worldviews more generally (Larbi, 2002). The focus of the strand of Christianity where most of these examples would largely be the Pentecostals and from Ghana but with inferences far reaching to other parts of the African continent where these practices are rife.

On the basis of transnationalism theory this influence of indigenous religions on Pentecostal churches in Ghana extends to Ghanaian-led Pentecostal churches in the UK. I postulate in this chapter that the differences in praxis between Pentecostal churches in Ghana and in the UK occur as a result of the socio-cultural milieu of Britain. And therefore the difference between practices at the places of origin and settlement become an indicator of the extent of contextualization as a tool of integration by African Pentecostal churches and consequently the relevance of these churches in British society. As already established from the previous chapter, integration from the perspective of the migrants begins and it's successful by integrating into their social groups which is the church, and the church as a microcosm of society becomes the channel into the larger society.

Prophetic Consultation

One of the principal responsibilities of pastors is counselling members of their churches through various life challenges on the basis of the teachings, principles and narratives of the Bible, which is usually upheld strongly by Pentecostals as the word of God. In many Christian circles this counselling involves the use of scripture and wisdom to bring suggestions of solutions to the problems that people face. There is evidence that there has been a tension in the past between forms of counselling that has a spiritual dimension and the psychotherapeutic techniques employed by 'secular' counsellors. Counselling that incorporates the spirituality of the individual and a person's belief in the spiritual is often central to pastoral counselling (Thorne, 2000). This type of counselling emphasises a form of dialogue and communication through the use of scriptures and scriptural narratives to alleviate the distress of a counselee within the context of pastoral ministry. Thorne underscores this, noting that:

> .... We are seeing the beginning of a great merger operation with increasing numbers of secular therapists acknowledging the importance of their clients' spirituality and many pastoral counsellors being only too keen to shake themselves free from the institutional or doctrinal straitjackets of their faith communities (Thorne, 2000).

As the clear demarcation between the two is being erased for a more inclusive approach, some pastoral counsellors seem to be finding ways of making the distinction even clearer by shifting to one end of the spectrum. Clinebell notes that;

> Pastoral counselling is the utilisation of a variety of healing (therapeutic) methods to help people handle their problems and crises in a more developmental way, and in doing so experience healing of their brokenness. Pastoral counselling is a reparative function needed when the growth of individuals is seriously jeopardised or blocked by crises (Clinebell, 1984).

This sums up the process of pastoral counselling. People tend to consult counsellors when life is difficult and they need direction, hope and even a solution. A new form of counselling is emerging which involves the use 'prophetic insight' delivered to men of God from the Spirit – as they claim – as bringing the authoritative instruction to solve a problem. In addition to what Clinebell describes as the nature of pastoral counselling, prophetic counselling places the crisis the individual faces within the context of the spiritual, claiming that the source of the crisis and the barrier to growth is in the spirit world. Within the context of this counselling the servant of God, as an agent of God is able to diagnose and give full instructions as to what needs to be done. In the instance of the latter, the counselee is somehow compelled to implement in full what they have been told: not carrying out the instructions in full would mean depriving oneself of experiencing a complete solution and ultimately disobeying the instructions of God. The down side as in many cases is that the counselee becomes subject to control not only by the 'Spirit' but also by the men of God.

In many Pentecostal churches, the counselling process begins with the member making an appointment to meet with the pastor at a chosen venue. As part of the process, the pastor is able to convey to the counselee a message from the Spirit about that particular situation. This practice of consultation and the subsequent solicitation of information from the Spirit has been a practice of the indigenous religions and have influenced Pentecostal church practices. However, this sits in contrast to assertions made by scholars such as Thorne that more and more people are choosing to go to secular therapists because most secular therapist acknowledges the spirituality of their clients. According to Thorne, the main reason for this disassociation from religious entities is that people feel more comfortable to be referred to as spiritual rather than religious (Thorne, 2000). For migrants, choosing a counsellor with a contemporary understanding of their spirituality is problematic: they are looking for something deeper than just an acknowledgement of their spirituality or even reaching deep within oneself for answers, as is the case with the secular-spiritual therapist.

Whilst there is no suggestion that Pentecostals completely reject 'secular' counselling, these new Pentecostal clients or members are looking for a deeper spiritual experience that involves action and a tangible response as evidence of having contacted the spirit world. Therefore any suggestion that this sort of pastoral-prophetic counselling is not patronised by people can be deemed inaccurate. In fact, evidence show that a lot of Pentecostals seek this sort of pastoral-prophetic counselling. And they refer to it as prophetic counselling.

The source of this kind of prophetic counselling practice by the African Pentecostal churches is embedded in the belief of spiritual causation. Spiritual causation is an inextricable part of most societies in sub-Saharan Africa and particularly the life of the Akan. As a result of the cosmology that everything originates from the spirit and every physical occurrence or event is set in motion by spiritual entities, the Akan, through the agent and agency of the spirit, seek to gain knowledge of this cause. This quest predisposes them to divination. Spiritual causation also becomes the framework with which most situations are interpreted. The question that is often asked in the diagnosis of a problem in the context of an African cosmology is 'who or what caused this?', rather than the questions 'what is this?' or 'why?' which characterise a western approach. It tends to be when a situation is recurring that spiritual knowledge is sought in order to deal with it. For the Akan a recurring circumstance is considered to have a spiritual cause, generating a demand for its remedy and future prevention. The actions normally taken involve the performance of rituals. It is now established that the corresponding practice of divination in the African and Ghanaian-led Pentecostal churches is what is described as prophetic consultation. The corresponding ritual actions that are undertaken in the indigenous religions to appease spirits or to avert evil are renamed as prophetic actions within the Pentecostal churches. It is worth noting that historically this is not entirely new in its essence as the AICs (African

Initiated Churches) introduced it into Ghanaian Christianity, and it was developed further at prayer camps where leaders, often referred to as 'Papa Odiyifo' or 'Maame Odiyifo', which translates as prophet or prophetess, have days of meeting one to one with adherents to enquire of the Spirit for them.

Prophetic Consultation in Ghana

Divination as practiced in African indigenous religions is done not only to understand negative events of the past but also to enquire into: present events whose causes cannot be explained; things unknown and hidden from the naked eye or even removed from one's cognitive recognition; determining the appropriate conduct of persons in critical situations such as the healing of illness or epidemics; determining the times and modes of religious worship; and making decisions about persons to occupy important positions of responsibility and about future events (Tedlock, 2001).

The practice of divination takes different forms among different communities within Akan states. Practitioners of different shrines administer the process of divination in its own unique form and this differs significantly from one area to another. The nature and role of the deity consulted also has a big influence on the process of divination. For instance in communities whose totem is a goat, a goat would not be prescribed and accepted for a sacrifice by the priest who sits as an agent for the deity being consulted at that point in time.

As part of the divination process, the priests who are agents of the deity use cowries; others use kola; ring bells; and chant. These items are just representative and used as mediums in soliciting information from the spirit. 'Others use certain herbs but one thing common to all of them is that the symbols they adopt to use at any particular time become the medium through which they access hidden knowledge present in the spirit world' (Appiah, 2019).

Prophetic Consultation in Britain

The practice of seeking the cause of evil occurrences and obtaining the relevant power and direction to deal with them and avert a similar future reoccurrence, as well as the search to know what lies ahead in one's life, (popularly referred to as destiny (*'hyɛbrɛ'*) through divination, as in the indigenous religions, has been referred to as 'prophetism' in Pentecostalism (Omenyo, 2011). 'Prophetism' is practiced and accepted in most African Pentecostal churches in Britain to a large extent although the leaders may deny and distance themselves from the use of this label due to excesses in these practices within the church body. However, the leaders of these churches at some point in their ministry lives tell counselees or the entire church about what God is indicating, requiring some kind of action from the members. These churches also invite other pastors recognised as prophets to their churches to speak at least once a year. The reason they would deny the label of 'prophetism' is to distance themselves from the earlier strand of Pentecostal churches that were referred to as *spiritual* churches or the *sumsum sore* as they are described in Akan, which had this practice as an integral part of their worship (Anderson, 2001). Meyer summarises the efforts of Pentecostals to break away from their past and notes that:

> Current Pentecostalist discourse clearly takes up this temporalising strategy. By emphasizing continuously that being born again entails a complete break with the past, Pentecostalists even celebrate the notion of rupture much more than nineteenth and early twentieth-century protestant missionaries (Meyer, 1998).

It is worth noting that in spite of this conscious effort being made by Pentecostals to break away from the past, there is overwhelming evidence that indigenous religions have provided the platform from which the Pentecostals have interpreted scripture to their members. They are closer in beliefs and practices to the *sumsum sore* that they vehemently seek to disassociate themselves from. So on one hand they are breaking away from the past and on the other they are making use of the indigenous cultural framework to highlight the biblical passages and narratives that speak to specific situations within their local contexts. This interaction and internal struggle reveals within the African Pentecostal self-understanding a theological concern that leaves the churches exposed to a theological debate about the place of their practices in scripture. This entanglement occurs where Pentecostals attempt to use scripture to explain their beliefs and praxis as against the traditional beliefs and practices of indigenous religions. Pentecostals would have to show their difference from the past as completely dissociated from the AICs to be considered as a new movement. It must be said however that this could prove difficult. Therefore it is reasonable to state that African Pentecostals would find it difficult to detach themselves totally from the indigenous religions.

The Theological Controversy Created by the Prophetic Consultations

The Pentecostals have given this practice of prophetic consultation, otherwise known in the indigenous religions as divination, a theological perspective by finding a way to locate their practices in scripture. In Pentecostal churches that are prophet–led, this is a welcomed practice and defended with scriptures such as Saul enquiring from the Prophet Samuel about his father's lost donkeys. In the biblical narrative of 1 Samuel 9: 1-8, Saul is advised by his accompanying servant to see Samuel, a Seer, to ask about the whereabouts of the donkey. They did this, and Samuel indeed told them that the donkey has been found.

Scriptures such as 2 Chronicles 20:20 are also quoted to support this practice. In this text, Jehoshaphat admonishes the people to believe in the prophets of God to be successful in their battle. This scripture has often been used to expand the influence and authority of these men of God over those who approach them in their office as men appointed by God. These individuals tend to make their voice heard through the media, and in some instance hold governments and heads of governments to ransom. They are convinced that their counsels have to be heeded for any individual who seeks them to be successful in their life's endeavours. For many who attend consultations with these men of God it is among other things to seek *akwankyerɛ (divine direction)* to negotiate through the difficulties of life successfully by means of knowledge of the future, through the agency of the Spirit.

In some of these prophet-led churches, prophetic consultations are held every day of the week depending on the nature of the solutions and prophetic directions being sought through the agency of the gifts of the Spirit. Whilst some members report finding this practice helpful, there are others who have been negatively affected, with families torn apart by reckless *akwankyerɛ* given to people that creates even more problems for them in the end. Some of the *akwankyerɛ* have been involved in pointing out family members who are behind the misfortunes of these people and therefore considered as evil. The practice of prophetic consultation in the churches is reminiscent of the divination process in indigenous religions, where sometimes, human agents of evil spirits are sometimes identified to be behind the struggles and failures of certain individuals. The practice of prophetic consultation as seen in the scripture from 1 Samuel 9:1-8 is practiced to the letter in some Pentecostal churches, in the following three respects:

  i.   Involves paying money as consultation fees
  ii.   Authoritative and compulsive declaration of the 'mind of God'; and
  iii. A dramatic result driven expectation – 'the person experience'.

These Pentecostals without any proper exegesis or even hermeneutical considerations take these three areas of practice verbatim from the scriptures. The scriptures are taken literally and practiced, in some cases to the detriment of the counselee. All the churches studies do subscribe to the (ii) and (iii) above, but do not collect consultation fees as part of the consultation process. However, there are African Pentecostal churches in Britain that practice prophetic consultation with consultation fees often referred to as a 'ministry gift'. Apart from the 'ministry gift' given before consulting the man of God, at the end of the consultation the counselee is also encouraged to give willingly according to the help they have received from the servant of God. There have even been occasions where individuals have been asked to give specific amounts for some specific solutions.

Those who receive these fees teach that what provokes a proclamation or prophecy is the gift that the counselee brings to the servant of God, based on the view that Saul's gift to Samuel caused the meeting to be a life changing moment for Saul. The veracity of this teaching is uncertain, as there are numerous examples where prophets in the Bible have proclaimed the word of God without a gift being traded for the prophecy. Indeed, when one looks at the passage from which these scriptures are extracted, this teaching becomes untenable because verse 15 states that the Lord had already spoken to Samuel before Saul came to him, therefore the gift that Saul gave to Samuel did not provoke the prophecy. Samuel had already received instructions from the Lord before any form of gift was handed to him. And with regard to Saul becoming 'another person' as a result of his encounter with Samuel, this was God's own sovereign act and had nothing to do with Saul himself or his action of giving. God let the people have their own way because they requested a new king, not because Saul fulfilled the requirements (Walwood and Zuck, 1985).

These actions on the part of Pentecostals represent a trend where scriptural narratives are translated into illustrations of a spiritualised understanding of the scriptures. This may not necessarily be a theological position, except that one takes the view that theology is the discourse of God in one's particular situation. Perceiving the scriptures as the word of God means taking verbatim what it says and making it speak into one's personal circumstances irrespective of the contextual issues that arise (Poirier, 2008). In that sense, individuals control the construction of their theologies on the basis of personal circumstances without recourse to scholarly theological analysis, and in the course of time those beliefs and practices are passed on to the church and are institutionalised. The result is a theological entanglement brought about by their controversial positions. This at times brings about isolation within the Christian community but at the same time, those for whom these practices work see themselves as the minority who hold the truth to liberate the majority. This whole phenomenon mimics the Akan indigenous religions as in their practice of *Okomfo*, where the priest holds the secret knowledge of gods, controls the interpretation and is positioned as a repository of knowledge of the oral narratives of their worship and its application in any given situation. There is a possibility that the current disposition of the African Pentecostal churches and their practice of prophetic consultation has been an influence of the indigenous religions, but they have found a way to place the practice in scripture through interpreting the narratives that speak to their situation. The discontinuity of this practice from the Ghanaian-led Pentecostal churches is that objects, such as live animals for instance, are not required, as is the case with the indigenous religions. However, in their place, money is collected. Another form of discontinuity is in the practice from the era of the boom of *sumsum sore* where in certain instances the priest or *odiyifo* as known then require candles and other objects as part of their performance of their prophetic actions. In essence there is not much within this practice of prophetic consultation in the Ghanaian-led Pentecostal churches that is different from the practice by the indigenous religions.

Libations and Libation Language in Pentecostal Prayer

Indigenous Libation Practice

One of the outstanding features of the indigenous religions is libation. Libation is the means by which humans stay in touch with the spirit world. Libation to the adherent of an indigenous religion is what prayer is to the Christian. Libation is an acknowledgement of the dependence of the living on supernatural forces that exist in the Akan universe (Appiah, 2019). The only difference would be that in libation there is a pouring out of drink to the ancestors whilst in prayer God is directly addressed and is the recipient of the request through Christ. Some indigenous religion adherents who are also members of various Christian churches, actually cannot tell the difference between the Christian prayer and libation as they are both forms of prayer ultimately to God. There are those who from a theological perspective consider Christ as an ancestor when the concept of place of ancestors is juxtaposed with Christianity (Beyers and Mphahlele, 2001). This is especially the case when ancestors are seen as the continuation of the family in the life beyond, and to the Pentecostals, the scriptures makes it clear that we are heirs of God and joint heirs with Christ. Most people who belong to both the indigenous religions and the

Christian church hold this position. In fact there are other prominent and popular priests of shrines like the Kwaku Bonsam, Obuotabiri, Ataa Ahia who argue the equality of the indigenous religions to all foreign religions, such as Christianity.

In most cases, libation pouring has involved the use of alcoholic drink or water or even both at times, or the offering of food to the spirit-beings, all this is done with prayer and incantation of words directed to God through the ancestors: it is a ritual action recognising their presence and continued participation in communal gatherings (Graveling, 2010). Interestingly, with the use of the alcoholic drinks, there are instances where the magnitude of help needed from the ancestors and gods determine the quality of the drinks that are offered. Very notable brands and expensive imported drinks such as Beefeater, Johnnie Walker, and Black Label Whiskey are sometimes offered in that regard, but usually it is a locally brewed gin often referred to as 'akpɛteshie' or palm wine that is used. The choice of the foreign brands to drinks for libation leaves one to wonder if the indigenous deities have acquired foreign taste. The fact that foreign products are used for indigenous rituals is indicative of the extent of globalisation and aids the contextualisation of religious beliefs.

For the Akan, the ancestors are invisible but play a major role in communities. This is the reason, the individual often pours libation for themselves or on behalf of the family to their own ancestors. Pouring libation to another's clan or family ancestors is considered most inhospitable, somewhat hostile and tantamount to gross disrespect and declaration of war on the ancestors of another clan or family. It has to be made clear however that depending on the kind of life that ancestor lived. They may have national ancestor status, and therefore can be consulted through libation pouring although they do not directly come from one's own family or clan. The act of libation pouring then becomes a reminder and an indication that the family consists of the living, the dead and even the unborn and that the living regard those who have moved on with much respect and consider them closer to the supreme being than the living and therefore able to help determine what the will or wishes of the supreme Being are at any point in time (Pobee, 1976).

Libation characterises almost every facet and aspect of life for the Akan. For instance, 'before and after travel, libation is poured to the ancestors to seek their blessings or in thanksgiving for the blessings on the journey. On such occasions there is no need for a ritual specialist or a priest to make the sacrifice' (Pobee, 1976). At the ethnic level a ritual specialist such as the chief linguist or priest mediates the cult of the ancestors through libation (Pobee, 1976). Apart from individuals who pour libations in clans and family gatherings it is the *abusua panyin* or the head of the clan or family that has that first privilege of pouring libation (Pobee, 1976). The established order is not merely an act of respect for the elderly or a quest to maintain order in the clan but it also holds spiritual connotations because whoever pours the libation must be well connected in the spirit to the ancestors and chosen by them to carry out the sacred act on behalf of the clan or family. Typically, libation pouring may involve invocations such as; *'Twereduapɔn Onyankopɔn Kwame, yɛ kyerɛ wo nsa na yɛn ma wo nsa, asase yaa nsa, nananom nsamanfo nsa; ɛnɛ daabɛn, ɛnɛ Awukudae, yɛ srɛ nananom banbo, nkwa, sika, ne ahoto ne yieyo.ɔkra tuntum biara a ɔbɛtwetwa yɛn nnantɛm anaase obibiara a obɛyɛ ne ho sɛ otwease nona bedidi yen ase na watoto yɛn ne mo nananom ntɛm deɛ yɛ samaran ma mo nananom sɛ mone won ndi no nwonwono; anaa sɛ ɔtamfo biara a ɔpe yɛn animguase de nananom mma wɔn anim nguase', anaase obibiara a onpe abusua yi ne oman yi yie deɛ won ma won dikan wo asamanndo'.*

Analysing the libation ritual prayer based on the translation set out in the footnotes, the prayer starts by addressing the one and only supreme and ultimate God Kwame (a name given to males born on Saturday among Akans), saying that we do not offer you drink but bring it to you to acknowledge it. Mother earth is also given drink, as are the ancestors. The occasion for the libation is then mentioned: in the instance above it is a sacred Sunday. They proceed to ask for protection from the ancestors and any other supplication they may have. They then curse their enemies and pronounce evil over their enemies. The section to do with enemies varies according to the circumstances the people may find themselves in at the time, and their cultural and linguistic ties to the area influence the person's choice of words. In some instances enemies are represented by the term 'any black cat or witch that will cross our path, or any individual as cunning as the serpent we subpoenaed it before you our ancestors; or any enemy who does not wish us well should have disgrace befall them... 'and so on.

Whilst the libation is being poured, those present utter their concurrence with the sentiments of the prayer being offered using words and statements such as *Ampaara* (it is the truth), or *Yonn*, (yes indeed); *Siompa*, (truly) or *wyiɛ*, (well spoken). These interjections to the spirit-beings by the participants and audience present at the libation are equivalent to the Amens used in Christian prayers, especially among Pentecostals, who also use words such as 'yes Lord' (Pobee, 1976). These interjections are considered an acknowledgement and agreement to the content of the prayer being offered by the individual performing the ritual. On some occasions the libation pouring is done whilst some of the adherents softly clap their hands as though they are stimulating or invoking the presence of the ancestors and gods (Appiah, 2019).

Libation Prayer Use in Church

Anyone who visits a Ghanaian-led Pentecostal church may realise that at their time of prayer people clap their hands. This mimics the clapping of hands that occurs when the libation is poured. This is also done when prayers are said in the Pentecostal churches. Acceptance of clapping during prayer may have stemmed from its introduction by Paul Owusu Tabiri who was the leader of the Bethel Prayer Ministry International in Sunyani, Ghana. They organised what was then known as 'breaking'. This is a deliverance session normally administered to a group of people simultaneously: the people are asked to follow certain instructions to be delivered from the demons that are considered to be tormenting them or from spirits that cause the problems they have. The deliverance process involves the invocation of curses against enemies through militant prayers with gestures and violent clapping.

In the process of pouring libation as illustrated above, it is important to note that the drink is not offered to the Supreme God but that this God is asked to acknowledge it as a blessing. It depicts the importance that the indigenous religion's adherents place on the Supreme God. However, another instance of the influence of Christianity on indigenous religions libation prayer is the use of the serpent to represent the devil or Satan, as in the Bible. The custodians of tradition and culture within the Akan areas do not question the use of the symbol of the serpent, as it is assumed that the audience and participants of libation understand the meaning of the symbol being presented quite clearly. Another reason for this is that many of the older people belong to mainline historical churches such as the Methodist Church, Catholic Church and the Presbyterian churches, either because they were born and baptised into those churches as infants or because they represent the families in those churches, but still practice indigenous religion in some sense, and participate fully in libation pouring. The representation of libation prayer in churches in forms and not in practice is quite common in certain areas of Ghana because a lot of people prefer Christian burials and therefore although they may not regularly attend these mainline historical churches, they pay their dues to maintain membership on their own behalf and that of their families. Such individuals would not question the use of the symbol of the serpent for instance because its significance is well understood due to its use in the church and in the biblical text in the book of Genesis.

As Christian prayers are said in the name of Jesus to denote the advocacy and mediatory role that Jesus plays for Christians and the Christian God, as the only son of God, libation in the form of pouring out drinks or in the form of offering food to the ancestors and gods is seen as drawing on the advocacy role of the ancestors between both God, the adherents, and the gods. The Akan believes the ancestors' play a similar role as Jesus does for Christians as advocates and mediators (Pobee, 1976). A key difference though is that the majority of Christians irrespective of their persuasions call on one mediator and advocate, Jesus Christ. However in the indigenous religions the ancestors differ from one area to another. One could therefore argue that Jesus and the ancestors are not on the same level, but there are ways in which the ancestors' roles may mimic some aspects of the role and work of Jesus Christ (Dickson, 1984).

Libation Language Use in the Churches in Britain

Most Ghanaian-led Pentecostals would assent to the argument put forward by Harry Sawyerr to distinguish the ancestry of Christ from the Akan ancestors by stating that 'unlike the ancestors of the Africans, Jesus Christ, once dead, now lives' (Sawyerr, 1968). On the other hand, as well as certain individuals resorting to libation pouring, the language used by some members of Ghanaian-led Pentecostal churches, can certainly be said to have been borrowed from the indigenous religions practitioners who pour libation at community and state functions. Whilst there may not have been a conscious effort on the part of the Pentecostals to adopt these forms of prayer from the indigenous religions, this practice is widespread and incessant denials of this form of prayer having been picked from the indigenous religions do not undermine the credibility of the claim. The petitions and supplications made through the ancestors and the gods to God during libation are often very rich in terms of the choice of words used; they carry with them a certain cultural flavour that reveals the rich cultural heritage of the community.

The Ghanaian Pentecostal churches employ this rich language, but claim that it is biblical jargon. However, this language illustrates the rich cultural backgrounds of these churches and the influence that indigenous religions have had on them. It is evident however, that this phenomenon is found among the churches with roots in Ghana more generally because most African indigenous religions pour libation and the churches used as case studies in this research are all led by Akans. It is clear that libation language influences the prayer vocabulary of the Ghanaian Pentecostal churches. For instance, a pastor of one of the churches observed led the members in prayer in English using these words: '...*in the name of Jesus Christ, may every power that is pursuing me; may every satanic plot against me; may every agenda of Satan against my destiny be aborted. As I clap my hands and pray, may they be bound, may they catch fire, and may they be confused. I declare that may shame and reproach be their portion, pray...*'. This is a prayer that would typically accompany a libation whilst the audience or participants clap their hands. Therefore this indigenous libation prayer has been contextualised for relevance for Christians in Britain. In the Christian practice those who are offering the prayer are encouraged to do the clapping themselves. It is believed that this enforces the power and resolve behind the prayer being offered. For these Pentecostals prayer is not only a request to God but also a way of enforcing one's spiritual power and authority in the world of spirits. It does not leave the onus on God, the supposed recipient of the prayer, for an answer but invokes the individual's resolve and determination to break into the world of spirits for an action as a response in the here and now.

There is a clear indication that not only is there continuity between the beliefs and praxis of indigenous religions and Ghanaian and African Pentecostal church practices. There is no indication of any difference in how the libation language is appropriated in Pentecostal Church prayers in Africa and in Britain, as traditional libation and Pentecostal prayer has more to do with meaning than form. In this sense they may be very relevant to the community of Africans who make up the majority of their members, but not necessarily to the wider host communities.

Naming (Din to) and 'Outdooring' Ceremonies

As with the elements discussed earlier in this chapter, the naming ceremonies and the accompanying rituals practiced by adherents of indigenous religions will now be analysed in comparison to the way that naming ceremonies are practiced within the Pentecostal churches both in Ghana and in Britain.

Practise of Naming (Din to) and 'Outdooring'

The life of the Akan is characterised by many ritual performances intended to create cosmic harmony at the various stages of human development and of the life cycle. Special ceremonies with accompanying rituals are performed when a person is born, when a person reaches puberty and then at their death. These ceremonies and rituals are taken seriously: they are not just treated as social events but are deeply rooted in the culture and the spirituality of individuals within the community. In most instances, when the rituals to be performed at these stages of an individual's life are omitted or refused, they carry consequences to the individual and the community at large. The naming ceremony, known by the Akans as *Din to*, is a ceremonial process where children are brought out on the eighth day after birth to be given a name. When a child is born, the child is often kept indoors, in the bedroom of parents and away from the eyes of the public apart from very close family. This tradition continues to this day although it is no longer as rigid as it used to be. For instance, the introduction of western medicine requires that a mother send the child to the hospital for various checks, making it impossible to keep the infant indoors for that duration.

To preserve the tradition mothers will often cover their un-named infants with a white cloth to make it impossible for anyone to see the child whilst they make their way to hospital. There are also instances where the mother is kept in hospital after birth for a medical reason; the naming ceremony is then held after they are out of hospital. On the day set for the ceremony and the rituals, 'the infant is taken out of isolation and privacy since birth to establish initial contact in the public realm with individuals and groups, families, and family friends-among whom he or she will grow, function, marry, die, and be buried. These are the individuals and groups who will also play significant roles in the child's life owing to his or her membership in specific cognatic descent social units' (Abarry, 1997). The whole process of the outdooring of the child is to affirm the responsibility of the child to the community and vice versa. It stresses that the extended family system has a role to play, particularly in the upbringing of the child, unlike most western societies where the raising of a child is the basic responsibility of the immediate family.

This has been altered somewhat because some of these traditional structures of society have been influenced by western ideals and definitions of the family and community. As part of the traditional protocols associated with the naming of a new born, it is the *abusua panyin* or head of the clan of the child's father that makes contact with the new-borns' mother's family to officially inform them about the new born and invite them to the ceremony. When the day of the ceremony arrives, elaborate procedures are followed to ensure that the ceremony conforms to the traditions of the father's family. With both of the baby's parents present, seated and given a traditional welcome, libation is poured to welcome the spirit of the ancestors and the gods. At that point the elders from the child's maternal family usher in the mum from her hiding place with the baby and hands him or her over to the *abusua panyin* or the leading elder of the father's family.

> Whilst seated the elders again offer libation to thank the gods and the ancestor for the safe delivery of the child and commit proceedings into their hands. He goes on to dip his hand in water and an alcoholic drink and drops it in the child's lips in succession and states 'sɛ wo hu nsu a kasɛ nsu'; na 'wohu nsa nso a kasɛ nsa', meaning: 'when you recognise water state it is water' and 'when you recognise drink state it is a drink (Appiah, 2011).

The significance of this is the introduction of the infant to the reality of life including choices between good and bad; it is making a declaration that the child opt for the good at all times. The elder who performs the ritual states clearly that they should choose to speak the truth at all times rather than telling lies. Thereafter, the elder who performs the ritual asks the child's father the name that he has decided to give the child. He is asked to explain the name he has decided, the rationale for that name and the meaning of the name. In the indigenous Akan context, the first name received, the *kra din* (soul name) is determined by the day of the week on which the child was born as well as the divinity that governs the day (Appiah, 2019). It is believed that *Nyame* or *Nyankopon* (the Supreme Being) ascribed different spiritual qualities and functions to seven of his children translated as divinities. Each is assigned to a day of the week. This spiritual quality of the divinities are believed to be correspondingly transmitted to and carried by the soul of the child along gender lines (Adogame, 2004). As a result each of these Akan weekday names given to a child have their '*mmrane*' – appellation. For instance a male born on a Wednesday is called Kwaku and his '*mmrane*' is *Bonsam*; a female born on a Sunday is called Akosua has the '*mmrane*' *Dompo*. Every Akan has kra *din* (soul names) given apart from the '*din pa*'- or the actual name, which is normally a name borne by an ancestor: the aim is that the child would emulate qualities of the ancestor to continue their good works in the community. When the name has been chosen by the *abusua panyin* to be placed upon the child, libation is poured to the ancestors to affirm the name upon the child. As a way to remember the child's name and to accept the child into the community, the *okyeame* or the linguist of the ceremony at that point passes around the drink used for the ritual for each present to drink portions of it. As part of the 'ritual participants of the ceremony mention the name and offer the child being named pleasant words of welcome. Thereafter the paternal, maternal family and guests present the child and mother with gifts' (Appiah, 2011). The 'symbolism, meaning, and power of naming and several elements of the indigenous naming ritual have been transposed within an African Christian worldview, although the agencies of propitiation have sharply altered' (Adogame, 2004).

The Pentecostal *Din To* Experience

Akan Pentecostals recognise the role of the *din to* traditions and rituals and accept *din to* as part of the traditions of the church. Ghanaian Pentecostals do not believe in infant baptism on the basis that a person is baptised after they have believed in Christ as Lord and personal saviour: since the infant is unable to make that conscious, informed choice they cannot be baptised. As a result they practice what they refer to as baby dedication and present certificates, as in baptism among the mainline historic churches. The baby dedication is practiced on the basis of Jesus being presented in the temple by his parents for certain rituals to be performed. The Pentecostals embracing the traditional *din to* alongside their biblical practice of dedication means that they are involved in introducing the infant into the world through *din to* and at the same time initiating the infant into the church. This is a classic example of the extent to which the Pentecostal traditions can contextualise to remain relevant to their communities. The naming ceremony and its rituals are adopted in Pentecostal churches, the *sunsum sore* with a few changes to certain elements of the indigenous practice but without changing the essence of it. The Pentecostal church's strength lies in their ability to place their system of beliefs, which they often claim to be biblical, within an indigenous framework to make it relevant to their members. This understanding seems to influence the practice of their beliefs a great deal as we will see from how they conduct their naming ceremonies.

The traditional naming ceremony begins with the husband of the new born informing his elders, and they in turn inform the elders of the mother of the new born of a set date to perform all the necessary rituals. The church does not take part in all these consultations that take place prior to the ceremony itself. The couple that belong to the church must communicate the date chosen and agreed by the families to the church for the church to also agree to come to the ceremony. When that is agreed it is expected that the church way of performing the *din to* rites over-ride the traditional practice. The church issues certain instructions such as a ban on libation. The church takes over the ceremony when all parties to it are seated. The traditional welcoming through the *okyeame* for the occasion is done. Thereafter the rest of the ceremony is handed over to the Pastor to continue with the proceedings. When the pastor is introduced, they would usually give the rationale for the 'Christian' naming and its relevance. Where the ceremony would have began with libation, the pastor prays. After the opening prayer, the pastor asks that the child be handed over to him. This is similar to the child being handed over to the elder of the child's paternal family who performs the rite. In Akan *din to* rituals, a drop of alcohol and water are placed in the child's mouth with certain instructions and declarations made to the child. At that point the child's name is taken from the father who mentions the name he wants the child to be known by and gives the meaning of the name.

Similar to the items used to perform the actual ritual, there are three items that the pastor uses in the place of items that would have normally been used by the elders: these are water, honey and salt water. The symbolism of the water is transparency, integrity and uprightness; the honey symbolises wisdom, hard work and (sweetness) enjoyable life; and salt water symbolises the child being the salt of the earth. They put a drop of each in the child's mouth and make declarations similar to those made in indigenous ceremonies. When that is done, the pastor prays and hands the child over to the father. To complete the ritual, the remaining honey is passed round to be tasted and as this is done the name of the child is mentioned, as in an indigenous ceremony. At that point, those who came with gifts for the baby are allowed to present them and the ceremony is brought to a close. This is the usual procedure in a Pentecostal church in an Akan speaking area in Ghana: certain aspects may differ from church to church, but the essence remains the same.

Naming (Din to) and 'Outdooring' in Britain

There is also a continuity of this practice in DC, RCI, ICGC and FCI. The only difference observed in the practice in Britain has been the use of white talcum powder as part of the ritual performance by FCI. The significance of the powder, according to Pastor Humphrey is that the whole biological process of conception and birth is a battle that an individual has to win in order to appear on this side of life. He goes on to say that, 'millions of sperms have to compete to fertilise an egg and it takes the fastest and healthiest to win that race'. Smearing white talcum powder on the child signifies that they are beginning life as victors and not as losers. This rhetoric is commonly heard in the sermons of the Ghanaian-led Pentecostal church preachers. Smearing of white talcum powder on individuals considered victorious in either a court case, an athletic event or some other form of competition is in itself an indigenous religious practice. This originates from the smearing of white talcum powder on the priest when the gods possess them and they are under the influence of the gods. The powder is smeared on the priests and blown on them supposedly to signify their authority through conquest the power they have over others. It is evident that the Ghanaian-led Pentecostal churches still seem to be attached to the aprons of their indigenous forbearers and the indigenous contexts provide them with the grounds for expressing their beliefs.

Another area of discontinuity in the practice of *din to* in DC, ICGC, RCI and FCI is the organisation of the 'baby shower' for expectant mothers prior to the delivery of their babies. These 'baby shower' functions are not organised by the church officially but are an accepted norm within the churches as friends of the expectant mother come together to organise them. Because of the baby shower not many people bring gifts to the baby at the naming ceremony according to the Ghanaian custom. There are those who see the baby shower a better option and chose to be absent on the day of the naming ceremony to attend to other matters. This is a modification of the naming ceremony since the practice of the baby shower is entirely a western concept and practice, traditionally known as *wetting the baby's head* in Britain. This is also in contrast to Akan tradition that a pregnant mother does not receive gifts from people and until the child is born there are no celebratory events involving the mother or the unborn. The 'baby shower' is therefore a departure from the cultural heritage of these people. 'Baby showers' I have attended have involved some persons from the white British community, alongside Indian and Brazilian work colleagues of the expectant mother. This is an important point for contextualisation because since the majority of the participants are from the church and the organisers come from the church, aspects of the function are Christianised as one can see and hear from the kind of vocabulary used, the songs sung and the merry-making without alcohol (although FCI sanctions the drinking of wine in moderation). I posit that those who attend these baby showers may only see subtle differences from ones they may have previously attended and through curiosity may become attracted to the church and eventually join as members.

Expelling Malevolent Spirits as Deliverance

Deliverance Practice in Pentecostal Churches in Ghana

After the child naming and all the rituals associated with it have been done, in case the child is born with any ailment or permanent disability or deformity it is attributed to malevolent spirits and those spirits have to be expelled to free them from their influence. Any other ailment or misfortune that the individual encounters sometime later in their lives is also treated in this way. Where rituals have to be performed to expel the spirits that are deemed to be responsible for the ailment, this fits seamlessly with the understanding of the individual's family's existential experience and it is therefore accepted. Assigning spiritual causes to explain an unfortunate event, ailment or disease is part of an indigenous religious cosmology, which has also found its way into Pentecostal thought and practice. Within the social and religious construct of the African, when a mishap occurs the question that is often asked is: 'why is this?' and 'who might have caused this?' In comparison, within the Western social and religious construct one might ask 'what is this?' Present beliefs that inform this practice in Pentecostal churches can be traced to the indigenous religions in that, they tend to attribute situations of difficulty or situations that cannot be easily explained to a spiritual influence and therefore seek some sort of spiritual interpretation and subsequently resort to a ritual performance to restore normalcy.

Within the indigenous religions the causes of such mishaps are identified either as the deities or the ancestors and they occur as a result of a wrong doing on the part of an individual, family, or indeed the whole community against the gods and the ancestors. The mishap or the unfortunate event is seen as a punishment, which is often interpreted as a temporary or permanent curse. In such instances there is a call to expel the malevolent spirits involved in enforcing the curse or for intervention to appease the gods or ancestor who has brought about the mishap and this is expressed by the indigenous religions and the Pentecostal churches as expelling the malevolent spirits and deliverance respectively. Expelling malevolent spirits as in deliverance, practiced by Ghanaian Pentecostals is similar to the practice of exorcism in the AICs in general as exorcism was practiced at a point when personal 'awareness' and consciousness of the devil and of evil increased among the churches in Ghana. However, scholars such as Onyinah and Forson have limited the practice of deliverance at the time of the AICs to an instance where individuals' depressed by the competing indigenous and Christian beliefs within leave the AICs exposing them to the Pentecostals for their form of deliverance (Forson, 1993).

However, while Onyinah and Forson make a very good historical contribution to our understanding of deliverance, in making this assertion they miss a very important reason why people seek deliverance: people are no longer seeking deliverance from association with the practices of indigenous religions, but rather Christians are regularly seeking deliverance from anything that restricts them from enjoying the abundant life given to them by God (Onyinah, 2002). The abundant life expressed here by the Ghanaian Pentecostals is not that envisioned from an evangelical perspective which proposes that once a person is saved by accepting Christ's salvific work they are free from all satanic influences, but rather an adaptation of the perspective of indigenous religions where interaction with the spirit world means that certain malevolent spirits can find their way to harm individuals. This means that there is the need for a ritual action to deal with this spiritual interference. To place this within the biblical discourse Pentecostals in Ghana would normally quote the story of Lazarus raised from the dead by Jesus. In this story, as presented in John 11: 38-44, after Jesus called the dead Lazarus from the tomb he came out still wrapped up in his grave shrouds. Jesus at this point turns to those who were with him to 'loose and let him go'. This narrative has been used to place the deliverance practice in scripture and to legitimise it among Christians. It is suggested therefore that one could accept Christ and be 'born again' but still be bound and experiencing what they claim are satanic attacks on their money, marriage, job, family. Deliverance is therefore needed to set them free from those influences considered to be brought on by malevolent spirits. If Onyinah's assertion was correct, then from what do the indigenous religions exorcise their adherents, because they also exorcise their adherents from spirits that bring mishap upon them? The validity of the question stems from the fact that the African Pentecostal understanding and practice of deliverance has borrowed much from the indigenous religions.

Obviously Ghanaian Pentecostals do not go through deliverance to be freed exclusively from demons but also from sickness, poverty, and other misfortunes, unlike the early Christian missionaries who regarded the gods and ancestors of the indigenous religions as demons and generally agencies and agents of the devil and may not consider issues such as poverty and sickness as demons (Bowdich, 1821). Pentecostals believe in the manifestation of demons into various debilitating human conditions. On this basis, they would regard social issues such as poverty to be spiritual, for instance, and anyone plagued by poverty would need to be delivered from the spirit of poverty.

The other problem that Onyinah and Forson's assertion raises is that it relegates the conditions for which individuals seek deliverance to the abstract and intangible, suggesting that they are only an internal struggle, which is not the case. The reason is that 'African Pentecostals, through the ministry of 'healing and deliverance', provide the ritual context within which such presumably "irreversible curses" on people's lives are broken by the power of the Spirit, in order that victims may be freed to enjoy the abundance of life that is available in Christ' (Asamoah-Gyadu, 2004).

As a result of juxtaposing the practice from the indigenous religions into Pentecostal churches there is an assertion that those who would have consulted the indigenous priests are now doing that through the Pentecostal church leaders. This is backed up by statistics from the 'Association of Religion Data Archive that states that 19.3% of the population in Ghana are adherents of Indigenous religions as against 61.2% being Christians' (Appiah, 2019). The data superficially shows a resurgence of Christianity. However, due to the rise of certain shrines' popularity as mentioned earlier this resurgence is being fiercely challenged. The resurgence and popularity of this type of beliefs and praxis within Pentecostal churches in Ghana has made it possible for its replication in other countries such as Britain, where Ghanaians and Africans generally can be found.

The appropriation of deliverance from the indigenous religions into Pentecostal churches is evidenced by the similar operations and motives around being set free from entities of darkness that seek to encroach on an individual's fortune, manifesting in poverty, sickness, confusion, lack of sleep, nightmares and generally anything an individual does not want in their lives. The aspect of individuals' wellbeing being encroached upon by powers beyond the human sphere makes the need for deliverance a bit subjective as the individual and what they consider as abnormal in their lives, as well as their ability to convince the practitioner or pastor that the events have a spiritual cause. There are also instances where the pastors or prophets they approach make their own independent diagnosis upon the statement of the client or member's situation and problem. Having said that there are those prophets who through their ability to see into the spirit (as discussed above) are able to diagnose with or without the client narrating their life's events and circumstances.

The vocabulary often used for the resulting condition of deliverance is freedom. Therefore the deliverance is for freedom from poverty, sickness and a host of misfortunes that are believed to have come into the life of the individual.

Deliverance practice in Britain

Among the churches studied in Britain, observations about the appropriation of deliverance showed that deliverance is approached differently by 75 per cent of the study sample, the exception being RCI, which was much closer to the praxis in Ghana. Special deliverance sessions are organised, where individuals are prayed for, with 'manifestations' of the demons behind their conditions. Some of these manifestations take the form of the said demons speaking through those individuals about the damage they have caused and intend to perpetuate in the victim's life. These manifestations are sometimes in the form of vomiting and the demons speaking through the individuals being delivered. These are an accepted occurence in the church, and church volunteer workers, especially ushers, are trained to deal with such manifestations when they occur in the service.

Different churches differ in their view and practice of deliverance from life's debilitating conditions and social issues such as poverty and sickness and so on, but the message of the process of the deliverance is not through the ritual action expressed by others, which is the normal practice in most Pentecostal churches in Ghana. Instead, people are encouraged through faith in the word of God and only in very limited sense people are called forward, prayed for and anointed with olive oil. Some pastors and leaders believe for instance that poverty is a spirit, but the agency through which you seek deliverance is not only through some form of 'spiritual ritual action but also through other common sense and specialised help such as financial planning, business start ups and giving to God, which the church has been providing to their members through various initiatives'.

My conclusion is that the subject of deliverance is very much present in all the sermons and activities of the churches, because of the composition of the membership, the majority being African migrants. The transnational status of the members makes the subject of deliverance relevant for the Pentecostal churches. However, the process of being freed, seen as the desired result of the deliverance does not depend too much on a ritual action, similar to that of the indigenous religions. The ritual solution to poverty is not always administered through prayer: each circumstance has its own tailor-made remedy. For example, when dealing with the issue of poverty members are told to give, as God will out-give them and give them opportunities to earn more money in return, and there have been testimonies from some members of these churches that the principle of giving as taught by their pastors works. This is also alongside other remedies of teaching them practical ways of saving money and making money through business start-ups. In my view these churches have been influenced by their current cultural milieu and are responding appropriately to the cultural demands to remain relevant: first internally to the younger generation of members who were born in Britain and have no experience and understanding of the African Pentecostal church heritage, and secondly to their host community. Observations about how these churches serve as agents of continuity or discontinuity of African Pentecostal Christianity suggest there are two ways that issues of beliefs and praxis peculiar to the Ghanaian Pentecostal Church have been approached. One way is orienting the younger generation of members born in Britain who come with their parents to the churches towards the beliefs, expressions of beliefs and praxis that represent the authentic way of Christian living and expression of worship to God, with the intention that this is the only form of Christian beliefs and praxis they would accept. The danger, however, is that this may be questioned later when they are exposed to other beliefs and praxis from other Christian traditions. There may then be a tendency for them to leave to other churches whose beliefs and praxis blend better into the culture of Britain.

The second approach is just focusing on their internal community of the younger generation of church members born in Britain who go back into their communities with these 'new' set of beliefs and praxis and influence the host communities of the churches. This is based on the perception that they may be much closer to the community than their migrant parents and can use the sub-culture being inculcated in them by the church to reach out to their communities. It is worth noting that there is not an over reliance on this group as the link to their communities, since there are various activities and programs that these churches run to maintain their relevance to their host communities. Although there have been controversies regarding the issue of deliverance in Pentecostal churches among the younger generation, where there has been allegation of death and child abuse in the processes of deliverance, this does not seem to be the case of the Ghanaian-led churches in Britain as the influence of British culture seems to slightly adulterate the forms, meaning and practice of deliverance as seen above.

The Youth, Music, Dance and Choreography

The Youth, Indigenous Music and Dance and Choreography

The churches give much attention to the younger generation's future representation and continued membership in the churches. In most Ghanaian indigenous communities, especially the Akans, succession planning is quite vital to the future growth and development of communities. Young men and women are groomed to grow through the ranks to take over from the present generation to perpetuate their culture and the governance of their various communities. So for instance you have chiefs, priests and priestesses, herbalists, town criers and announcers who have apprentices who understudy them. Within these African indigenous communities, youngsters are taught the traditional dances and music because these arts define their community's culture. Akan music and dances are often expressive, with expressions that involve movement of the whole body with a combination of lyrics and rhythm. The lyrics often tell a story of an accomplishment of past warriors or the community as a whole. Examples of this traditional music are; *Kete, Adowa, Fontomfrom*, and *Nnwomkoro*. There are some of the music types such as the *fontonfrom* music and dance that does not involve lyrics. Body movements are made in line with the rhythm of the *fontomfrom* drum, which is a huge cylindrical drum often played at state functions and at the funeral of very important members of the community.

The music and dance are non restrictive to gender in the community; both males and females with the ability and training are able to perform them. In some cases, special attire needs to be worn for particular music and dance. For instance, during the time of war, the warriors had to put on special clothing and adorn themselves to look very fearful and their march may or may not include any dancing at all. If there was a dance accompaniment, it was to express the mood of the chief, the chief warrior, the warriors and the entire community. That is to say that the music and dance was not only meant for pleasure but also as part of domestic events by individuals and families and community functions of high importance. It was more often than not used as an expression of the mood of the individual and the community as a whole and could serve as a switch between times of pleasure and times of seriousness in a situation of war, famine or atrocity (Appiah, 2011). To further illustrate this point, the music and dance of the Akan has always got meaning and function whether in its domestic application as festival celebration or public appropriation as in time of war. There is an extra-musical context that gives meaning and significance to the music and dance. For instance there are songs sung by fishermen during boat rowing and during fishing, which are meant to help them synchronise the movement of the oars and also to motivate produce the energy required for the job at hand. The singing does not end on the sea: it continues at the shore whilst the fishermen are pulling the net out of the sea. Farmers do the same, singing whilst on the farms and when they bring in their produce to the harvesting grounds ready to be sent to the community or sold. It is a common sight in parts of Africa to see members of the police academy on their routine marches, do their march with songs, which came to define the courage and the bravado of the police force. It somehow distinguishes them as a serious group of people with a serious assignment.

There are dances and specific movements that are reserved for certain important members of the community such as the kings and chiefs of the community who sometimes in dancing *Kete* or *Adowa* can open their arms wide and then bring them together with the fingers to hit their chest to signify their ruler-ship and ownership of the land. This expression of authority and power to rule is limited to one's own area and in an instance where the chief of a particular traditional area hosts the *Omanhene*, the traditional chiefs or the sub-chiefs cannot make such a gesture in his presence, as he himself is under the authority of the *Omanhene*. To this end, music and dances are performed together to convey a message to the audience and community at large. Apart from the mundane and specialised use of music and dance in the community, music and dance is considered to have a spiritual function as it is used as a medium for invoking the spirits of the ancestors and the gods. During most indigenous religious rites at *Awukudae, Akwasidae, Ohum, Odwira* festivals or community celebrations, drumming and music are a central part of the ceremonies from start to finish: they are believed to be the medium that causes the transition of the ancestors or gods from the spirit to possess priests or others who they may choose as spokespersons for the moment (banks, 2011). Some communities have special drums they beat sometimes without lyrics to a particular rhythm for the invocation of a particular god in response to a need that may have arisen in the community. Those spirits are invoked with the use of music and sometimes for intervention purposes. In this case, the music and the subsequent spirit possession in itself becomes a means to an end and an opportunity to hear from the gods and for the community to convey their supplications to them (Appiah, 2011).

Due to the importance attached to music and dance in the communities there are elders who are charged with the responsibility of training the young men and women of the communities in music and dance to perpetuate culture and the indigenous religions. Music is very central to the life of the African and for that matter the Akan, as it becomes the expression of the hopes, fears, joys and sorrows of individuals and the community (Nketiah, 1963). Christian songs sung in some parts of African and the African diaspora (which have been incorporated into the Asempa Hymnal used in secondary schools in Ghana in the 1990s) include a lot of what were described as 'negro spirituals', commonly referred to these days as 'spirituals', which were mainly songs composed by African slaves whilst they worked on the plantations in the Caribbean and the Americas. The content and rhythm of these songs were inspired by African music, with some of them referred to as 'shouts' accompanied with typical dancing, hand clapping and foot taping. The content of most of these spirituals expresses the hopes, fears, joys and sorrows of these slaves at the time. These spirituals have become part of church music across Christian traditions in Africa.

A Legacy Continued In Churches in Ghana

The influence of traditional African cultures is evident in the spirituals in the African American context and has also in the music of the African Pentecostal churches, in their appreciation of music and dance, with a modern twist. In most of these churches the only difference between some of the music and dance of the indigenous religions and the church, is the insertion of the name Jesus and God and the use of biblical narratives in the music, as well as the fact that these dances are now said to be performed unto the Lord. The Pentecostal tradition that comes closest to the use of indigenous music and dance are the sumsum sore among whom Musama Disco Christo Church (MDCC), Nakaba, Divine Healers Church are very much notable. Due to the influence of western music there has been a slight modification of the type of music and dance used by the Pentecostal–Charismatic churches. This is actually a move away from the indigenous religions' type of music and the early AIC's. As seen from the previous paragraph, music and dance permeate every aspect of life of the Ghanaian, and neo-Pentecostal churches have fully taken advantage of this phenomenon (Appiah, 2011). It is therefore not surprising at all that 'gospel music' constitutes 75% of all music recorded in Ghana for instance and the rapid growth of the gospel music industry is said to have coincided with the proliferation of neo-Pentecostal churches in Ghana

(Atiemo, 2006). The kind of music learnt, choreographed and performed in these churches includes reggae, R & B and rap music with the lyrics being made up of a biblical narrative that prominently features the words God and Jesus. An example of this occurrence is the song by *Mɛsom Jesus* by Daddy Lumba, a popular Ghanaian highlife musician. The focus of the music, as in the indigenous music, is about telling the accomplishments of God and Jesus and their encounters with these personalities. These persons of the Godhead are their warriors as the Supreme Being and the ancestors in the indigenous religions and have become the embodiment and the reflection of the individuals' and the entire church community's accomplishments. The lyrics are mostly testimonial in nature which in itself reflects the preaching content and style of most Pentecostal–Charismatic sermons. The lyrics are musical personal testimonies about accomplishments with God and the audience are encouraged to believe in God and Christ, and remain firm in the faith irrespective of their personal challenges.

Also through these music and dances, the times and seasons of the church, the mood of individuals and of the church and the community as a whole can be set, expressed and gauged. A typical example is the use of this kind of music at political rallies of political parties to galvanise support and whip up support for their parties by creating awareness of the state of the nation through the music and to tell where the nation is heading, therefore providing a basis for the message of the political parties. During Ghana's return to Democratic rule in 1992, Jewel Ackah, a previously high-life singer turned gospel singer, was contracted to compose a song as an anthem for the National Democratic Congress which was a party formed by the sitting head of state. Jewel Ackah chose to use the rhythm and lines from the hymn 'Stand stand up for Jesus' originally composed by George Duffield jr. (1818-1888). This was a very crucial time for the siting president Jerry Rawlings who had resigned from the military as military dictator in order to continue under a democratic rule. Interestingly, the head of state had been hailed, as a Junior Jesus during his 1979 coup and therefore the lyrics of the song was a call to remembrance for Ghanaians not to dump their one time saviour. As it happened, Rawlings won and was inducted into office as democratically elected president of the fourth republic of Ghana. Once again during the 1998 elections the then main opposition commissioned a song written by Cindy Thompson, titled *Awurade Kasa* translated as 'Speak Lord'. The message of the song was a call to God to speak in the midst of all the difficulties they were facing. This captured the mood and attention of the nation at a time of economic difficulties and hardship, with some participants shedding tears. This according to observers was a game changer for the opposition and handed them victory in the 2000 election. This resembles the way indigenous religions use music to set the mood of the nation through their war songs by *Asafo Companies* in the communities. Music transcends religions and traditions in Ghana and the nature of the non-restrictive flow of music in between traditions and religions has provided the platform for certain socio-political agencies to carry out their agendas on the back of this sociological phenomenon.

Pentecostal churches in Ghana have taken advantage of the role of music and dance within the indigenous culture to maintain relevance to their communities. In some of these churches in Ghana, certain women are trained to play the tambourine and dance to its music. ICGC Ghana has a band called Zama and a choreography group made up of the youth who perform in the church on Sundays and special occasions. This is commonplace in many of the Pentecostal Churches and there is a set day and time where music and dance is taught as part of the church's weekly activities. Those interested in learning the musical instruments are given free tuition and the churches musical equipment is at their disposal for practice when they need it.

Youth, Music, Dance and Choreography in Britain

The practices described above in terms of the involvement of youths with music, dance and choreography in the Pentecostal churches in Ghana are the same in Ghanaian-led and other African Pentecostal churches in Britain, except that the context differs and the choice of music genre may be more diverse due to the youths exposure to different music genres in electronic and digital media. The prominence given to youth development by the Ghanaian-led Pentecostal churches through the arts, namely music, dance, and choreography, is not only a legacy of their transnational status but is also a way of keeping their youth in their churches and making the church relevant to them. Also having in mind that music from a cultural perspective can serve as a pathway to integration among younger people. This is especially important when statistics show that '16 per cent of young people detained in Young Offender Institutions in England and Wales in 2011/12 were black'. Parents and pastors through the church want to do their bit to keep the kids off the streets and subsequently out of crime. The churches also become the place for discovering and developing the

talents and abilities of these young people who sometimes feel let down by the state, because of the lack of the opportunities to realise their dreams as young black people through the development of a career alternative to the academic route. Forty four per cent of young black people capable and available for work in the twelve months to September 2012 did not have jobs compared with the national average of 24 per cent for all young people for instance. In addition, potentially only three per cent of the 44% are able to get into apprenticeship in England. In some ways the odds seem to be against these churches whose leaders turn out to be the role models of these youngsters: the responsibility falls on these leaders to work hard and creatively to develop programs that will change the life chances of black children in Britain. They therefore use music, dance and choreography as vehicles to deliver their program.

In so doing, the church accommodates music that was not previously considered to be traditionally 'gospel' as a means to retain their youth. Readiness to adapt to the changing needs of a dynamic group of people who are also in some instances upwardly mobile is seen as the means by which the churches to can remain relevant and secure their future membership, unlike the historic mainline churches they met in Britain, whose membership is now mainly the elderly. There is a deliberate attempt to provide a church environment that would be a good fit for these young people.

Making room for the current interest of street dance and rap music in Britain within the church, for example, would mean that the youth would stay in the churches. Rap music itself is said to have West African roots and therefore its appreciation by these African youth is not a novelty. Those that might have joined their parents and been exposed to the myriad of genres of the Ghanaian music industry, might have come across hip-life which a fusion of Ghanaian high-life and western pop music. Therefore rap music is not entirely new to those groups either. As mentioned earlier, historically the Akan *Nnwomkoro* contains rap-style music, which has been a music genre of the Akan people. This rap-style music only gained popularity in the US in the 1970s as a kind of street art in African-American communities.

As such, the church becomes relevant without necessarily diluting its message. This has been the trend among most African Pentecostal churches. Most African migrant parents who belong to these Pentecostal churches in Britain want their children to remain in the churches and welcome any activity that will keep their children off the street and out of trouble. This is especially so since some of them work very long hours, meaning that the church becomes their unpaid remote nanny. Common to all the churches are defined activities aimed at bringing the youth up to succeed the current generation through music and dance, as music has historically been part of the worship of the church in general. As a result the performances of these youth groups during their week of celebration, a week set aside by the church to recognise the youth, showcase what they have been learning from their mentors and patrons in the church. Music, dance and drama play a very prominent role in the line up of the program. The type of music has ranged from Reggae, Rap and R&B, and it's likely that the leadership of the church would accept other types of music for the youth to perform, so long as it carries a message of the gospel. In recent times for instance the rhythm and tune of a Bob Marley song, *No Woman No Cry*, has been used for another music title *No Jesus No Life,* which is an example of how 'secular' music has been adapted by the youth and accepted so long as the lyrics project the gospel.

In some of the African Pentecostal churches there are new dances called *Azonto* that is claimed to have been invented by a popular Ghanaian hip-life 'secular' musician called Sarkodie; and *Shaku Shaku* and *Shoki* which is originated from Nigeria. The popularity of these dances in Britain has grown beyond the African migrant community when an African volunteer

at a Homeless Centre in South London was seen to be teaching Prince William and Kate, the Duke and Duchess of Cambridge the Azonto dance moves, which its adaptation has come to be known overtime in Britain to as the 'swag dance'.This dance craze has gained much popularity in African Pentecostal churches and has been re-named *Christo-zonto* for the *Azonto* to reflect it's christening into the church as a Christian dance, whilst the *Shaku Shaku* and *Shoki* has remained the same. This has come about as a result of the transnational links these churches and members have with their country of origin, establishing their transnational status. Taking something that the young men and women outside of the church can becomes a tool for contextualising the gospel, and assisting the youth of the churches through music and dance to be ambassadors for the church and to bring other white members of the community into the church. As discussed earlier, apart from seeking solutions to the socio-economic problems of black youth in Britain, this group is also used as a tool to reach out to the communities and consequently integrate. The church has focussed on this means of maintaining relevance to the host community, because public perception of the African Pentecostal churches as a whole makes it difficult for the older Christian migrant parents to reach out to their communities.

The Public Perception Discourse of the African Churches

The public here refers to the host community who are predominantly white, members of ethnic minorities who are non-Africans and of course other Africans who belong to different Christian traditions, whose beliefs and praxis may not have been influenced by the African indigenous religions and may therefore lack understanding of the socio-cultural paradigm of the African Pentecostal churches' beliefs and praxis. The perception discourse have included criticisms that have often arisen from how the group has interpreted through the media, as well as the impact of public policy on different aspects of the migrants' lives in Britain.

Most migrants who arrive in Britain come with burdens of poverty, deprivation and in some instances the trauma of political tyrannical pursuit, it is the case that some migrants sacralise their migration and place minimal emphasis on the economic motivation for their migration (Adedibu, 2003). As a result of the background of most of these migrants, African migrants are viewed with much sceptism, in spite of the substantial contributions that some make to British society. Instead a section of the media largely considers migrants to be scroungers and is usually excluded in consultation processes in the drafting of policy that affects the migrants themselves. The pastors of these churches in my view witness the lives of the migrants from the time they come into the country through to their integration and independence of any form on social and welfare support, in a way that no UK Border official will, at any border post in the country. Previous research on migrants has marginalised the church as one of the most important places where migrants congregate for spiritual nourishment on a weekly basis and are supported through their difficulties by the initiatives the churches as discussed in previous chapters. The leaders and pastors of the churches, however, are excluded from any serious consultation in forming and forging meaningful immigration and integration policies. This may be because the host community do not regard these pastors, who have daily contact with the migrants and witness their struggles and have to develop schemes to assist them, as themselves being integrated enough to understand British culture to make a meaningful contribution because they have also come here as migrants.

This is in spite of the fact that the Life in the UK Test was supposed to help with the process of integration, where every individual seeking to settle in Britain would have to gain a basic understanding of British history and life. The lack of public approval of these pastors creates confusion within the migrant communities because the young people in the churches look up to the men and women who lead these churches as their role models. The lack of recognition that results from the public perception of these leaders and their churches means that most of these pastors have been limited in reaching out to the public and instead project a section of young members born in Britain as their agents of contextualisation. This is also because of the fact that the role models that the state agencies, policy makers and the host community leaders would like to project as models are mainly those born in Britain. Some African Pentecostal churches have outsourced their customer service organisation, including virtual receptions and administrative assistants, to companies owned and managed by whites in order to appear British, integrated and therefore to be accepted. There are other instances where the church employs white staff to handle their receptions to give them an appeal to the public beyond their immediate black communities. Even those who play certain vocal roles in the church services such as MCs, and Announcers must sound British or have an accent that is close to the British tongue. Such is the daily and systemic struggle of the African Pentecostal churches to contextualise in order to remain relevant.

The downside to this occurrence is that those role models outside of the churches themselves, who are projected and received the approval and recognition of the host community leaders, often want to disassociate themselves from their compatriots who were born outside the country and have migrated with their parents. Those born in the country hardly describe themselves as Africans and the result is that those they could have potentially influenced within as role models are left outside of their circles. This could also be as a result of their own struggles with acceptance as black people in the community. Due to the fact that 'young people's multifarious identities are, therefore, implicated in the nature of their social networks and the resources which they acquire from those connections', the disconnection from those who they consider one of them or with whom they share an identity, leaves them in a limbo, in their definition of self (Weller, 2010).

Arguably, notions of multiple identities are rife among these young people and they would shift towards one end of the identity spectrum provided there are positive effects of their connection to any identity they allude to, at any point in time. Weller and Kuusisto admit that there are some difficulties in trying to understand young people's religious identities through their religious praxis (Kuusisto, 2007). What they overlook, however, is the fact that religious praxis in itself is shaped by the culture of the parents; therefore, to reinforce the argument I made earlier, young people would find it much easier to look up to role models from their socio-cultural surroundings, whose identities they can trace and identify with. The result of this is that there is distrust of some of the institutions that have state recognition. There are highly educated migrants who are working in jobs below their capabilities and below their academic attainments; they are not in the top echelons of society because they lack the opportunity to reach the top, in order to 'qualify' as role models.

There is a systemic failure in the approach of British society as a whole in dealing with migrants and until there is a change, highly skilled and educated migrants would continue to voluntarily sit on the fringes or remain within their zones of marginalisation. This has and will continue to develop inertia in the process of contextualisation and contributing to their host community. If this phenomenon continues without being attended to, African churches would remain African as they would have no choice but limit their influence to the African community. They would want to maintain the status quo to preserve their identity as Africans in order not to get lost in their attempt to gain recognition within the wider sphere of society.

The other public perception of the African Pentecostal churches is that they are often referred to by their origins. This does not only affect the Pentecostal churches; for instance, the Presbyterian Church formed by members of the Presbyterian Church from Ghana is called Ghana Presbyterian Church; there is also the Ghana Wesleyan Methodist church. The challenge for these churches and the tags they are given is a result of the cultural infusion into the general identity of the churches because of where they have come from. In spite of boasting of other nationalities, members of these churches still consider themselves primarily Ghanaian but generally multicultural. The differences of the experiences and the praxis of the African churches from those of the other churches, coupled with the background of the migrants that are the majority in these churches, makes people from the host communities not give them the needed recognition.

The applied content of what these churches do and the positive effects of their ministry to young marginalised people are often glossed over because of the minute differences they have from predominant white churches. It seems as though the proverbial 'can anything good come out of Nazareth' is often applied due to the context these churches have originated from, forgetting that there are people that these churches attend to who may be missed by the state or other state sponsored agencies in providing them with assistance in their time of need.

Some of these African churches take their ritual performances to the extreme, such as the use of the anointing oil; some of them have been alleged to extort money from their poor migrant members; pastors have been accused of aiding and abetting the abuse of children; and providing false hopes for the sick they pray for as being healed when not passed and signed off by medical professionals. These allegations notwithstanding, there are often generalisations in the mass media, which use isolated cases to brand these African churches as all being scandalous. For those who may never visit or attend an African church this may produce a negative perception of the churches, which could affect those individuals' acceptance of these churches in their communities as agents of change or spiritual vitality, which most of these churches believe they bring to the host community in the context of reverse mission. The pastors of these churches consider these negative public perceptions as impediments from

the devil to resist the work of God and to slow down the process of reverse mission.

In addition to issues of differing perceptions, whilst the level of contextualisation will determine the extent of host communities' acceptance of African churches, they have a 'divine mandate' to revitalise the spirituality of their host communities, and therefore can only make marginal changes in the message and approach. For instance the British perception of the church as a registered charity would be to provide support to the vulnerable in society and generally in doing good works in the community: the Ghanaian-led churches and for that matter the African churches believe that the priority is the preaching of the gospel that 'saves' people and that doing charity work is only a by product of the preaching of the Word of God. The difference in the theological approaches is that the British public would rather accept the faith on the basis of works to humankind whilst the churches approach is based on accepting the word and the works would follow.

Summary and Discussion

Within the context of reverse mission the purpose of the African Pentecostal churches' agenda would be to bring the gospel of Jesus to the white British community. The process by which they can get the gospel to their host community would be to put the gospel in a familiar package to make it relevant to them and easier to accept. This becomes of utmost importance because African Pentecostal Christianity in Britain has cultural orientation, which influence the interpretation of the Bible, and the praxis that follows from this. The practice of deliverance; naming ceremonies; libation prayer language and its use in Pentecostal prayer;

prophetic consultation; and music and dance have special characteristics that leaves little doubt that they have been influenced by the Pentecostal churches in Africa, which have in turn been heavily influenced by the indigenous religions. It can be agreed that some of the practices of the churches in Britain have been overhauled from their original form in Africa but by and large they still have those distinctive features traceable ultimately to the indigenous religions.

The process of contextualisation in the case of the African Pentecostal churches would involve balancing the weight of its' cultural baggage to make their Christianity relevant within the British cultural context. That would also mean that it adds African flavour to the interpretations of scripture and its subsequent practice. This enables it to and remains relevant and appealing to the African in Britain, who is familiar with this kind of Christianity. Asa result, and due to bad public perception arising from negative representations in the mass media these churches have resorted to focussing on their own community to whom they are relevant. Their practices of the principles of scripture have been derived by their own scriptural interpretations through the lens of their culture. Since the indigenous religions are part of the culture of the people, it makes their type of Christianity African; this is sometimes difficult for the predominantly white host community to appreciate or accept. In order to pursue their reverse mission agenda and carry their message into the host community, they use the young members of their churches born in Britain to reach out. The host communities find it easier to accept these young people, whereas the leaders – although they are role models to the youngsters – do not have the recognition and approval of the host community. This lack of recognition has nothing to do with the contribution of these churches to the social-economic or cultural development of Britain, but rather is because the kind of Christianity of the Ghanaian-led Pentecostal churches is different and has not as yet been vey well understood.

CHAPTER SIX

TRANSNATIONAL STATUSES AS A DERIVATIVE OF SOCIO-THEOLOGICAL POSTURE OF THE CHURCHES

Introduction

As the previous chapter showed, the fluid socio-cultural dynamics of relations between the Pentecostal churches and their host community somehow pushes the African Pentecostal churches to first focus on themselves. As a result, the integration strategies adopted by churches to assist members to integrate into the larger host community are managed internally within the churches through varied initiatives. These initiatives assist members to internally fit into the churches and to co-exist through helping the individuals to be productive but at the same time providing them with the tools for integration into the larger society. In spite of these churches being pushed into obscurity and often designated by the public as 'specific ethnic churches' such as 'Ghanaian churches', Nigerian churches or even 'Congolese churches', some have managed to make significant, recognisable contributions to their host communities, and these have aided their integration into these communities. These contributions include changes to the religious landscape and social and economic infrastructural development as part of community regeneration. These contributions are discussed in depth in the sections that follow in this chapter. Following through the argument that the characteristics of the churches give them a transnational status, not only do the churches contribute to the British communities in which they are located, but they also contribute to communities where they have ties elsewhere in Africa. These ties are usually ethnic ties defined by the pastors' and leaders' origins in Africa, covering the areas where the pastors and leaders start with their ministries; they are also generally areas where there is a notable need that draws national attention.

In this chapter, the contributions described in the paragraph above will be used as the framework to analyse simultaneously and concurrently, the churches' individual contributions both in Britain and in their places of origins in Africa.

Changes to the Religious landscape

Due to the influx of migrants from various African nations from the 1960s onwards, there has been a significant change to the religious landscape in Britain, and London has become the melting point of these cultures. A walk through parts of London on a Sunday would reveal church-going people from different parts of the world in different church uniforms that identify them to specific cultural origins. For instance a walk along Old Kent Road would reveal the myriads of churches especially from sub-Saharan Africa. This is so at a time when there is a general decline in the membership of African-Caribbean initiated churches and the mainline historic churches (Burgess, 2009). There seems to be a resurgence of the 'noisy' African Christianity that is far from the solemn and 'quiet' church services held by the mainline historic churches in Britain. The fact that these churches are springing up everywhere in classrooms, theatres, leisure centres, libraries and disused warehouses, shows that purpose built facilities to hold a body of believers to be equipped to profess their faith is not always the norm. These migrant's believe that they have been sent by God to bring the gospel back to those who first brought it to them, they are the body of Christ and for that matter the church, and the church is not necessarily the bricks and mortar infrastructure in which they hold their meetings; they do however underscore the importance of the buildings for their church, hence the purchase of landmark buildings for services. These communities argue that the presence of God is anywhere His people represent Him and the kind of infrastructure in which they hold their services in itself testifies of the revival that God is in the process of bringing to Britain through their churches, and that churches are not only meant to be purpose-built beautiful edifices with stained glass windows. They argue that before this time this was not how churches were organised and generally looked like in Britain: this is a patronising statement from the migrants as most 'non-conformist' churches in Britain at their beginning had similar histories regarding meeting places. Holding church services in unconventional buildings such as classrooms, and theatres for instance by Pentecostals, has changed the face of Christianity in its organisation in Britain, as borough councils across Britain have in recent years been granting planning permission for the change of use of various buildings to be converted to churches. The issue of infrastructure will be analysed adequately in this chapter.

These Pentecostal Christians of West African origin believe that very soon British Christianity will be defined on the basis of the Christianity of the African-led churches and not the mainline historic churches, in two main ways. Firstly, that there will have been a transformation of the beliefs and practices of the mainline historic churches to reflect a new age of spiritual vigour that the church has received from the Lord. To buttress this point, they cite an instance where some parishes of the mainline historic churches of Britain in areas with quite a large number of African migrant population have introduced a style of worship which is characteristically African, or borrowed from the African Pentecostal churches probably because of the Pentecostalisation of African Christianity in general. It is not clear from what perspective these churches have introduced those 'African aspects of worship' into their worship but due to the unverifiable nature of the information provided, it is probable that the strategy is to attract the

African community in general because of the cultural constituents of those particular communities. However, if this is the case, there is a question as to whether it could be adopted by other parishes, as has been the case in some African-Caribbean churches (Morrison, 2014).

Secondly, the respondents believe there will arise the situation where the presence of the African Pentecostal churches generally, will continue to reinvigorate the other mainline historic churches back to growing membership and to a prominent place as a significant Christian voice in the nation. They assume that the success of these churches will challenge the mainline historical churches to spiritualise their services and Christianity a bit more to provide the public with a genuinely alternative lifestyle. Some scholars have described this kind of Christianity with its beliefs and praxis as African Christianity but for many of these African migrant Christians, it's just a pragmatic, biblical way of serving God and enjoying the benefits of this service to God. Highlighting differences between the types of Christianity is met with scepticism as a way of denigrating the success of these churches in Britain because for a long time the main British Pentecostal churches have not done so well in consistently attracting huge numbers of people to their services compared to the African–led churches, in since the time of George Jeffreys of the Elim Pentecostal Church, and in more recent times Paul Scanlon of the Abundant Life Church, now known as Life Church UK who attracted a significant number of worshippers. For these churches, the focus of their message, beliefs and praxis is a Christianity that works. A biblical explanation often used to characterise this modus operandi is the fact that 'the God who created the heavens is the same God who also created the earth', in other words the God of the spiritual is the God of the physical and therefore the spirit must have expression in the worship services, such as healing, prophesying among others. This perception is in line with the theological basis adopted by

the Pentecostals to back their expressions of worship, which also gives the churches their distinctiveness in comparison to others, especially the Christianity of the mainline historical churches. And in as much as Pentecostalism generally embraces that belief that is consequently expressed in their worship, for African Pentecostals it has become even more imperative, as their indigenous cosmology and religious beliefs enforces those forms. These forms are so inextricably intertwined with their culture that it's impossible to perceive otherwise or consider any other way of worshipping as authentic, apart from the way that they do it.

Ninety per cent of all respondents believe that the African Pentecostal churches have changed the landscape of Christianity and the organisation of church services as a whole. Some cited open public advertisement of church conferences in the mass media as an example. This is in addition to the advertisements shown on the Christian TV and radio stations owned by the churches. The advertisements for instance have gone as far as posting huge paper posters at public places, advertising on double decker London buses, hoardings at public places, and placing flyers in supermarkets. These initiatives are not something entirely new to the British scene as some of the mainline historic churches do the same but it is the consistency, conviction and dependence on it as a strategy of outreach. Some of these churches resort to advertising on their church commuting buses which mainly picks up members from specifics stops to church during days of services. On these buses they have the names of the church and their service times and phone numbers written. On occasions they would stick posters of conferences on the bus to advertise their conferences and conventions. This and many other innovative strategies are used to attract worshippers and those who also feel that the churches have got answers to their problems. This, to an extent, is a bit further from the advertising campaigns that most of the mainline historic churches would be prepared to do. As unconventional as it may be according to these churches, it is an attempt of the churches to make use of innovative mediums of reaching out to the communities of their churches. Other methods have included writing to members of their communities through details obtained from the edited electoral register for their local areas.

Access to these personal details enables them to write personal letters to appeal to residents with their message and also to extend a hand of fellowship to those who may want to visit them and worship with them. In some cases some vulnerable and needy people have been visited because of their response to the churches' initial contact. The church in these cases has provided support to these persons. The strategy has been to bring the church to the homes of the people through charitable work. However, what changes landscape is not only the provision of support to people in their homes but also the modes of contact itself. There are instances churches pay visits to the vulnerable in their local communities sustain and maintain a relationship with these people, anticipating that that they will one day make the decision to come to the church. This goes to illustrate the important role the churches play in providing support to members of their communities irrespective of their ethnic lineages, having dared to position themselves as dependable community assets.

Apart from the above humanitarian outreaches, there have been instances where, permission has been sought from authorities to have little gigs in market places to create the opportunity to preach the gospel, as people are attracted to the music and singing in town centre areas. All these aggressive strategies of reaching out to the communities by the African churches have dramatically transformed the landscape of Christianity in Britain. Some scholars claim there is a general decline in Christianity, but it depends on where one is looking, as through these African churches Christianity is made ever more visible. The question that arises however is whether they are recognised as having an impact on Christianity as a whole or are they only seen by those who are a part of those churches, affirming the suggestion that these churches have become somewhat inward looking.

From the perspective of the African churches there is the need for the church to have an independent voice that arises from its convictions rather than being propped up by those who are given their place through the recognition of the state. There is the belief among some of the leaders of the churches mentioned state quite categorically that the current economic woes of Britain are due to the fact that the country has rejected God, resulting in a decline in the prosperity of its people and that a change will only occur when the nation return to the Lord. Some would narrow this phenomenon down to globalisation through migration but the changes that African churches in general and African Pentecostal churches in particular are affecting in the landscape of Christianity in Britain is happening because of the spiritual invigoration, brought into Britain by these churches. It is clear from the perspective of some of the members and leadership of these African churches, that the spiritual impact and effect of their presence and contribution in Britain has been very important in reshaping the landscape of Christianity in contemporary Britain.

The changing landscape: contra-flow of the transnational influence

Apart from these churches changing the landscape of Christianity in Britain, they have also changed the landscape of Christianity in their places of origin. This change has occurred in two ways: first through the access of the pastors and leaders of churches in their places of origin in Africa to the churches in Britain. Within the African cultural paradigm, people have respect for anything that comes from their colonial masters for historical reasons. As a result, this raises their status in their homelands and brings respect to their churches' standing. A visit to the Facebook accounts of some of African pastors reveal pictures proudly published of pastors posing by famous monuments in London and other parts of the world, with famous African pastors who they call on whilst in Britain, as well as pictures of them preaching in churches. There is a perception that ministers invited to minister abroad from these homelands are successful, due to their recognition by the churches in the diaspora. In fact, the pastors may only be friends of these pastors in the diaspora or might have been introduced by other friends of the pastors to them; they have not necessarily been invited for a special or peculiar ministry they have to deliver to the church. Having said that, some of these pastors are sought-after popular speakers within their nation's Pentecostal church circles and speak at conferences organised by the churches, as mentioned in chapter three.

The second change has been the influence from the British and African churches and their leaders on the church organisation strategies and practices of churches in their places of origin. These ranges from ancillary influences that include the type of songs used as part of their worship services and, relatedly, the use of the English language for the services. Over the years, music within Pentecostal churches has been used as the means to invoke the presence of Spirit to enable them to worship and praise God (Jennings, 2008). Songs were used to set the atmosphere for the working of the Spirit and for personal encouragement, as some of the songs are mainly used to minister to one another. The motive and style of songs used in African Pentecostal churches shares some affinities with the way music is used in African indigenous culture, as discussed in the previous chapter, although in African indigenous worship the songs are used for the invocation of the gods and deities.

The songs from the west that most influenced worship by the Pentecostal churches were primarily from Maranatha! Music, a group from the United States who had much influence in Pentecostal churches in Britain. However, it seems as though this has lost ground to Integrity Music, which is another American label that produces artists mainly from the Pentecostal Charismatic stream and lately Hillsong from Australia. These songs which are widely used in Pentecostal churches in Britain are exported to Africa, where they are considered by many to be British Gospel Music. These have been adopted by most of the churches in Africa and the songs are reproduced live for the worship services. This has not only been a result of African church leaders' direct contact with churches in Britain or the western hemisphere but also through the work of Nigerian music pirates who produce cheap copies of this Christian music for the African market. Without discussing the ethical implications of their actions for the record labels and artist, most worship leaders in the churches have access to this pirated music and teach their church members, choirs and praise teams to sing the songs. In addition to this style of music, youthful rap gospel music has also caught on very well with the Pentecostal churches in Africa, mainly because they have been accepted by the churches in Britain.

In the last ten years, there is also an export of African gospel music in the main stream of white Pentecostal churches, performed by western artiste. Examples of these African artiste include, Uche (Nigeria), Sonnie Badu (Ghana), Winnie Mashaba (South Africa), Mercy Chinwo (Nigeria), Nathaniel Bassey (Nigeria), Sinach (Nigeria), Joe Mettle (Ghana), and Benjamin Dube (South Africa). These artiste have recorded with popular western gospel artistes and held live concerts together. In part, the successful adaptation to this is due to its unique style and also the fact that this type of music is used for the invocation of the Spirit, which is an element in Pentecostal worship with influences from the African indigenous religion. Currently most of the songs are in English and this makes it easier for other parts of the services to be conducted in English. The appeal for these songs and style of worship is as a result of the growth of the middle-income sector of the population and young members who have had contact with churches abroad, especially during their time as students. In addition to this ancillary transnational influence there are two significant areas of influence: the strict adherence to time, and the use of the mass media in advancing the cause of the pastors, their churches and the gospel.

Strict Adherence to Time

In the early stages of the emergence of the Pentecostal church in Ghana sand parts of Africa, worship services were conducted over several hours. For instance at ICGC Ghana, RCI Ghana, Action Chapel, Global Revival Ministries and the Full Gospel Evangelical Ministry, in the late 1980s and 1990s church services were held from 9am to about 3pm. The length of time the churches spent in worship services was itself underpinned by the whole African concept of time, which according to Mbiti is 'time is simply a composition of events which have occurred, those which are taking place now and those which are immediately to occur' (Mbiti, 1969). Therefore, time to the African is a continuum of events with no specific point for commencement and completion: this amounts to what most westerners would regard as a disregard for time.

Due to the influence of western lifestyles on migrants, this has changed and a post-migration attitude to time has emerged among those who have spent a period of time in the west. The insurgence of foreign direct investments into parts of Ghana especially during the fourth republic also saw these foreign firms demanding a certain level of efficiency of their labour force, which includes a change in attitude and conceptions of time. Amongst other factors, such as the level of education for pastors, this has given rise to this wave of change not only among Africans but also among African-Caribbean (Roberts, 2009). However, there are still some Pentecostal churches that have very lengthy church services. At the time of the emergence of the movement, many of their congregants were students and had time on their hands (Kalu, 2007). The then student congregants are now the cream of the labour force and can no longer afford to spend the whole day in church. The growth of the country's economy to a middle-income status also means that people in certain firms and industries have to work longer hours to meet employers' targets (IMF, 2013). They also have young families to spend time with after being away for work most part of the week. Another factor is that holding multiple services in the same building means that services have to be relatively short to accommodate the second group of congregants. Even more important is that some of the congregants who had migrated to Britain for further studies were exposed to the British way of life due to their interaction with some of the churches they attended whilst in Britain, giving them the post-migration attitude described above. They have therefore developed a consciousness for saving time at church to be spent on other areas of life. Most of the pastors of the churches have also been exposed to the way church is organised and run in the Northern hemisphere, particularly Britain (Roberts, 2009).

These visits have shown these pastors alternative ways of saving time and making judicious use of time for their services. Not only is this innovative for these churches but it is also necessary to keep their members, especially those within the middle income bracket who can only make it to Sunday services due to work commitments. There are cases where pastors have returned to homelands from Britain or elsewhere after their studies and have introduced changes to the strict adherence to time. Although the churches in Britain are not perfect in their adherence to time, strict adherence to time is promoted using strategies such as stating the time in African time and 'GMT', jokingly keeping members on their toes to adhere to time. Another factor affecting the churches in Britain are also that because some of the places of worship are rented premises, caretakers and landlords strictly enforce the time. In effect some of the changes that have taken place on the religious landscape in Ghana have been both transnational and local factors feeding into each other to produce the changes now experienced. It has become a cycle where local indigenous factors shape African Pentecostalism, these affect African Pentecostal churches in Britain, which in turn are also shaped by contextual factors in Britain. These changes then affect the Pentecostal churches in Africa because of the continued ties there. In another way, local factors push people to study in Britain, whilst in Britain they imbibe the British/African religious culture and on their return effect changes that produces transnational results. The relationship between both individuals and churches does not actually cease with the movements of individuals across the countries but it is rather strengthened further by the continuous movements of these same people or their other associates. Apart from the physical movement across borders for contact between the migrants' current place of abode and place of origin, there is the use of various mass media and social networking platforms with which contact is made and information is disseminated.

Use of Mass Media and Social Networking Platforms by African Churches

The transnational influence of African Pentecostal churches in Britain, in the area of media use has been phenomenal. The process of globalisation and the technological revolution has made it possible for churches to be able to disseminate information across borders without going through physical borders. This has aided the sharing of information from one church to another and enabled churches to develop cultures that can be easily seen somewhere else on the planet. Therefore one can visit a church in Britain with an African pastor whose church worship style looks American; and one can also visit a church in Ghana, Nigeria, and South Africa that looks like a church in Britain or the United States. This is understood in the context that they are not a corporate group but have different organisational forms yet forged for themselves, a specific religious identity that makes them identifiable to a larger global movement.

These churches either in America, Britain or Ghana use the media to share their desirable cultures some of which are applicable in other contexts, therefore creating some form of connection with others in other places (Hackett, 1998). This amalgamation and unification of church ideas and cultures has made some churches transnational, to an extent. For example churches copy infrastructure designs or styles of worship and pastors even copy-preaching styles from others they admire and consider more successful. In effect, some become surrogates of others somewhere that they may not necessarily be connected to culturally, therefore creating ambiguous transnational relationships around the world. The transfer of ideas transculturally has been referred to by Wilson as a 'new kind of relativism in men's thinking' (Wilson, 1982). These churches, their pastors or congregants are not necessarily from the same places of origin and yet they have a strong bond through a shared common church culture (Schiller et al, 2006). This is because the ideas espoused by these global church actors are well 'transportable and transposable to different cultural contexts' (Csordas, 2007). The strategies they use to reach out to the public globally are also shared. It's worth mentioning, there are a lot of similarities shared among churches' use of media technology in Ghana and African churches generally in Britain, apart from the similarities with African Pentecostal churches. This has taken the connections between the churches and the resulting networks to new global levels as they are set to increase and become widespread as technological advances are made (Hackett, 2009).

The participation of the churches in globalisation has revealed their apt use of technology such as multi media and social media to reach out beyond their immediate confines to make disciples of the nations. It's worthy of note that this occurrence lacks a deliberate design or framework, the extent of usage of the media has been dependent on the results that individual churches are able to derive from the media use and their willingness to invest more to exploit it even more.

The African churches in Britain use the mass media to advertise the God they worship, to promote their pastors within their church organisation and to show the world that they are. These motives for the use of the mass media are all encoded in an ideology that works within the framework of their theology, and this ideology is also transferable across borders (Fiske, 1987). The churches in Africa use the media and social networking platforms with the same motives. The overriding aim is ultimately to increase their following not only locally but also globally. From a transnational point of view they seek to incorporate their converts into a global community of believers and to use these relationships to influence and to be influenced in the playing field of global Christianity (Schiller and Caglar, 2008). Considering that this is the motive for the use of the mass media by the Pentecostal churches in Africa and the African churches in Britain, one is tempted to ask where this influence on the churches in Britain has actually come from. This question arises from an Akan ideological saying that 'ahenepa nkasa', literally translated: 'very good beads do not make noise when they rub against each other'; meaning that any good thing does not announce itself. This is a prevalent cultural ideology in most Ghanaian communities, so one might ask the question as to whether the use of mass media is a noise-making platform and therefore constitutes a foreign influence and for that matter its use a recent phenomenon in the African Christian community. The answer to this question may lie in globalisation, in that mass media use occurs not only among the churches but also among practitioners of indigenous religions and their shrines (Appiah, 2011).

A trip to Ghana, from Accra in the Greater Accra Region to Koforidua in the Eastern Region, one could come across about eight big sign boards advertising the services of the priests of these shrines, in the small towns and villages along the main roads. This is a recent development in Ghana due to the rise to fame of Nana Kwaku Bonsam who had regular appearances on the mass media to represent the indigenous religions in religious debates. He seems to have taken over from where Osofo Komfo Damoah, the leader of the Afrikania Mission left off with his weekly broadcast (Clark, 2006). Therefore not only has Pentecostals' use of the mass media become part of Pentecostal self-definition as a strand of African Christianity, but it has also become part of the self-definition of religion in general through globalisation (Maxwell, 1998). The mass media is exploited by the Pentecostal churches in both Africa and in Britain because it is regarded as an 'icon of modernity' (Asamoah-Gyadu, 2005). In spite of the fact that some rather low standard and shoddy representations in the mass media (such as TV, Radio, Internet and the social media) exposes the ill-preparedness of some of these churches to venture into a global playing field, they are determined to stay there as they feel its use maintains their relevance to the public, in the same way as their physical infrastructure, such as buildings gives them a presence in the areas where they are situated.

Community Regeneration through Socio-Economic Infrastructural Development

Church buildings are the focal point of the communities in which they are built. In most societies most of the rites of passage of members of the community, namely christening, first communion, confirmation, weddings and funeral services are all held there. This is even more important especially among the migrant communities who consider the church as a major source of support for them and their families. Therefore the building up or the destruction of a church building can bring joy or can be devastating (Carter, 1999). For African migrant Pentecostals, this is even more important as the church serves as the place of their social integration into wider British society: it also serves as a place for economic empowerment; as a place for religious education and worship; as a place they consider entirely theirs; and as a place where they reaffirm their identity as people of African descent. As a result of the migrants' perspective on the church, 'the church and community continue to be highly integrated, and religious practices of the church often affect other areas of community life' (Boyd-Franklin, 1989). Apart from the migrant members' individual benefits from the churches, the acquisition of permanent places of worship can be considered as a sign of social regeneration of the communities. Firstly, because of the programmes and activities of the churches which are geared towards empowering individuals of the church. And secondly, because these churches rarely have land on which to build new churches so they resort to buying disused warehouses and dilapidated cinema halls and refurbish them and turn them into places of worship. The result is that economic activity in the area is boosted because the churches draw a lot of people into the area and there is a possibility that some members may decide to relocate closer to the location of the church at some point. There is also significant economic activity on the premises of theses churches. Some of the churches operates snacks shop where members make purchases after their worship services; they also have a book shops which sells popular Christian literature to members and the public, generating income for the church and employment for the bookshop attendants who are also members of the church. In instances where these churches have no place of worship of their own, these members sell their merchandise merchandises from their car boots after service. The items sold included, men and women shirts, children's wear and African food items such as yam, plantain, palm oil, chin chin and gari.

This orientation towards social engagement is in itself transnational and is adopted from other earlier independent churches in Africa as Turner points out. In the past, some of the African independent churches in Africa set up economic initiatives as a means of self-support for the inhabitants of the deprived areas where they were located (Turner, 1980). This transnational element of social engagement within the context of economic regeneration assists the migrants to overcome locally bounded traditions of church organization to find unique ways of being (Krause, 2008). This helps them to meet their own most urgently felt needs of spiritual and economic independence from their colonial churches under their own kind of leaders (Turner, 1980). As a proof of their willingness to contribute to social and economic development of their host country, as they seek to consolidate visible outcomes of the gospel in their communities, with reference to reverse mission. This reverse mission rhetoric 'signifies the appropriation of a new position for black Christians within the global power geometry' where these African Pentecostal churches seek to establish themselves as major players in the religious arena in Britain (Assey, 1993). This has led to the acquisition of buildings to pursue this objective. Not only does the acquisition of these buildings reveal how powerful these churches have become, but also for some the ownership re-writes the history of the buildings themselves, to include their current occupation by a predominant minority group. The church in turn gains public recognition for regeneration they bring to the area by bringing back to life a derelict public building. The power rhetoric also includes the financial power of the churches to earn their respect and place in society not only as receivers but also as givers to the localities and society in which they find themselves.

Considering the fact that 'it is religion, more than anything else, which colours their understanding of the universe and their empirical participation in that universe, making life a profoundly religious phenomenon', completing the often-laborious process - including getting planning permission- of purchasing a place of worship that can also be used for the church's ancillary activities, is a spiritual experience in itself. It is often characterised by special prayer during services because for them it is about the Lord creating room for them in the land where they are migrants. The biblical narrative often used to describe this experience is Isaac's experience of hostility and strife over the wells he dug, recorded in Genesis 26. The appropriation of the experience within the context of scripture further deepens the spiritualising of the migration experience. This then in the minds of these African Christians decriminalises illegal immigration on the basis that the claims of Gods are superior to those of people, in the sense that God can move people from one place to the other to accomplish an assignment for him. In that instance, the factors that precipitates migration encompass religious and spiritual factors. Also for some, the acquisition of buildings by the churches is a reminder to the members that God can also do great things for them. Apart from collectively claiming ownership and taking pride in their collective enterprise, the buildings serve as a reminder of the results of personal commitment and faithfulness towards God. Therefore the building stands as a monument of the faith of the people.

Summary and Discussion

People carry their faith with them wherever they go and its expression is often subject to the context within which it is expressed. Within a new social context, existing forms of faith tend to influence that particular faith in diverse ways as the 'new' faith also influences existing faiths and their expression within that particular context. African Pentecostal migrants bring their faith and its expression to Britain, and their faith influences and are influenced by the existing conditions within the host community in diverse ways. The introduction of elements of transnationalism means that not only are the host community's form of Christianity and the migrants' Christianity affected but the Christianity of the place of origin of the migrants is also affected. There are specific areas that can be identified as the derivative of the socio-theological posture of the churches.

Firstly, due to the presence of the African churches in the host communities, there are visible changes to the religious landscape. The face of Christianity has changed in several ways; there are infrastructural changes to accommodate the churches and the nature of worship services even in mainline historic churches and British Pentecostal churches have adopted liturgy styles to make migrant worshippers feel at home.

The phenomenon of migrants influencing worship styles of the churches in the host community also extends to the place of origin as even the music is shared to reflect the influence of the indigenous religions; church organisation strategies and practices are also shared in both directions. A significant example of this is the strict adherence to time in running church services which is a departure from the norm in most of the Pentecostal churches of African origin.

In addition, the African church has adopted and become embedded in the trend of using technology to reach out to people, including through mass media and social media platforms which are considered as 'icons of modernity'. This has enabled churches in the host community and the place of origin to become global and local players at the same time. Both churches in Britain and homelands can participate in the churches in real time in spite of the spatial differentials to location and conditions.

Finally, the churches deliberate community regeneration initiatives involving the transformation of derelict public spaces into sacred edifices of worship have strengthened their place in their communities and given their members – most of whom would otherwise be considered voiceless - a voice in society. These initiatives tend to portray the economic power these churches have, making them noticeable and recognisable in their communities as the gospel bearers, thereby solidifying the reverse mission agenda to bringing the gospel back to the country from which they first received it. The effect of this is that they are better able as local actors to go beyond their communities to making a global impact. The relationship between African churches in Britain and churches in Africa cannot be under-estimated considering the fact that on the grounds of transnationalism each flows into the other, shapes its beliefs and praxis, and also its responses to the global influences of other forms of Christianity. The resulting 'new' form of faith is then consciously and unconsciously transported via transnational ties to the places of origin of the migrants.

EPILOGUE

The African Church in Britain: The future

This book is an analysis of the trajectories of African churches with a focus on the Pentecostal strand, and the religious and social change they have brought about in the host communities of Britain. It has discussed and illustrated innovative ways by which Africa churches from a socio-theological perspective, contextualise their beliefs and praxis through the influence of their indigenous religions; integrate into British society; and subsequently contribute to both their place of settlement and of origin. The analysis adds to the broader debate on the place of African churches and the processes that ultimately lead to them forming and forging a transnational statuses in Britain. The key question which the research underpinning the content of this book set out to explore were how and why the African Christian migrants and the churches they belong to have assumed transnational statuses.

In doing so, the enquiry identified internal micro-level integration strategies adopted by the African churches within the context of macro-level national and governmental integration policies, as well as exploring specific areas of the socio-cultural interface of indigenous religious beliefs and praxes in the churches in Britain which give rise to the contextualisation of their faith. I have postulated that this process has strongly been shaped by the church communities' socio-theological perspective to issues.

It have argued that the churches and members are ultimately both transnational entities, and that the process of integration is made easier for migrant members through the initiatives of the church. Since its members embody the church, the beliefs and praxis of their faith from their place of origin influence the expression of their faith in their present context and that is enforced by their regular interaction with their places of origin.

The broader perspective of the study discusses the religious, cultural and socio-economic aspirations and to some extent the political aspirations associated with migrants coming to Britain. With my approach to the study, I looked at religion through the lens of socio-cultural and theological change in migrants' lives, but more importantly explored how religious institutions and their members interact with their past, present and future. Investigating the internal integration and contextualisation rhetoric opens up the study of small-sized African Pentecostal churches in Britain in relation to the making of transnational churches. Aside from the religious sphere, the study also takes into account the wider local, national and global surroundings of the churches and how they fit into a phenomenon that may be traceable to other parts of the world with similar religious, cultural, economic and political circumstances.

The book contributes new information to the existing knowledge in this field in three areas: firstly, regarding the internal integration initiatives and interventions of the churches as social units; secondly, the socio-cultural interface of African Pentecostal belief and praxis leads to its contextualisation in Britain; and thirdly, exploring the influences of the churches on the social strata of both places of settlement and origin. Most of the literature on African Pentecostal migrants and churches in general overlooks how intertwined the churches are with the migrant community: the onus on both sides to ensure their continued existence as entities and conduits of expression in the private and public sphere. The churches and members work together in providing a place of communion with other believers and in the process help the migrants to integrate into the wider society through their initiatives. This subsequently provides the platform to remain in constant touch with their places of origin.

As I describe through the chapters of the book, the constant interaction of church and membership produces an inseparable mix, which helps us to analyse both members and church separately, but also as a unit, to understand their impact on their community and vice versa. I argued at the outset that understanding the transnational migrant status of any group of people or institutions begins with understanding the factors that gives rise to migration. Existing theories on migration, stress factors of economics, politics, and socio-cultural change in a generalised sense. These theories are put forward without reference to religious factors, other than where religious persecution is a factor of migration. I assert that from the perspective of some migrants, their migration is precipitated by a perceived command from God. There are also those who migrate initially for economic reasons only to realise after some time that there has been a 'spiritual' factor to their migration: they may consider themselves as the modern day archetypes of Joseph and the biblical patriarchs. This is referred to as a 'spiritual factor' due to difficulties in its measurability and the subjectivity of individuals' own religious experiences.

This changes the face of migration, and means that whether migration should be considered positive or negative on the part of sending and receiving nations can only be properly analysed when the religious factors are considered. Consequently there is a need to develop a new theory that encompasses the 'spiritual' factor. It has to be noted, however, that apart from the command from God as a reason for migration, there are several other reasons subsumed under this religious dimension. Where individuals realise there may have been a spiritual dimension to their migration before leaving their countries of origin, this presents a particularly complex situation to explain. Church communities who consider themselves highly spiritually inclined most often claim this 'spiritual factor', and these are typically the leaders and pastors of the churches. It is clear throughout the book that, according to the perspective of the migrants and leaders of the churches, where religious factors precipitate migration, positive changes to the religious landscape result, both at places of origin and in their settled communities. I therefore maintain that people migrate on the basis of a supernatural commission although in some cases, like that of Abraham in the Bible, migrants have been told to leave their country for a different country without being sure of their mission until they arrive at their destination and discover the reason for the supernatural prompting to move. Within the context of Pentecostal relationship to the scriptures, where the Bible is read literally and certain experiences are traced to other biblical narratives, such observations are problematic for existing theological discourses. But at the same time they are verifiable by the experiences of the migrants who attribute their migration to a supernatural commission. The ambivalence about this spiritual factor of migration is eliminated by the verifiable narratives of the migrants *vis à vis* their current placement within society as a result of their claims. Some, against all odds, have been able to confront the challenges of coming to Britain without the requisite resident permits and yet have become relatively well placed within society and use their experiences to help others.

The pastors and leaders of some of the churches that started in Britain without a parent church in Africa that I examined as case studies in this book believe they came to Britain by a supernatural commission. They represent the many African Pentecostal pastors and Christians alike who have started churches and have a strong connection to their previous churches in their place of origin. Besides these pastors who started churches in Britain as a result of the supernatural commission, there are many such migrants who have different assignments besides starting churches. But these migrants also maintain that they are in Britain by a supernatural commission; and as a result they maintain strong connections to the churches, partly due to the similarities in experiences they share with the leaders of those churches. So strong is the connection and belief in the pastors and leaders of the churches and communities, that some have assumed an important status in their communities, with airtime purchased on various radio and television stations to project them as role models within the migrant communities. The projection of these pastors on TV and radio is also partially in response to the marginalisation of sections of the communities who feel voiceless due to the stratification of society into a hierarchical order. Certain people considered to share a very close affinity to the British way of life are given the recognition to represent others within the community. And yet within the community itself those appointed who are normally from the Caribbean or are of mixed race are also not considered African or black enough. Such occurrences influence the wider debate on migration and on transmigrants' lives in communities, which is not usually captured in the various theories cited as giving rise to migration. This offers a perspective on migration theories not previously captured by theories of migration and it makes a contribution to the existing literature on migration. Within the context of migration it is expected that migrants move to their places of settlement taking their religious and cultural beliefs and practices with them. Conditions in their new context determine to a large extent how those beliefs and praxis are continued or discontinued.

Continuity and Discontinuity of African Pentecostal Beliefs and Praxis in African Churches

The observation of African Independent Churches (AICs) and various strands established in the northern hemisphere have led scholars to conclude that African churches are organised in a particular way, with beliefs and practices that are akin to the belief and practices of their mother churches in their places of origin. This is therefore described as African Christianity. Appiah, Adogame, ter Haar, Daswani, from previous researches identifies that the African Pentecostal churches in Africa carry with them cultural nuances from their indigenous religious context which makes the beliefs and practices of the churches wherever they are found easily identifiable to their roots. This kind of Christianity and its expressions lie in the Pentecostals' literal translation and application of the scriptures. In some instances data analysis demonstrates that the Pentecostals bring their spiritual experiences to bear on scripture and make relevance of it without a much wider consideration to the contextual issues that arise. An analysis of some common practices such as deliverance; naming ceremonies; libation prayer language and its use in Pentecostal prayers; Prophetic consultation; and Pentecostal Music and dance concludes that

African Pentecostal churches in Britain, whether they started in Britain or as a branch church, share some affinity with Pentecostal churches in Africa. However, those churches that began here in Britain at the initiative of their migrant pastors without a parent churches in Africa tend to be more moderate in the practices mentioned above. It has been observed and noted in this book that these churches are moderate in terms of an aggressive and militant approach to prayer for instance.

In addition to this, the way the spirits are invoked in some African indigenous religions is not very different from how the spirit is invoked through 'praise and worship' in the African Pentecostal churches in Britain. Similarly, African churches associated with other cultural contexts invoke the Spirit in a way that fits their cultural interpretation of the presence of the spirit. The perspective of African Pentecostal migrants is that in some burgeoning 'white' British Pentecostal churches, the invocation of the Spirit and the subsequent move of the Spirit appears very minimal or even non-existent. This viewpoint does not mean that the Spirit is absent in the 'white' Pentecostal churches, rather it is the militancy attached to invocation and expression of the presence of the Spirit found in the African church that differs.

However, from the perspective of the African Pentecostal migrants, the Spirit is not present in the churches. If expressions of the presence of the spirit in the churches and in the lives of the people are indeed absent, as the African Pentecostals claim, then unless 'white' British Pentecostals become awakened to this, very soon African Pentecostal Christians (i.e. those from an ethnic minority with British society) will shape the interpretation and experience of Christianity in Britain to an extent that is beyond what has been predicted. In other words, based on current trends, African Christianity will be the dominant type of Christianity in Britain in a quarter of a century. This is partly due to the fact that these Christians are loud and conspicuous and use various multimedia platforms to connect with the public. However, the downside is that most of these Christian TV and radio stations are largely patronised by the African migrant communities and therefore are unlikely to be making significant inroads into white Christian communities. However, the migrant communities perceive that they represent the present and future of Christianity in Britain. There seems to be a deliberate strategy on the part of the African Pentecostals to perpetuate their cultural values across the generational divide making sure that the second and third generation members of the churches continue in the beliefs and praxis of the present, although there are bound to be some modifications because a section of the second and third generation of members have been born and raised in Britain. Their cosmology would therefore be marginally influenced by the culture perpetuated by the churches. These younger generations consider Britain to be their home. In spite of the inculcation of the values of their cultural heritage, these second and third generation migrants will someday free themselves from the beliefs and praxis of the older generation. This process has already begun in the churches where youth choirs and youth groups run programmes that contrast with their parents' cultural stereotypes. The use of rap music and other contemporary music genres in church exemplify this. This path was chosen because discrimination of the older generation of migrants in wider society meant that there was mistrust and, as Chapter Four showed, churches preferred to use the younger generation, most of whom have been born and raised in Britain, to lead its programmes and activities in order to gain acceptance by the larger host communities.

Other factors contributing to the reliance o the younger generation African Pentecostal beliefs include their educational attainment. Most often the educational attainment of these younger generation places them in a different and sometimes a better social groupings unlike the older generation in their churches. British societal values and culture imbibed through education would ultimately influence the perpetuation of this new culture would eventually feed into the beliefs and praxis of the churches. It is possible that this would not sustain the African-led churches in Britain. It is probable that the face of African Christianity in Britain may be that of the second and third generation, carrying similarities from the previous generation but also being somewhat different. As such, this new African Christianity could still be the strongest numerically, if the younger generation find it to be relevant to their lives.

There is currently a perception within the migrant community that the pastors and role models are being overlooked in favour of others in society who look and behave in a more British way than they do. The pastors are considered by their own communities to be stalwarts who through their struggles and leadership have paved the way for migrants to integrate into the wider communities. The African youth in these churches feel that they are not adequately represented in the public arena and feel marginalised. It is the struggle for space within British society and the stereotyping of migrants as scroungers by the public that makes the process of integration an uphill task. I have suggested that the struggle for acceptance even within the fraternity of African Pentecostal believers besides the wider society is partly due to the fact that they are of a different culture. The main difference is in the expression of their faith. Their faith has been particularly influenced by the African indigenous religions that are embedded in the culture of the migrants and carried over to their new contexts. Their Christianity is African, and is sometimes not easily appreciated and accepted by the predominantly white host community, giving rise to the need for internal strategies to assist with integration.

The Internal to External Integration strategies

Since the end of the Second World War, Britain has been allowing migrants into Britain at various stages of its development, to fill job vacancies. Most migrants from Africa arrived in the 1970s. Under Tony Blair's government the Immigration, Asylum and Nationality Act 2006 was established to make ensure that those migrants who would contribute to Britain's prosperity and fill employment vacancies were allowed into the country, via a Points Based System, and that these migrants could become part of British society. In response to this government directive, various policies were initiated. The first of these was a policy of assimilation, which involved the redefinition of migrants' identity to be able to look like the majority. Over time, the policy of assimilation was considered unworkable and a new rhetoric of integration emerged. However, there are difficulties in defining exactly what is meant by integration and, without a proper definition, this approach has not been operationalised into practical programs. As part of the integration agenda, a 'Life in the UK Test' was instituted to ensure that every migrant who wants to stay in Britain permanently has knowledge of life in the UK. Unfortunately, from the perspective of the migrant, this program has not lived up to expectations in relation to integration into British society.

In 2013, English testing has been added as a further requirement for permanent residence under the broad umbrella of integration. From the migrants' points of view, state programmes and activities that come at a cost such as the English test and the 'Life in the UK Test' do not recognise their learning and or assist their subsequent integration as intended by the state. It is questionable whether the huge sum of money spent on the programme, which involves answering questions about the culture and political history of Britain has been worthwhile. Not all British nationals born and raised in Britain know all of the answers to the questions included, and this has not prevented them from owning businesses, buying houses, getting jobs and making a meaningful contribution to the communities in which they live. Based on my analysis of the macro-scale processes of integration initiated by the government under the definitions given for those policies, I posit that Britain in practice pursues an assimilation policy, although integration may be the intent. The misuse of the term integration means that although macro-level indicators may point to the success of policies and initiatives, in practice, these are practically useless for those they are meant to integrate. The bottom line is that these policies have been drawn up by policy makers, some of whom do not understand the whole migrant experience, including the privileges of living in Britain and the struggle to find space within their chosen settled communities to live out their dreams and accomplish their lives' aspirations and visions.

It is however understandable that the state does not want to be seen to promote illegal migration or to create imbalances in communities by creating states within the state, where there is a total transfer of the culture of a people to their receiving communities and where they live as if they were in their countries of origin. The territorial and cultural integrity of the country has to be protected somehow. The misconception underlying existing policies of integration and the initiatives accompanying them is that the longer a person lives in the UK the more British the person will become and therefore the more easily they will integrate. However, it is not being in the UK for a long time that ensures an individual becomes integrated but rather through their understanding the operations of the state and feeling a part of its processes. To the migrants, this is where the role of their churches comes to the fore, because unlike the state, the churches' programs help them to feel a part of the community. Unlike the national level policy initiatives with huge budgets, the churches provide tailor made solutions to migrants to ameliorate their daily struggles and the challenges they face.

It is this that makes the churches a safe haven and popular amongst the migrants because the services support their continuing stay in the country. Previous studies by Funmati, Krause, Werbner, Leroi, Giles, and Mazzucato captured certain arrangements within the migrants' communities outside the church that in some cases provided economic support for their members, but these were not framed within the context of integration. A further contribution to the body of knowledge on this subject, is that the internal integration strategies adopted by the churches are motivated by their faith and the need to assist those in need, whether this is through a social welfare intervention, an immigration and nationality forum, or personal development or leadership training. The speakers, facilitators and trainers used for these initiatives are usually pastors or practising Christians, as chapter three showed. This study fills a gap in the existing body of knowledge by demonstrating that the churches use their initiatives and programmes strategically to support the integration of their migrant members into the settled community using tailor-made internal models designed by the pastors and leaders or sometimes by committees set up in the churches. From the migrants' perspective, these learning processes provide them with a perfect setting to integrate into the society. In some instances these initiatives involve providing the migrant members with information and knowledge about how to integrate into wider society. Such information may include giving them information about how to come together to buy houses, or about immigration rules and how to be compliant with these, as discussed in the chapter three. The second is the affective domain: this refers to growth in feelings or emotional areas of one's life. The personal development and leadership training the churches provide for their migrant members prepares them to go through the difficulties of migration and creates a sense of community and support networks for people who attend the programs. In a pragmatic sense, the churches become the places in which migrants gain hands on experience: they are placed in leadership positions and made to serve on various committees in the churches and in the ministries of the churches. In this way they are given the opportunity to put into practice what they are taught in the training programs. Those who believe they have a supernatural commission to come to Britain to bring the nation back to Christ, consider this to be a process of self-actualisation and part of their fulfilment of the commission to migrate.

A prominent contribution of the integration strategies to the churches is that, the initiatives help the African Christian migrant and the churches create a new identity, both in private for their own sustenance, and in the public sphere for a new sort of engagement with their communities. Although to some extent, they remain African in their cosmology, the migrants are made to see a new perspective that is influenced by British values, and the programmes assist them in contextualising their faith and lifestyle in general to accomplish their goal of spreading the gospel. At the same time the training gives them a strong place in their settled community and helps them make use of that as a platform to maintain their ties to their places of origin. This process eventually develops further into the adoption of a transnational status.

Assuming the Transnational Status

Previous research by Schiller, Gulbrandsen and Schanton (as discussed in chapter one) on the transnational engagements of migrants overlooks certain issues, which this study examines critically. This book reveals that it is the internal processes through the integration initiatives of the church that assist migrant members to settle, before assuming a transnational status through their engagements with their places of origin. These internal integration strategies are much more effective than any government policy for integrating migrants into Britain. Transnationalism is not limited to the transfer of lifestyle and cultural traits to the place of origin, but more importantly concerns the processes that prepare migrants to engage with their places of origin. The churches were flexible in obtaining the required material and human resources to accomplish their purposes and brought in 'experts' who shared the same identity as their migrant members. These 'experts' and facilitators come to enforce the inculcated cultural ideals and values and move their audience from a familiar knowledge base to a new knowledge base, helping them in their process of change.

I maintain that transnational engagement by migrants is not only a coping mechanism but also an indication that migrants have crossed the barriers that migration imposed on them with regard to being themselves. This study has shown that assuming a transnational status is not a one way process: influences from the homeland are at the same level, if not greater, than influences from the new settled communities, on the places of origin. There is a flow and a contra flow of religious convictions, cultural ideals and values, perception changes and outlook on life, socio-economic changes, political rhetoric and economic capital flows which have been captured quite well by most researchers in previous research in this field. The churches are influenced by both local and global factors, meaning that the African churches we see in British communities are both a local and a global.

A further finding that this study contributes to the existing knowledge base is the fact that there are direct economic capitals flows to churches in Britain and parts of Africa. In the past support was given to African churches by European and American church and para-church organisations. In the course of time due to the wave of Pan-Africanist and nationalist ideologies that swept through the churches in Ghana and in sub-Saharan Africa in the late 1980s to 1990s, churches were wary of Western financial ties as they considered them an opportunity for control by these donors. As a result they would rather accept money from their African sister churches in the West. This wave was championed by Mensa Otabil the leader of the International Central Gospel Church Ghana, who, promoted the idea of self-governing churches independent of Western donor assistance through his 'Heritage Series' held twice in a year in the cities Accra and Kumasi. This was in a bid to raise the image of the 'black man' in reference to the African and to tell the world the 'black man' is capable of managing his own affairs, the ideological statement that was very popular during the days of the nationalists' struggles for independence in sub-Saharan Africa in the 1950s and 1960s. As discussed earlier in this book, at the commencement of ICGC Ghana's Central University, it rejected a set of computers donated by a Western para-church organization in the late 1990s. However around that same period it accepted donations of computers from ICGC Treasure House that is an ICGC branch church in South East London and also from the Leader of KICC London, Matthew Ashimolowo. The Pan-Africanist disposition of the African churches in Britain is an attempt to demonstrate that African Christianity is unique and to create an 'African Diaspora Voice' for Africans in Britain and in Africa. The message from this Pan-Africanist ideals is that, African Christianity has come of age and is ready to revitalise Christianity wherever it find itself. This research has shown that the churches' see the acquisition of various landed properties in their settled communities as proof that they are capable of 'managing their own affairs' and are not dependent on the parent host community. These acquisitions are normally places of worship and also centres for community-wide projects that address specific social issues. As well as providing physical space, they also encouragement those migrants who have suffered or been badly treated due to bad publicity about immigrants, helping them believe that they are capable of accomplishing anything they set out to do. For those who consider their migration to be a supernatural commission, the accomplishment of purchasing property to them serves as proof of having been instructed and sent forth by God, as in the case of the biblical narrative of Abraham in the Book of Genesis who ended up being wealthy and influential in a land where he was initially a stranger. I therefore advance the idea that the strength of the transnational ties built by migrants is usually dependent upon the level of integration of migrants with their places of settlement.

Some areas that present the opportunity for further related research can be identified. Firstly, the fact that the African churches currently rely on the influx of migrants from Africa suggests that analysis of current and predicted trends in migration from Africa to Britain should be investigated, with a view to understanding their implications for the scale and social-economic and political power of these churches in future. Secondly, a critical examination of the migrants' socio-economic and political status in their communities of residence would be valuable; this could explore to what extent their integration has helped them to achieve their status. Thirdly, there is the need for further investigation into the role of second and third generation migrants in upholding the cultural values of their parents' heritage, since that will inform beliefs and praxis in the churches in the future. Finally, an in-depth comparative study could be undertaken of the Pentecostal churches in other countries of Africa and Britain, including research into their transnational relationship, which might help establish in which direction the flow of influence is stronger. This could also assist in projecting or forecasting the future of these churches in Britain.

This project has contributed to the on-going debate of understanding of African-led migrant churches in the Northern hemisphere and the close relationships they have with their parent churches and the nation in country of origin. These relationships have implications for the intercultural approach to studying Pentecostal churches, where there is a fusion of the local and the global in the identities of churches as organisations and of their members. Although their membership are from one predominant culture, through their beliefs and praxis these churches showcase the process of integration, and the process of contextualisation within a diverse globalised unit, where nuances from different cultures and nations are exhibited in one place and at one time. The processes that help form these diverse globalised units, also develop the capacities of the churches and individuals to participate in negotiations in the global religious market. And in the process strengthen the churches' interconnection of their ecclesiastical and theological framework with the various sociological perspectives.

Notes

Chapter One

1. The British Minority Ethnic directory holds information on churches from the African-Caribbean community. Not many African-led churches are noted on the website. The BME directory is updated with information from the Evangelical Alliance and Churches Together England. Further information could be obtained from http://www.bmcdirectory.co.uk/index. php.

2. There were informal discussions with some congregants and members at the Eternal Sacred Order of the Seraphim and Cherubim Church at Tottenham, London. They revealed that the proliferation of the 'New Pentecostal Churches' have led to a decline in membership, as member's children prefer the flamboyant 'New Pentecostal Churches'. This branch of the church began on the 5th June 1965 and claims to be the oldest branch in Britain. The Eternal Sacred Order of Cherubim and Seraphim was one of the earliest African Initiated Churches from the Anglican Church Community in Western Nigeria and was founded in 1925 by Moses Orimolade Tunolase.

3. Examples of collaboration of churches and other charitable organisation in offering services to assist migrants was a PMP & Helping Hands Initiatives with International Central Gospel Church and Praise Harvest Community Chapel to offering Prince 2 Project Management Training without cost to participants. The initiative was to train people after the 2012 Olympics was awarded to London as it was anticipated there would be jobs for Project Management Professionals.

4. In the transnational discourse, there is a trend where pastors invite prominent pastors and prophets from Ghana, to speak in their churches and these speakers somehow provide the link between their host community of churches and their places of origin. Pastors I spoke to maintain ties with their place origin by inviting prominent pastors and prophets from the place of origin.

5. Krause, "Transnational Therapy Networks among Ghanaians in London," 235-251; Also Schiller and Krause subscribe to the use of the word incorporation instead of integration as used in this study. A discussion of the development of the concepts is analysed in book.

6. The settled status as would be described in the book unlike Schiller's definition covers those who irrespective of their legal residence status consider their present abode as home.

Chapter Two

7. A definition of Sociocultural anthropology as given by the American Anthropological Association: social anthropology examines social patterns and practices across or within a particular culture with a concern to ascertain similarities and differences among and within societies. Even more important is the fact that social anthropological studies emphasise participant observation, which involves placing oneself into the research context for a first-hand feel. For further information see http://www.aaanet.org/about/whatisanthropology.cfm

8. The growing number of Ghanaian-led Pentecostal churches in London also makes them significant since they form approximately 8% of all black majority churches in Britain. This percentage calculation was based on a count done by the researcher from the website directory of the Black Majority Churches in the UK. Please see http://www.bmcdirectory. co.uk/index.php

9. An unpublished resource material provided by Prof David Killingray on the diary entries of Thomas Brem Wilson, a Pioneer Ghanaian Pentecostal church leader in Britain from 1899-1925. This catalogues the history of the African-led Pentecostal churches in Britain.

10. Trinity Baptist Church is part of the Baptist Union of Great Britain and a predominantly Ghanaian church led by Kingsley Appiagyei. Although officially a Baptist church, its outlook, beliefs and practices are Pentecostal in nature.

Chapter Three

11. A focus group in an African church was of the view that, besides the 'organised religious migration' through the churches and other religious agencies, there are also individuals who migrate because they feel 'led' by God to migrate as missionaries. Although these individuals' mission may not preclude making economic gains through secular work at their destination, they believe God has sent them. Others have also found the motive and a 'higher calling' of God for their migration upon arrival although their initial desire to travel was mainly economic.

12. Tony Blair was Prime Minster held that regular, large-scale legal immigration was necessary to the prolonged prosperity and international competitiveness of the UK economy. Indeed, David Blunkett, the cabinet minister who was responsible for immigration policy declared that he saw 'no obvious limit' to immigration. For further information see http://newsvote. bbc.co.uk/mpapps/pagetools/cmail/news.bbc.co.uk/1/hi/uk_politics/3265219.stm.

13. "UK government agrees on skilled migration cap" BBC News item published on 23 November 2010. The government announced a cap of 21,700 on the number of skilled workers from outside the European Economic Area allowed into the UK. The figure represented a reduction of 6,300 on the equivalent figure for 2009. It excluded employees transferred by companies from abroad - in the future they will be allowed to stay for up to five years if their salary exceeds £40,000. For further information see http://www.bbc.co.uk/news/uk-politics-11816979.

14. The 2001 census counted 55,000 Ghanaians living in the UK, an increase of 72 per cent since the last count. Other sources such as MigHealth UK estimate there are about 96,900 Ghanaians in Britain. This is an estimate of Ghanaians living in the UK as published by MIGHEALTH, an organisation co-funded by DG SANCO, the Health and Consumer Protection Directorate-General of the European Commission. http://mighealth.net/uk/index. php/African_Migrants_in_the_UK#Ethiopia.

15. The International Central Gospel Church was founded by Mensa Otabil in Accra, Ghana on 26th February 1984.

16. The Vision is a document detailing the vision of the ICGC, Ghana. Also further information on the ICGC philosophy of ministry can be found at www.centralgospel.com/?root=about&t=64, accessed on 8 August 2012.

17. Ankrah. S K, The Rising of the Sun: Shining from Obscurity, First ed. (Accra: Royalhouse Chapel International, 2010). This was the autobiography of the founder and Apostle General of the Royalhouse Chapel Churches Worldwide. The Royalhouse Chapel began as the International Bible Worship Centre (IBWC) in Accra Ghana on 19th June 1991.

18. The vision of the Royalhouse Chapel is displayed on their website. Vision of the Royalhouse Chapel London can be found at www.royalhouse.org.uk/vision accessed on 17 July 2014.

19. Freedom Centre International (FCI), formerly South London Temple (SLT), was birthed in 1997 out of Universal Prayer Group (UPG) Ministries. Samson Kwaku Boafo, who came to

Britain as a law student, founded the UPG Ministries in the 1960s. He left in the 1970s to practice law in Ghana and upon his departure, the church collapsed. However he returned in 1986 to seek political asylum from persecution by the Provisional National Defence Council (PNDC) government, the military junta in Ghana. The church has another satellite branch called the Dominion Centre located at Woodgreen also led by a Ghanaian Pastor. For further information please see DC www.dominioncentre.org, and www.freedomcentreinternational. org accessed 14 July 2011.

20. An architectural and design firm who specialises in the refurbishment of churches with a portfolio of conversion of warehouses into places of worship. Richmond was formed in 1984 by Sam and Mavis Stewart, who had identified a niche in the marketplace for a specialist company to design, construct and install new corporate interior schemes for pubs, restaurants, hotels and clubs. See http://www.churchdesign.co.uk/portfolio1.htm, accessed on 25 July 2012.

21. The struggle to stabilize the British economy during the recession, politicians pursued a rhetoric of focusing on citizens in employment as against migrants. A newspaper article quoting Gordon Brown as saying 'British Jobs for British People', obtained from www.theguardian.com/politics/2009/jan/30/brown-britsh-jobs-wprkers, accessed 21 November 2014.

22. The Home Office from time to time publishes an occupation shortage list. See a working document that outlines the shortage occupation list and the criteria for eligibility. http://www.ukba.homeoffice.gov.uk/sitecontent/documents/workingintheuk/shortageoccupationlistnov11.pdf, accessed 20 July 2013.

23. A speech delivered by Tony Blair on 8 December 2006, 'Our Nation's Future - Multiculturalism and Integration', http://www.itnsource.com/shotlist/ITN/2006/12/08/R08120603/?v=1#sthash.l0mKQJ7y.dpuf R08120603/?v=1, accessed 21 July 13.

24. Trevor Phillips, Chair of the Commission for Racial Equality, argued that the existing policies and strategies were merely treating 'integration' as an alternative word for 'assimilation': practically, nothing had changed because the definition of integration still required some form of uniformity in the way 'we speak, look, dress and act'. See for more information Phillips, "After7/7: Sleeping to Segregation" a speech delivered on 22 September 2005, at http://www.humanities.manchester.ac.uk/socialchange/research/social-change/summer-workshops/documents/sleepwalking.pdf, accessed on 19 October 2012.

25. Policy makers argue that 'Life in the UK Test' which was introduced in 2007 would enable migrants to feel at home when they become British citizens due to their mastery of the English language and their basic knowledge of British life. Anne-Marie Fortier argues (very persuasively) that the real motivation behind the requirements of the UK citizenship policy is not to achieve integration for immigrants but rather to alleviate the anxieties of 'natives'. The policy sends a signal to people worried about immigration: we hear you, and we're doing something about it. For further reading see https://blogs.lse.ac.uk/politicsandpolicy/life-in-the-uk-marginalisation/

26. The Government website provides an overview of the content of the 'Life In The UK Test' at https://www.gov.uk/life-in-the-uk-test/overview; and a downloadable pdf version of the 'Life in the UK Test', http://www.tsoshop.co.uk/bookstore.asp?FO=1240167&ProductID=9780113413553&Action=Book&TRACKID=002353, accessed on 12 September 2012.

27. İpek Gocmen, "The Role of Faith-based Organisation in Social Welfare Systems," Nonprofit and Voluntary Sector Quarterly 42, 3 (2013): 495-516. Abrahamson, P. Changing welfare

mixes in Europe. (Copenhagen: University of Copenhagen. 1999).; Baines, S., Hardill, I., & Wilson, R. "Introduction: Remixing the economy of welfare? Changing roles and relationships between the state and the voluntary and community sector," Social Policy and Society 10, (2011): 337-339.

28. The six largest ethnic minority groups in Britain today and in descending population size order are: Indian, Pakistani, Black Caribbean, Black African, Bangladeshi, and Chinese. These groups differ in the timing of their arrival. While the majority of immigrants from the Caribbean arrived in the period between 1955 and 1964, the main time of arrival of Black African, Indian and Pakistani first generation groups was between 1965 and 1974.

29. The difficulties that migrants go through: Borteley, a Ga was raised by her uncle and his wife, because she had lost her dad when she was just six years old. Her working life started as an apprentice at a hair beautician salon in Mamprobi, a suburb of Accra. In the course of her apprenticeship, at around the age of twenty, one of their regular customers, a woman about sixty years old told her she had a daughter abroad who was a nurse and had just had a baby and wanted someone to baby sit her child whilst she went back to work.

30. The Ga ethnic group inhabits the plains along the coastlands of the Gulf of Guinea in the Greater Accra Region. The Ga ethnic group comprises mainly of the Ga-Mashie groups occupying neighborhoods in the central part of Accra; http://www.kwabla.com/ga.html, accessed on 13 January 13.

31. The Highly Skilled Migrant Programme (HSMP) was discontinued in November 2006 and replaced with a new Tier system with those that previously applied for the HSMP being allowed to switch to Tier 1 General of the new Tier system. It came with its attendant problems with HSMP Forum limited, winning a high court case to reverse the new route established for those who wanted to settle in Britain permanently after working for 5 years. For further information see http://www.hsmpforumltd.com/index.html, accessed on 14 January 2013.

32. See the autobiography John Maxwell at http://www.johnmaxwell.com/about/meet-john/, accessed on 14 February 2013; Autobiographical information of Myles Munroe can be found at https://mylesmunroeinternational.com/?page_id=107, accessed on 14 February 2013; A brief biography of Mensa Otabil can be found on the website of one of the branches of ICGC in Virginia USA found at http://www.icgcva.org/overseer.asp, accessed on 14 February 2013.; Autobiography of Bill Winston http://www.billwinston.org/bwinston/, accessed 15 February 2013.; Biographic data on Celia Appiagyei-Collins on her organisation's website at http://www.rehobothfoundation.com, accessed on 15 February 2013; biography of Bishop Michael Hutton-Wood is found on the House of Judah's website at http://www.houseofjudah.org.uk/Pages/who-we-are.html, accessed on 15 February 2013.

33. Richard Black, Khalid Koser and Karen Munk, with Gaby Atfield, Lisa D'Onofrio, and Richmond Tiemoko, "Understanding Voluntary Return," Sussex Centre for Migration Research, Online Report 50/04,http://webarchive.nationalarchives.gov.uk/20110220105210/rds.homeoffice.gov.uk/rds/pdfs04/rdsolr5004.pdf. accessed on 14 February 2013.

Chapter Four

34. Transnational pulpit sharing among popular pastors of African decent: a cassette tape-recording of Myles Munroe; "Understanding the Power of Purpose," part 1 and 2, Altar Tapes, 1992. Altar is the audio-visual and print department of the International Central Gospel Church, at the Baden Powell Memorial Hall, in Accra, Ghana.

35. Tithing features very strongly in Pentecostal teaching, except that from 2018 there has been

difference in the theology and interpretation of the practice in African-led churches: Tithe is a principle drawn from the Old Testament Biblical narrative Malachi 3:1-10 where a tenth of once produce is presented to priests in the temple in exchange for God's promised blessings. This is a scripture most Pentecostals base the act of collecting tithes from their members.

36. HCF has been a pioneer in the development and the facilitation of the mortgage industry in Ghana. They are considered the number one mortgage provider. Further information can be found at http://www.hfcbank.com.gh, accessed on 17 February 2013.

37. HCF has been a pioneer in the development and the facilitation of the mortgage industry in Ghana. They are considered the number one mortgage provider. Further information can be found at http://www.hfcbank.com.gh, accessed on 17 February 2013.

38. Further information on houses being let in very good neighbourhoods in Accra. All prices are quoted in US Dollars (USD), http://www.ghanafind.com/search_r-textfield1-houses-category-houses%20for%20rent.html. Also see additional information on the prices of houses and letting at http://www.modernghana.com/GhanaHome/estates/show_estate.asp?cat_id=189&cat_which=4&sub_cat_id=195&item_id=5844&menu_id=37, accessed on 18 February 2013.

39. An interview with Shola Lana, on the role of Nexgen Initiatives in assisting churches in empowering their members, conducted on 19 January 2013. Background, mission and vision statements, Aims and Objectives of the Nexgen Initiatives found at http://www.nexgenlimited.org/aboutus.html, accessed on 20 February 2013.

40. Chartable organisations that work with churches in training their leaders in compliance issues: Information on the work of Stewardship with churches, http://www.stewardship.org.uk/money/about-us/about-stewardship, accessed on 21 February 2013.

41. The Charity Commission allows churches to register with the HMRC to claim GiftAid. 'Gift Aid is a way for charities or Community Amateur Sports Clubs (CASCs) to increase the value of monetary gifts from UK taxpayers by claiming back the basic rate tax paid by the donor on the donation. It can increase the value of donations by a quarter at no extra cost to the donor. Gift Aid is worth nearly £1 billion a year to charities and their donors'. The above is information on Gift Aid found on the HMRC website at http://www.hmrc.gov.uk/charities/gift_aid/basics.html, accessed on 21 February 2013.

42. Information on the Identity of the Charity Commission found at http://www.charitycommission.gov.uk/About_us/About_the_Commission/Our_status_index.aspx, accessed on 03 May 2013.

43. Describing the African marriage from http://www.africanholocaust.net/news_ah/africanmarriageritual.html, accessed on 11 May 2013.

44. Baby-Momma Syndrome is a street term widely in African-Caribbean communities to refer to a woman who has the child of a man she's unmarried to and there is no intention to marry.

45. The changing rhetoric on mirage by politicians: See an article by Ian Dunt, 'Tories Call for Pregnant Teenagers to lose Housing Benefit Right' at http://www.politics.co.uk/news/2013/07/15/tories-call-for-pregnant-teenagers-to-lose-housing-benefit-r, accessed on 18 July 2013.

46. Examining the sermon and message of the African preachers: a sermon by Mensa Otabil on the title; "Fruitful in Affliction," at the Breakthrough Extraordinary Conference at the Word Miracle Church in 2011. The sermon is found at http://www.youtube.com/watch?v=4R_CfjCj4yI, accessed on 12 May 2013.

47. A discussion of the financials undertakings of the KICC in an Article titled, "Richer than St Paul's: church that attracts 8,000 congregation to a disused cinema" 'http://www.guardian.co.uk/world/2009/apr/11/kingsway-international-christian-centre, accessed on 12 May 2013

Chapter Five

48. Papa Odiyifo and Maame Odiyifo titles are normally given to accomplished spiritual leaders who are claimed to possess the ability to enquire of the spirit on behalf of people. This was much prevalent in the AICs which some have referred to as 'spiritist' churches or sumsum sore.

49. Stories from those who have undergone 'deliverance' by a prophet invited to their church. A Ghanaian-owned Internet radio that hosts a show that discusses the problems of Ghanaians in the UK, had a caller call to complain about how a prophet told her that her Aunt who brought here to the UK was possessed with a Maame Water spirit and was the cause of her barrenness.

50. Obuotabiri is the main and revered deity of Koforidua in the Eastern Region of Ghana and Ataa Ahia is a popular shrine situated in Bubiashie in Accra with international connections outside of Ghana and operates like the Akonnedi of Larteh- Akuapem in the Eastern Region; Kwaku Bonsam's stand against Pentecostal pastors seem to have given boldness to other shrines to operate more openly even in places where some of the Pentecostal churches are very prominent. He also has a regular TV broadcast on Metro TV in Ghana and on a local radio station in Kumasi in Ghana. For him, the supreme God of the Indigenous religions is no different from the God of the Christians. He has debated with other Pastors from Pentecostal churches on various issues which includes libation on different public media platform.

51. I witnessed the pouring of libation on numerous occasions in Ghana. (Translation of the Twi libation prayer) 'Almighty God acknowledge our sacrifice, god of the earth, ancestors, today is the great Sunday feast, we ask for protection and life. Any witch or evil spirit who will attempt to sabotage our gathering is subpoenaed before you for judgement. Any enemy that seek the destruction of the community should suffer disgrace and must die'.

52. The Ashantis celebrate Akwasidae every six weeks according to the Akan annual calendar that is nine months in a year. The Adaekese which a grand Akwasidae and normally the last Akwasidae of the year.

53. Paul Owusu Tabiri was a Presiding Elder of the Church of Pentecost Estate Assembly in the Brong Ahafo Region of Ghana. In 1995 Bishop resigned from the Church of Pentecost to form the Bethel Prayer Ministry International to propagate the gospel in the whole world. The real reason however was as result of a misunderstanding with the hierarchy of the church over some of his beliefs and practices. Further information can be found at http://www.bethelprayerministrylondon.com/bishop.html, accessed on 08 July 2013.

54. Testimonies to authenticate 'spiritual instructions' given by Kyeiwaa, regarding receiving unexpected sums of money from HMRC for over-paying taxes. According to her the miracle of it was the timing of the money's coming because that she had to meet a deadline to pay her school fees which was four days to the time. Meaning that she could pay in the HMRC cheque and have it cleared on the fourth day and on that same day pay the school fees. Testimony given at an all night held on 7 December 2012.

Chapter Six

55. For further information see www.negrospirituals.com, and Jackson, Buckwheat Notes, pp. 392-401. Also the Asempa Hymnal is a hymn book put together with the initiative of the Historic Main line churches in Ghana to aid worship and praise during their school times of

worship or devotion as some refer to it. It is printed by the Asempa Publisher which is owned by the Christian Council of Churches of Ghana.

56. The Asafo Companies are the traditional warrior groups within Akan communities.

57. Statistics obtained from the website of Black Training and Enterprise Group (BTEG); The statistics cover mainly African youth and African-Caribbean youth. www.bteg.co.uk, accessed 23 August 2013.

58. Soul Winners, are a music group of young men from Ghana who have composed the song, No Jesus, No Life which follows the rhythm of Bob Marley's No Woman , No cry.

59. Pastors of the Ghanaian-led churches argue that the older historic churches have projects for humanitarian purposes but have lost the primary responsibility to preach salvation to save lost souls. They argue that there would be no use to feed a person and watch them go to hell. You must snatch them from hell fire and also feed them. Discussions from first round of interviews conducted from July 2012 to January 2014.

60. A Brief Biography of George Jeffreys of the Elim Pentecostal Church found at http://healingandrevival.com/BioGJeffreys.htm, accessed on 15 June 2014.

Bibliography

Abarry, A. S., 'The Naming Drama of the Ga People', *Journal of Black Studies* 27: 3 (1997), 366.

Abrahamson, P., *Changing welfare mixes in Europe*. Copenhagen: University of Copenhagen, 1999.

Obadare, E., and Wale Adebanwi, 'The Visa God: Would-be Migrants and the Instrumentalisation of Religion', in A. Adogame, J. Spickard (eds.). Religion Crossing Borders: Transnational Religious and Social Dynamics in Africa and the New Africa Diaspora, Brill, 2010.

Adedibu, B., 'Origin, Migration, Globalisation and the Missionary Encounter of Britain's Black Majority Churches', *Studies in World Christianity 19:1* (2003), 93-113.

Adogame, A., 'Contesting the Ambivalences of Modernity in a Global Context: The Redeemed Christian Church of God, North America', *Studies in World Christianity. Vol. 10: 1* (2004), 39.

_____, A., 'African Christian Communities in Diaspora', in O. Kalu, J. Hofmeyr, P. Maritz (eds.). *African Christianity: An African Story*, University of Pretoria, 2005, 498.

_____, A., *Celestial Church of Christ*, Peter Lang, 1999.

_____, A., 'Betwixt Identity and Security: African New Religious Movements and the Politics of Religious Networking in Europe', *Nova Religio* 7:2 (2003), 24 -41.

_____, A., 'African Instituted Churches in Europe, Continuity and Transformation', in Klaus Koschorke (ed.), *African Identities and World Christianity in the Twentieth Century*, Harrassowitz Verlag, 2005.

_____, A., *African Christian Diaspora: New Currents and Emerging Trends in World Christianity*, Bloomsbury, 2013.

Anarfi, J. K., 'International Labour Migration in West Africa: A Case Study of the Ghanaian Migrants in Lagos, Nigeria', *Regional Institute for Population Studies, University of Ghana*, 1982.

_____, J. K. and K. Awusabo-Asare, et al. *Push and Pull Factors of International Migration*. 2000/E(10).

Anderson, A. H., *African Reformation: African Initiated Christianity in the 20th Century,* Africa World Press, 2001.

_____, A. H., 'The Origins of Pentecostalism and Its Global Spread in the Early Twentieth Century', *Transformation* 22: 3 (2005), 182.

_____, A. H., *Spreading Fires: The Missionary Nature of Early Pentecostalism,* SCM, 2007.

_____, A. H., *To the Ends of the Earth: Pentecostalism and the Transformation of World Christianity,* Oxford University Press, 2012.

Ankrah, S. K., *The Rising of the Sun: Shining from Obscurity*, First ed, Royalhouse Chapel International, 2010.

Appiah, B. 'Moving Survival into Blessing: The Search for the Spiritual-Material Path for Prosperity by the Pentecostal Charismatic Church. A case study of the International Central Gospel Church, *Koforidua'*, BA Dissertation, Central University College, 2001.

_____, B. 'Christianity in Indigenous Cultures: African Religious Worldviews in Neo-Pentecostal Churches in Ghana', MTh Thesis, University of Edinburgh, 2011.

_____, B. 'Convoluted Pentecost? An Analysis of Akan Indigenous Worldviews in Ghanaian Pentecostal-Charismatic Praxes', Journal for the study of the Religions of Africa and its Diaspora, 4:1, (2018), 82-98.

Arhinful, D. K., "We Think of Them': Money Transfers from the Netherlands to Ghana', in I Van Kessel (ed.), *Merchants, Missionaries and Migrants: 300 Years of Dutch-Ghanaian Relations*, Sub Saharan Publishers, 2002.

Arthur, L. W., 'Economic development with unlimited supplies of labor', *The Manchester School of Economic and Social Studies,* 22 (1954), 139-191.

Asamoah-Gyadu, J. K., 'Pentecostal Media Images and Religious Globalisation in Sub-Saharan Africa', in Peter Horsfield, Mary Hess and Adan Medrano (eds). *Belief in Media: Media and Christianity in Cultural Perspective*, Ashgate, 2004.

_____, J. K., "Mission to "Set the Captives Free': Healing, Deliverance, and Generational Curses in Ghanaian Pentecostalism', *International Review of Mission*, 93 (2004), 391.

_____, J. K., *African Charismatics: Current Developments within Independent Indigenous Pentecostalism in Ghana*, Brill, 2005.

_____, J. K., 'Anointing through the screen: Neo-Pentecostalism and Televised Christianity in Ghana', *Studies in World Christianity*, 11:1 (2005), 13.

_____, J. K., "Get on the Internet!' Says the Lord': Religion, Cyberspace and Christianity in Contemporary Africa', *Studies in World Christianity*, 13: 3 (2007), 225-242.

Assey, D., 'Power-geometry and a progressive sense of place,' in Jon Bird et al. (eds), *Mapping the Futures: Local Cultures, Global Change*, Routledge, 1993, 59 – 69.

Atiemo, A., '"Singing with Understanding': The Story of Gospel Music in Ghana', *Studies in World Christianit.*12: 2 (2006), 142.

Baines, S., Hardill, I., & Wilson, R., 'Introduction: Remixing the economy of welfare? Changing roles and relationships between the state and the voluntary and community sector', *Social Policy and Society*. 10, (2011), 337-339.

Banks, W. D., 'Spirit-Possession Rituals in Southern Ghana: Priests, Musicians, and Ritual Efficacy', *Western Journal of Black Studies*, 35:1 (2011), 45.

Barrett, D. B., 'AD 2000: 350 Million Christians in Africa', *International Review of Mission*, 59 (1970), 41 -50.

Bauman, Z. *Wasted Lives : Modernity and Its Outcasts*, Polity, 2004.

Becher, V., *Black Christians: black church traditions in Britain*, Centre for Black and White Christian Partnership and Westhill RE Centre, 1995.

Bediako, K., 'African and Christianity on the Threshold of the Third Millenium: The Religious Dimension,', *African Affairs,* 99 (2000), 311.

Bell, B. D., 'The Performance of Immigrants in the United Kingdom: Evidence from the GHS', *Economic Journal,* 107 (1997), 333–344.

Bellah, P. Tokugawa Religion. New York, NY: Free Press, 1957.

_____, P. Beyond Belief: Essays on Religion in a Post- Traditional World. New York, NY: Harper and Row. 1970.

Berger, P. and Langman, T. The Social Construction of Reality. New York, NY: Anchor Books. 1967.;

Berger, P. Religions in Global Society. London, UK: Routledge. 2006.

Beyer, J. and D. N. Mphahlele, 'Jesus Christ the ancestor: An African Christian Understanding' *Theological Studies*, 65:1 (2009), 1-5.

Bimrose, J. and McNair, S., 'Career Support for Migrants: Transformation or Adaptation', *Journal of Vocational Behavior*, 78:3 (2011), 325-333.

Blackaby, D. H, Leslie, G, Murphy, P. G. and O'Leary, N.C. "Born in Britain: How are Native Ethnic Minorities Faring in the British Labour Market." *Economic Letters.* 88, (2005): 370–375.

_____, D. H, Leslie, D. G, Murphy, P. D. and O'Leary, N. C., 'White/ Ethnic Minority Earnings and Employment Differentials in Britain: Evidence from the LFS', *Oxford Economic Papers,* 54 (2002), 270–297.

Blanc, C. S., Basch, L., and Schiller, N. G., 'Transnationalism, Nation-States, and Culture', *Current Anthropology*, 36: 4 (1995), 683-686.

Bode, I., 'Disorganized welfare mixes: Voluntary agencies and new governance regimes in Western Europe', *Journal of European Social Policy*, 16, (2006), 346-359.

Bosch, David, *Transforming Mission: Paradigm shifts in Theology of Mission*, Orbis, 1991.

Bowdich, T. E., *An Essay on Superstitions, Customs, and Arts, Common to the Ancient Egyptians, Abyssinians, and Ashantees*, Peter Smith, 1821.

Boyd-Franklin, N., *Black families in therapy*, Guilford Press, 1989.

Bruce, S. *Secularisation: in Defense of unfashionable Theory*. Oxford: Oxford University Press, 2011.

Bryman, A. *Social Research Methods* 2nd ed., Oxford University Press, 2004.

Burgess, R, 'African Pentecostal spirituality and civic engagement: the case of the Redeemed Christian Church of God in Britain', *Journal of Beliefs & Values*, 30:3 (2009), 255–273.

Cain. G. G., 'The challenge of segmented labour market theories to orthodox theory: A Survey', *Journal of Economic Literature*, 14 (1976), 1215-1258.

Campbell, H., 'Who's got the power? Religious authority and the Internet', *Journal of Computer-Mediated Communication,* 12:3 (2007), 1043-1062.

Carter, C. S., 'Church burning in African American communities: Implications for empowerment practice *Social Work', .44: 1.* (1999), 62-68.

Carling, J., Marta Bivand Erdal and Rojan Eati, 'Beyond the insider – outsider divide in migration research', 2 (2014), 36-54.

Castles, S., and Mark Miller, *The Age of Migration: International Population Movements in   the Modern World* (3rd ed), Guildford Press, 1993.

Chike, Chigor, *African Pneumatology in the British Context: A Contemporary Study*, PhD Thesis, University of Birmingham, 2011.

Chiluwa, I., 'Online Religion in Nigeria: The Internet Church and Cyber Miracles', *Journal of Asian and African Studies,* 47:6 (2012), 734-749.

Chiswick, B. R., 'The Earnings of White and Coloured Male Immigrants in Britain', *Economica,* 47 (1980), 81–87.

Clark, K. and Drinkwater, S., *Ethnic minorities in the Labour Market: Dynamics and Diversity.* Joseph Rowntree Foundation. 2007.

Clark, K. and Lindley, J., 'Immigrant Labour Market Assimilation and Arrival Effects: Evidence from the UK Labour Force Survey', *IZA Discussion Paper*, 2228 (2006).

Clarke, P. B., (ed), *Encyclopedia of New Religious Movements*, Routledge, 2006 .

Clifford, J., 'Diasporas', *Cultural Anthropology*, 9: 3 (1994), 302-338.

Clinebell, H. *Basic types of Pastoral Care Counseling: Resources for the Ministry of Healing and Growth*, Abingdon, 1984.

Coleman, D. and Robert Rowthorn, 'The Economic Effects of Immigration into the United Kingdom', Population *and Development Review,* 30: 4 (2004), 582-583.

Corten, Andre and Marshall-Fratani, Ruth. (eds.), *Between Babel and Pentecost: Transnational Pentecostalism in Africa and Latin America*, Indiana University Press, 2001.

Cox, P., 'Movements and Migratory Processes: Roles and Responsibilities of Education and Learning', *in Zvi* Bekerman and Thomas Geisen (eds.), *International Handbook of Migration, Minorities and Education: Understanding Cultural and Social Differences in Processes of Learning*, Springer Science, 2012, 1.

Csordas, T. J., 'Introduction: modalities of transnational transcendence', *Anthropological Theory*, 7:3 (2007), 261.

Daft, R. L., *The leadership experience*, Harcourt College Publishers, 2001.

Daly, M., 'Governance and social policy', *Journal of Social Policy*, 32: 1 (2003), 113-128.

Dickson, K., *Theology in Africa*, Orbis, 1984.

Dijk, R. A. V., 'From Camp to Encompassment: Discourses of Transsubjectivity in the Ghanaian Pentecostal Diaspora', Journal *of Religion in Africa*, 28:1 (1997), 135- 159.

Dijk, R. A. V., 'The soul is the stranger: Ghanaian Pentecostalism and the Diasporic contestation of 'flow' and 'individuality', *Culture and Religion*, 3 (2002), 49- 65.

Durkheim, E. *The Elementary Forms of Religious Life. Translated by Joseph Ward Swain*. New York: The Free Press, 1915.

Edward, T. J., 'Differential migration networks information and risk', in Oded Stark (ed.), Research in Human Capital and Development *4, Migration, Human Capital, and Development*, JAI Press, 1986, 147 – 171.

Ekem, J. D. K., *Priesthood in Context: As study of Akan Traditional Priesthood in dialogical relation to the priest-Christology of the epistle to the Hebrew and its implications for a relevant functional priesthood in selected churches among the Akan of Gh*ana, Verlag an der Lottbek, 1994.

Fiske, J., *Telelvision Culture*, Routeledge, 1987.

Forson, M. K., *Split-Level Christianity in Africa: A Study of the Persistence of Traditional Religious Beliefs and Practices Among the Akan*, Ph.D. Asbury Theological Seminary, 1993.

Fumanti M, and Werbner, Pnina, 'The Moral Economy of the African Diaspora: Citizenship, Networking and Permeable Ethnicity', *Transnational Journal of Culture, Economy & Society*, 3:1 (2010), 7.

_____, M. "Virtuous Citizenship': Ethnicity and Encapsulation among Akan-Speaking Ghanaian Methodists in London', African Diaspora: *Transnational Journal of Culture, Economy & Society*, 3:1 (2010), 12 - 41.

Garton, L. and Wellman, B., 'Social impacts of electronic mail in organizations: A review of the research literature', *Communication Yearbook*, 18 (1995), 434–53.

Gerloff, R., 'The Significance of the African Christian Diaspora in Europe: A Report on Four Meetings in 1997/8', *Journal of Religion in Africa*, 29:1 (1999), 116.

_____, R., 'Editorial', *International Review of Mission*, 89:354 (2000), 276- 277.

_____, R., 'An African Continuum in Variation: The African Christian Diaspora in Britain', in Black Theology in Britain, *A Journal of Contextual Praxis*, Sheffield Academic Press, 2000.

Gifford, P. *Ghana's New Christianity: Pentecostalism in a Globalised African Economy*. Indiana: Indiana University Press, 2004.

_____, P. "Trajectories o in African Christianity", *International Journal for the Study of the Christian Church*, 8 :4 (2008), 275-89.

Gocmen, İpek, 'The Role of Faith-based Organisation in Social Welfare Systems', *Nonprofit and Voluntary Sector Quarterly*, 42: 3 (2013), 495-516.

Graveling, E., 'That is not religion, that is the gods': Ways of conceiving religious practices in rural Ghana', *Culture and Religion*, 11:1 (2010), 31–50.

Groot, A. E. D., 'Methodology; Foundations of Inference and Research in the Behavioural Sciences', in *Methodology; Foundations of Inference and Research in the Behavioural Sciences*, Mouton, 1969.

Gustav, R. and Fei. J.C. H., 'A theory of economic development', America *Economic Review*, 51 (1961), 533-565.

Gyekye, K. *African Cultural Values: An Introduction*, Sankofa Publishing Company, 1998.

Hackett, R. I. J., 'Charismatic Pentecostal Appropriation of Media Technologies in Nigeria and Ghana', Journal *of Religion in Africa*, 28 (1998), 259.

Hammersley, M. and Atkinson, P. *Ethnography: Principles in Practice*. London: Tavistock Publications, 1983.

Hanciles, J. J., 'Mission and Migration: Some Implications for the Twenty-first Century', *International Bulletin of Missionary Research*, 27: 4 (2003), 150.

_____, J. J, 'African Christianity, Globalization, and Mission: Marginalizing the Center', in *Interpreting Contemporary Christianity: Global Processes and Local Identities*, O. U. Kalu, (ed.), William B. Eerdmans Publishing, 2008, 89.

Harris J,.R., and Michael P. Todaro, 'Migration, unemployment development: A two-sector analysis'. *American Economic Review*, 60 (1970), 126-142.

Helland, C., 'Diaspora on the electronic frontier: Developing virtual connections with sacred homelands', Journal *of Computer-Mediated Communication*, 12:3 (2007), 956-976.

Hiebert, R. E., D. F. Ungarait and T. W. Bonn, *Mass Media IV: An Introduction to Modern Communication*, Longman, 1985.

Hollenweger, W. J., 'The Black Roots of Pentecostalism', in *Pentecostals After a Century: Global Perspective on a Movement in Transition*, Sheffield Academic Press, 1999.

Hunt. S. and Lightly, N., 'The British black Pentecostal `revival: identity and belief in the `new` Nigerian churches', *Ethnic and Racial Studies*, 24, (2001), 104-124.

Idowu, E. B. *Olodumare: God in Yoruba Belief.* London: Longmans, 1962.

Jackson, G. P., 'Buckwheat Notes', *Musical Quarterly*, 19:4 (1933), 392-401.

Jenkins, R., 'Racial Equality in Britain', in *Essays and Speeches*. London: Collins, 1967, 267.

Jennings, M., "Won't you break free?' An ethnography of music and the divine-human encounter at an Australian Pentecostal Church', *Culture and Religion: An Interdisciplinary Journal*, 9 (2008), 162.

Johnson, T. M, Barrett D. B, Crossing, P. F, "Status of Global Mission, 2012, in the Context of Ad 1800-2025," *International Bulletin of Missionary Research*. Vol. 36, 1 (2012).

Jorgensen, D. L. *Participant Observation: A Methodology for Human Studies.* London: Sage Publications, 1989.

Juergensmeyer, M. and Sheikh, M. K. "A Sociotheological Approach to Understanding Religious Violence," *The Oxford Handbook of Religion and Violence, Oxford University Press,* 2013.

Kalu, Ogbu, 'The Andrew Syndrome: Models in Understanding the Nigerian Diaspora', in Olupona, J.K., Gemignant, R., (eds.). *African Immigrant Religions in America,* New York University Press, 2008.

_____, Ogbu, 'Preserving a Worldview', *Pneuma,* 24: 2 (2000), 110-137.

_____, Ogbu, 'Pentecostalism and Mission in Africa', *Mission Studies,* 24 (2007), 9-45.

_____, O., *African Pentecostalism: An Introduction,* Oxford University Press, 2008.

Katz, E. and Stark. O., 'Labor migration and risk aversion in less developed countries', *Journal of Labor Economics,* 4 (1986), 131-149.

Kay, W. K., 'A history of the charismatic movement in Britain and the United States of America', *Journal of Beliefs & Values,* 32 (2011), 363-364.

Kietzmann, J. H., Hermkens, K., McCarthy, I. P., Silvestre, B. S., 'Social media? Get serious! Understanding the functional building blocks of social media', *Business Horizons,* 54:3 (2011), 241-251.

Knibbe K. and van der Meulen, M., 'The Role of Spatial Practices and Locality in the Constituting of the Christian African Diaspora', African *Diaspor,* 2 (2009), *125-130.*

Krause, Kristine, 'Transnational Therapy Networks among Ghanaians in London', Journal *of Ethnic & Migration Studies,* 34:2 (2008), 238.

Kritz, M. M., L. L. Lim and H. Zlontik (eds). Kritz, *International Migration Systems: A Global Introduction.* Oxford University Press, 1992.

Kuusisto, A., 'Religious identity based social networks as facilitators of teenagers' social capital: a case study on Adventist families in Finland', in H. Helve and J. Bynner (eds), *Youth and Social Capital,* Tufnell Press, 2007.

Landes, D. *The Unbound Prometheus: Technological Change and Industrial Development in Western Europe from 1750 to the present.* Cambridge: Cambridge University Press, 1972.

Larbi, E. K., *Pentecostalism: The Eddies of Ghanaian Christianity.* CPCS, 2001.

_____, E. K., 'The Nature of Continuity and Discontinuity of Ghanaian Pentecostal Concept of Salvation in African Cosmology', *Asian Journal of Pentecostal Studies,* 5: 1 (2002), 88.

Layder, L. and Sung, J., 'The Emperical Correlates of Action and Structure: The Transition from School to Work', *Sociology,* 25 (1991), 447-464.

Leach, W. H., 'Financing the Local Church', *Annals of the American Academy of Political and Social Science,* 332 (1960), 70-79.

Lehikoinen, T., *Religious Media Theory: Understanding Mediated Faith and Christian Applications of Modern Media,* University of Jyvaskyla, 2003.

Levitt, P., Levitt, 'Local-Level Global Religion: The case of US Dominican Migration', *Journal for the Scientific Study of Religion,* 3 (1998), 74-89.

Lindley, J.K., 'Race or religion? The Impact of Religion on the Employment and Earnings of Britain's Ethnic Communities', *Journal of Ethnic and Migration Studies,* 28:3 (2002), 427–442.

Mabogunje, 'A. L., Systems Approach to a Theory of Rural-Urban Migration', Geographical Analysis, 2 (1970), 1-18.

MacAndrew, S. and Voas, D., 'Immigration generation, religiosity and civic engagement in Britain', *Ethnic and Racial Studies,* 37: 1 (2014), 99-119.

Mccauley, J. F., 'Africa's new big man rule? Pentecostalism and patronage in Ghana', *African Affairs,* 112: 446 (2013), 1-21.

McNeill, P. *Research Methods* (2nd ed.) London: Routledge, 1990.

Manning, A. and Georgiadis, A., 'Cultural Integration in the United Kingdom', in Yann Algan, Alberto Bisin, Alan Manning, and Thierry Verdier (eds.). *Cultural Integration of Immigrants in Europe,* Oxford University Press, 2012.

Manuh, T. "Efie' or the meanings of home among female and male Ghanaian migrants in Toronto, Canada and returned migrants to Ghana', in Koser, K. (ed.), *New African Diasporas*, Routledge, 2008.

Marsh, C., 'The Survey Method: The Contribution of Surveys to Sociological Explanation', in Martin Bulmer, ed. *Contemporary Research Series*, George Allen & Unwin, 1982, 146.

Marx, K. and Engels, F. *The German Ideology*. Ed. R. Pascal. New York: International Publishers, 1939.

_____, K. Critique of Hegel's Philosophy of Right'. Translated by Joseph O'Malley and Annette Jolin with an introduction by Joseph O'Malley. Cambridge: Cambridge University Press, 1970.

Mason, A., 'Integration, Cohesion and National Identity: Theoretical Reflections on Recent British Policy' *British Journal of Political Science*. Vol. 40, (2010): 857-874.

Massey, D. S. et al, 'Theories of International Migration: A Review and Appraisal', *Population and Development Review,* 19: 3 (1993), 456.

_____, D. S. et al., *International Migration: Prospects and Policies in a Global Market. International Studies in Demography*, Oxford University Press, 2004.

Maton, K. I. and Wells, E. A., 'Religion as a Community Resource for Well-Being: Prevention, Healing, and Empowerment Pathways', *Journal of Social Issues*, 51: 2 (1995), 177-193.

Maxwell, D., 'Editorial', *Journal of Religion in Africa*, 23: 3 (1998), 255.

Maxwell, J., *Becoming a Person of Influence*, Thomas Nelson Publishers, 1997.

Mazzucato, Valentina, 'The Double Engagement: Transnationalism and Integration. Ghanaian Migrants' Lives between Ghana and the Netherlands', *Journal of Ethnic & Migration Studies*, 34: 2 (2008), 205.

Mbiti, J. S., *African Religions and Philosophy*, Heinemann, 1969.

Menjiver, C., *Fragmented Ties: Salvadoran Immigrant Networks in America,* University of California Press, 2000.

McLeod, H. *Secularisation in Western Europe 1848-1914.* New York: St Martin's Press, 2000.

_____, H. 'Introduction' in Hugh McLeod and Werner Ustorf (eds), *The Decline of Christendom in Western Europe, 1750-2000.* Cambridge: Cambridge University Press, 2003.

_____, H. *The Religious Crisis of the 1960's.* Oxford: Oxford University Press, 2007.

_____, H., and Ustorf, Werner (eds.). The Decline of Christendom in Western Europe, 1750-2000. Cambridge: Cambridge University Press, 2003.

Merton, R. K., *On Theoretical Sociology*, Free Press, 1967.

Meyer, B., 'Make a Complete Break with the past. 'Memory and Post-Colonial Modernity in Ghanaian Pentecostalist Discourse', *Journal of Religion in Africa, 28: 3* (1998), 316-349.

_____, B., 'Pentecostalism, Prosperity and Popular Cinema in Ghana', *Culture and Religion*, 3:1 (2002), 69-70.

_____, B, "There is a Spirit in that image': Mass-produced Jesus pictures and Protestant-Pentecostal animation ain Ghana', *Comparative Studies in Society and History*, 52:1 (2010), 100-130.

Middleton, A., Murie, A., Groves, R., 'Social Capital and Neighbourhoods that Work', *Urban Studies*, 42 (2005), 1711-1717.

Mitchel, Nathaniel D., 'Ritual and New Media', in Eric Borgman, Stephan van Erp and Hille Haker (eds), *Cyberspace - Cyberethics - Cybertheology Concilium*, SCM, 2005, 90-98.

Morawska, E., 'The sociology and historiography of immigration', in Virginia Yans-McLaughlin (ed.), *Immigration Reconsidered History, Sociology, and Politics* Oxford University Press, 1990, 187-240.

Morrison, D., *Reaching for the Promised Land: the role of culture, issues of leadership and social stratification within British Caribbean Christianity*, PhD Thesis, University of Birmingham, 2014.

Mundey, P., Davidson, H., Snell Herzog, P., 'Making Money Sacred: How Two Church Cultures Translate Mundane Money into Distinct Sacrilised Frames of Giving', *Sociology of Religion*, 72: 3 (2011), 303 – 326.

Munroe, M., *In Pursuit of Purpose*, Destiny Image Publishers, 1992.

Nieswand, B., 'Charismatic Christianity in the Context of Migration', in A. Adogame, C. Weissköppel, ed., *Religion In The Context of African Migration,* Bayreuth African Studies Series, 2005, 256.

_____, B., 'Ghanaian Migrants in Germany and the Social Construction of Diaspora', *African Diaspora: Transnational Journal of Culture, Economy & Society* 1:1 (2008): 28-52.

_____, B., Nina, G. S., Gunther, S., Tsypylma, D., Lale, Y., Laszlo, F. 'Pathways of Migrant Incorporation in Germany', *Transit*, 12:2 (2004).

Nketia, J. H., *Drumming in Akan Communities*, University of Ghana Press. 1963.

Okoṛọcha, C. C., *The Meaning of Religious Conversion in Africa: The Case of the Igbo of Nigeria*, Avebury, 1987.

Olofinjana, I., *Reverse in Ministry and Mission: Africans in the Dark Continent of Europe*, Author House, 2010.

Omenyo, C., 'Man of God Prophesy Unto Me: The Prophetic Phenomenon in African Christianity', *Studies in World Christianity*, 17: 1 (2011), 30-49.

Onyinah, O., *Akan witchcraft and the concept of exorcism in the Church of Pentecost*, PhD Thesis University of Birmingham, 2002.

Otabil, M., *The Vision: Making Plain God's Purpose for the International Central Gospel Church*, Altar International, 1995.

Pajo, E., *International Migration, Social Demotion, and Imagined Advancement: An Ethnography of Socioglobal Mobility*, Springer, 2008.

Panayi, P., *An Immigration History of Britain: Multicultural Racisim since 1800*, Pearson Education: 2010.

Parrinder, E. G., *West African Religion: Illustrated from the Beliefs and Practices of the Yoruba, Ewe, Akan and Kindred Peoples*, Epworth Press, 1949.

Peach, C., Black-Caribbeans: class, gender and geography', in C. Peach (ed.), *Ethnicity in the 1991 Census: the Ethnic Minority Populations of Great Britain*, Vol. 2., HMSO, 1996, 25-43.

Petras, E. M., 'The global labor market in the modern world-economy', in Mary M. Kritz, Charles B. Keely, and Silvano M. Tomasi (eds.), *Global Trends in Migration Theory and Research on International Population Movements*, Center for Migration Studies, 1981, 44-63.

Pobee, J., *Toward an African Theology*, Abingdon, 1979.

Pobee, J., 'Aspects of African Traditional Religion', *SA. Sociological Analysis,* 37:1 (1976), 1-18.

Poirier, J. C., 'Narrative Theology and Pentecostal Commitments', *Journal of Pentecostal Theology*, 16: 2 (1985), 17.

Portes, A. and Walton, J., *Labor, Class, and the International System*, Academic Press, 1981.

Portes, A and Borocz, J., ' Contemporary Immigration: Theoretical Perspectives on its Determinants and Modes of Incorporation', *International Migration Review*, 23 (1989), 606-630.

Ranis, Gustav et al. 'A theory of economic development'. *America Economic Review,* 51 (1961), 533-565.

Roberts, G. J., *Entrepreneurship : an African Caribbean perspective Doctoral*, Ph.D. Thesis University of Birmingham, 2009.

Robbins, J., 'The Globalization of Pentecostal and Charismatic Christianity', *Annual Review of Anthropology*, 33 (2004), 117–143.

Robin, B., 'Atlas of West African Migrations to Europe 1985-1993', in *Atlas of West African migrations to Europe 1985-1993*, Orstom, 1996, 109.

Rogers, E. M., *Diffusion of Innovations, (4th ed.)*, Free Press, 1995,

Ryan, K & Oestreich, D., *Driving fear out of the workplace; How to overcome the invisible barriers to quality, productivity, and innovation*, Jossey-Bass, 1991.

Sabar, G., 'Witchcraft and Concepts of Evil amongst African Migrant Workers in Israel', *Canadian Journal of African Studies*, 44 (2010), 110-141.

Sawyerr, H., *Creative Evangelism*, Lutterworth, 1968.

Schiller, N. G, Ayşe, Çağlar and Thaddeus, C. G., 'Beyond the Ethnic Lens: Locality, Globality, and Born-Again Incorporation', *American Ethnologist*, 33:4 (2006), 612-633.

_____, N. G.,L. G. Basch, C. Blanc-Szanton, *Towards a Transnational Perspective on Migration,* Academy of Sciences, 1992.

_____, N. G, Basch, Linda, and Blanc, C . S., 'From Immigrant to Transmigrant: Theorizing Transnational Migration', *Anthropological Quarterly*, 68:1 (1995), 1053–1067.

_____, N. G. and Caglar, A., 'And ye shall possess it and dwell therein': social citizenship, global Christianity and nonethnic immigrant incorporation', in Deborah Reed-Danahay and Caroline Brettell (eds), *Immigration and Citizenship in Europe and the United States: Anthropological Perspective*, Rutgers University Press, 2008, 201-225.

_____, N. G., 'Transmigrants and Nation-States: Something Old and Something New in the U.S. Immigrant Experience', In *The Hand- book of International Migration: The American Experience,* Charles Hirshman, Philip Kasinitz, and Josh DeWind, (eds.), Russell Sage Foundation, 2009, 94 -119.

Schreiter, R., *Constructing Local Theologies*, Orbis Books, 1985.

Scott, K. and Liew, T., 'Social Networking as a Development Tool: A Critical Reflection', *Urban Studies*, 49:12 (2012), 2751-2767.

Senge, P., *The fifth discipline*, Doubleday, 1990.

Shenk, W. R., *Changing Frontiers of Mission*, Orbis Books, 1999.

Singleton, A. *Religion, Culture and Society*, Sage Publications, 2014.

Spinks, C., 'Panacea or Painkiller? The impact of Pentecostal Christianity on women in Africa Critical Half', Annual *Journal of Women for Women International*, 1: 1 (2003), 20–25.

Stark, O. and Levhari, D., 'On migration and risk in LDCs', *Economic Development and Cultural Change,* 31 (1982), 191-196.

_____, O. and David E. Bloom, 'The new economics of labor migration', *America Economic Review,* 75 (1985), 173-178.

Stewart, M. B., 'Racial Discrimination and Occupational Attainment in Britain', *Economic Journal*, 93 (1983), 521–541.

Stogdill, R. M., *Handbook of leadership: A survey of the literature,* Free Press, 1974.

Sturgis, P., Brunton-smith, I, Kuha, J., Jackson, J., 'Ethnic diversity, segregation and the social cohesion of neighborhoods in London', *Ethnic and Racial Studies*, (2013), 1-21.

Taylor, J. E., 'Differential migration networks information and risk', in Oded Stark (ed.), Research in Human Capital and Development *Vol.4, Migration, Human Capital, and Development*, JAI Press, (1986), 147-171.

Tedlock, B., 'Divination as a Way of Knowing: Embodiment, Visualisation, Narrative, and Interpretation', *Folklore,* 112:2 (2001), 189.

Ter Haar, Gerrie, *Religious Communities in the Diaspora*, Acton Publishers, 2001.

_____, Gerrie, *Halfway to Paradise: African Christians in Europe,* Cardiff Academic Press, 1998.

Thorne, B., 'The prophetic nature of pastoral counselling', *British Journal of Guidance & Counselling* 29:4 (2000), 435-445.

Tschannen, O. "The Secularisation Paradigm: a systemisation", *Journal for the sceitific Study of Religion,* 30 (4): 395-415.

Turner, H. C., 'African Independent Churches and Economic Development', *World Development,* 8 (1980), 523–533.

Van der Ven, J. A., *Practical Theology : An Empirical Approach*, Kok Pharos, 1993.

Viney, R., 'Religious Broadcasting on UK Television: Policy, Public Perception and Programmes', Cultural *Trends*, 9:36 (1999), 1-28.

Währisch-oblau, C., 'From Reverse Mission To Common Mission… We Hope', *International Review of Mission*, 89:354 (2000), 467-483.

Walwood, J. F. and Zuck, R. B., *The Bible Knowledge Commentary: An Exposition of the Scriptures*. Chariot Victor Publishing, 1985.

Ward, P. D., 'The Flooded Earth; Our Future in a World without Ice Caps.', *Arctic Antartic And Alpine Research*, 42:4 (2010), 498-499.

Warnes, A. and Williams, A., 'Older Migrants in Europe: A New Focus for Migration Studies', Journal *of Ethnic and Migration Studies,* 32:8 (2006), 1266-1277.

Weber, M. *The Protestant Ethic and The Spirit of Capitalism. Translated by Peter Baehr and Gordon C. Wells*, New York: The Free Press, 2002.

_____, M. *The Religion of India: The Sociology of Hinduism and Buddhism*. New York: The Free Press, 1951.

_____, M. *The Religion of China: Confucianism and Taoism*. New York: The Free Press, 1958.

Weller, S., 'Young people's Social Capital: Complex identities, dynamic networks', *Ethnic and Racial Studies*, 33:5 (2010), 874.

Wet, C. J. D., 'Development-Induced Displacement: Problems, Policies and People' in Chris De Wet (ed.), *Studies in Forced Migration,* Berghahn Books, 2006,

Whitfield, L., 'The State Elite, PRSP's and Policy Implementation in Aid-dependent Ghana', Third World Quarterly, 31:5 (2010), 721-737.

Wickes, R., Hipp, J. R, Zahnow, Mazerolle, R. L., 'Seeing' Minorities and Perceptions of Disorder: Explicating the Mediating and Moderating Mechanisms of Social Cohesion', *Criminology*, 51:3 (2003), 519-560.

Wilson. B., *Religion in Sociological Perspective*, Oxford University Press, 1982.

Witte, M. D., 'Altar Media's *Living Word:* Televised Charismatic Christianity in Ghana', *Journal of Religion in Africa,* 33: 2 (2003), 172-202.

Yin, R. K., *Case Study Research : Design and Methods,* Sage Publications, 2009.

Internet Sources

Asamoah-Gyadu, J. K., 'African-led Christianity in Europe: Migration and Diaspora Evangelism', http://www.lausanneworldpulse.com/themedarticles. php/973?pg=all, accessed 22 December 2010.

Black, R., Koser, K., and Munk, K., with Atfield, G., D'Onofrio, L., and Tiemoko, R., 'Understanding Voluntary Return', Sussex Centre for Migration Research, Online Report 50/04, http://webarchive.nationalarchives.gov. uk/20110220105210/rds.homeoffice.gov.uk/rds/pdfs04/rdsolr5004.pdf, accessed on 14 March 2013.

Conolly, H and White, A., '*The Different Experiences of the United Kingdom's Ethnic and Religious Populations*', www.ons.gov.uk, accessed on 10 January 2013.

Del Granado F. J. A., '*Ghana's Advance to Middle-income Status Requires Firm Policies*', IMF African Department, http://www.imf.org/external/pubs/ft/ survey/so/2013/car061213a.htm, accessed on 12 October 2013.

Glaniel, G., '*21st Century Faith: Results of the Survey of Clergy, Pastors, Ministers and Faith Leaders*', Irish School of Ecumenics, Trinity College Dublin, http:// www.ecumenics.ie/wp-content/uploads/Clergy-Survey-Report.pdf, accessed on 16 January 2013.

Home Office, *Strength in Diversity: Towards a Community Cohesion and Race Equality Strategy*, HMSO, 2004, http://dera.ioe.ac.uk/5009/, accessed on 18 October 2012.

Jenkins, P., 'The Next Christianity', An article in the Online Atlantic Magazine published on 01 January 2002, http://www.theatlantic.com/magazine/ archive/2002/10/the-next-christianity/302591/, accessed 03 May 2014.

Johnson. T and Kim, S., 'The Changing face of Global Christianity', http://www.bostontheological.org/assets/files/02tjohnson.pdf, accessed 10 February 2011.

Mitton, L. and Peter Aspinall, 'Black Africans in the UK: Integration or Segregation?' http://www.restore.ac.uk/UPTAP/wordpress/wp-content/uploads/2011/01/uptap-findings-mitton-jan-11.pdf, 1-5, accessed 18 March 2012.

Mkwaila, Andrew, 'Contextualization and the Challenge of Contemporary Pentecostal Missions from Africa to the Northern Hemisphere', *Ethne Online Journal For Pentecostal and Missional Leadership* 1 (1), www.antslnline/article2v2i1.html, accessed 10 January 2011.

Mona Kanwal Sheikh, "Sociotheology: The Significance of Religious Worldviews", E-International Relations, the world's leading open access website for students and scholars of international politics. See https://www.e-ir.info/2015/12/14/sociotheology-the-significance-of-religious-worldviews/#_edn5. Accessed 02.07.2018.

Phillips, Trevor, 'After7/7: Sleeping to Segregation', A speech delivered on 22 September 2005, http://www.humanities.manchester.ac.uk/socialchange/research/social-change/summer-workshops/documents/sleepwalking.pdf, accessed on 19 October 2012.

Shukor, S., 'African children at risk of ritual abuse', http://news.bbc.co.uk/1/hi/england/london/6177001.stm, accessed 20 December 2010.

Unknown Author, Black Majority Churches website directory at http://www.bmcdirectory.co.uk/index.php, accessed 20 December 2011.

Unknown Author, 'About Us', Royalhouse Chapel International, www.royalhouse.org.uk, accessed on 12 July 2012.

Unknown Author, 'About Us', http://www.freedomcentreinternational.org/our-history.php, accessed on 01 August 2012.

Unknown Author, 'Life In The UK Test', https://www.gov.uk/life-in-the-uk-test/overview; and a downloadable pdf version of the 'Life in the UK Test', http://www.tsoshop.co.uk/e.p?FO=1240167&ProductID=9780113413553&Action=Book&TRACKID=002353, accessed on 19 October 2012.

Unknown Author, 'Biography of Mensa Otabil', http://www.icgcva.org/overseer.asp, accessed on 14 February 2013.

Unknown Author, 'Biography John Maxwell', http://www.johnmaxwell.com/about/meet-john/, accessed on 14 February 2013.

Unknown Author, 'Biography of Myles Munroe', https://mylesmunroeinternational.com/?page_id=107, accessed on 14 February 2013.

Unknown Author, 'Biography of Bishop Michael Hutton-Wood', http://www.houseofjudah.org.uk/Pages/who-we-are.html, accessed on 15 February 2013.

Unknown Author, 'Biography of Bill Winston', http://www.billwinston.org/bwinston/, accessed 15 February 2013.

Unknown Author, 'Biography of Celia Appiagyei-Collins', http://www.rehobothfoundation.com, accessed on 15 February 2013.

Unknown Author, 'Census Data', http://www.ons.gov.uk/ons/rel/census/2011-census/key-statistics-for-local-authorities-in-england-and-wales/rpt-ethnicity.html#tab-Ethnicity-in-England-and-Wales, accessed on 21 March 2013.

Unknown, 'Boys Used for Human Sacrifice', A BBC news item published on 16 June 2005, http://news.bbc.co.uk/1/hi/uk/4098172.stm, accessed on 12 May 2014.

Unknown Author, 'The Evaporation of the African-Caribbean Community', An article on a Carribbean Community Online forum, http://www.intermix.org.uk/forum//forum_posts.asp?TID=2285, accessed on 06 June 2014.

Unknown, For further information on Paul Scalon of the Life Church, UK and its history see http://www.lifechurchhome.com/store/teaching/paul-scanlon.html, accessed on 15 June 2014

Unknown, A Brief Biography of George Jeffreys of the Elim Pentecostal Church found at http://healingandrevival.com/BioGJeffreys.htm, accessed on 15 June 2014.

Unknown Author, A speech delivered by Tony Blair on 'Our Nation's Future - Multiculturalism and Integration', http://www.itnsource.com/shotlist/ITN/2006/12/08/R08120603/?v=1#sthash.l0mKQJ7y.dpuf R08120603/?v=1, speech delivered on the 8 December 2006, accessed 21 July 2013.

Unknown Author, 'Shortage occupation list and the criteria for eligibility', http://www.ukba.homeoffice.gov.uk/sitecontent/documents/workingintheuk/shortageoccupationlistnov11.pdf, accessed on 21 July 2013.

Unknown, History of rap music', www.plasticlittleraps.com/history-of-rap-music.html, accessed on 23 August 2013.

Unknown, 'Story of the hymns', www.hymnsite.com/lyrics/umh514.sht, accessed on 23 August 2013.

Unknown Author, Black Training and Enterprise Group (BTEG), www.bteg.co.uk, accessed 23 August 2013.

Unknown Author, 'Story of the Negro spirituals', www.negrospirituals.com, accessed on 23 August 2013.

Unknown Author, 'The Ama Sumani Story', http://news.bbc.co.uk/1/hi/wales/7305963.stm and also http://www.theguardian.com/uk/2008/mar/20/immigration.immigrationandpublicservices, accessed on 29 September 2013.

Unknown Author, 'Census Data', http://www.ons.gov.uk/ons/interactive/vp2-2011-census-comparatively/index.html, accessed on 14 October 2013.

Unknown Author, A definition of Sociocultural anthropology, http://www.aaanet.org/about/whatisanthropology.cfm, accessed on 13 December 2013.

Appendix 1

Church Documents and Other reports

Dominion Centre London, 'Constitution of the Universal Prayer Group Ministries.' UK.

Freedom Centre International, Program of activities for the grand opening of the Building on 15th February 2011.

International Central Gospel Church, *The Vision: Making Plain God's Purpose for the International Central Gospel Church* (Altar International: 1995), 1- 24.

International Central Gospel Church, 'Annual General Church Council Report, 2011.

Audio-Visual Sources

Bishop Michael Hutton-Wood, 'Keys to exemption from economic holocaust.' House of Judah, UK. Pre-recorded audio CD.

Bishop Michael Hutton-Wood, 'The force behind divine accomplishments.' House of Judah, UK. Pre-recorded audio CD.

Dr Bill Winston, 'Speak the Word only.' Bill Winston Ministries, USA. Pre-recorded audio CD.

Dr Bill Winston, 'Heaven on Earth' Bill Winston Ministries, USA. An MP3 download from ministry website.

Rev 'Dr' Mensa Otabil, 'The Dominion Mandate.' Pre-recorded DVD, obtained from the International Central Gospel Church, Ghana.

Rev 'Dr' Mensa Otabil, 'Generational Thinkers'. International Central Gospel Church,

Ghana. Pre-recorded 25th Anniversary message preached at the Accra Sports stadium, Ghana.

Rev 'Dr' Mensa Otabil, 'Breaking the spirit of inferiority.' International Central Gospel Church, Ghana. Pre-recorded audio CD.

Rev 'Dr' Myles Munroe, 'Maximising your potential' Bahamas Faith Ministries, Nassau. A pre-recorded audio CD.

Rev 'Dr' Myles Munroe, 'Discovering the Kingdom' Bahamas Faith Ministries, Nassau. A pre-recorded audio CD.

Rev 'Dr' Shadrach Ofosuware, 'Wealth Exchange.' Freedom Centre International, Welling. Pre-recorded audio CD.

Rev ' Dr' Shadrach Ofosuware, 'Breaking Ancestral Curses and invoking ancestral blessing.' Freedom Centre International, Welling. Pre-recorded Audio CD.

Rev ' Dr' Shadrach Ofosuware, 'Wisdom for Successful Living.' Freedom Centre International, Welling. Pre-recorded audio CD.

Rev Celia Appiagyei Colins, 'In pursuit of Destiny.' Rehoboth Foundation, UK. Pre-recorded audio CD.

Rev Celia Appiagyei Colins, 'The Church, Its Mandate and Influence.' Rehoboth Foundation, UK. Pre-recorded audio CD.

Rev Sam Ohene-Apraku, 'The God of Abundance.' Dominion Centre, London. Pre-recorded DVD.

Rev Sam Ohene-Apraku, 'Sowing and Reaping.' Dominion Centre, London. Pre – recorded Audio CD

Rev Sam Ohene-Apraku, 'The Audacity of Faith.' Dominion Centre, London. Pre-recorded Audio CD.

African TV Stations on Sky Digibox

TV Station	Channel	Ownership
Olive TV	593	Zion Church
OHTV	199	Redeemed Christian Church of God
Believe TV	592	Victorious Pentecostal Assembly
Faith World TV	590	UK World Evangelical Church
KICC	591	Kingsway Int. Christian Centre
Love World TV	586	Christ Embassy Church

Index

B

baakofo ntiti abofra, 123
baby dedication, 158
baby-mama syndrome, 125
baby shower functions, 161
baby showers, 161
background, 45, 85–86, 98, 177, 180
Baden Powell Memorial Hall, 46
baggage, cultural, 182
Bahamas, 86
Baines, 221
Bangladeshi, 80
banks, 62, 96, 170, 221
  private, 62
  state-owned Ghana Commercial, 96
baptism, 36, 158
Barrett, ix, 221, 227
barriers, 121, 140, 215
  invisible, 234
  racial, 62
Basch, 8, 222, 234
Basic types of Pastoral Care
    Counseling, 224
Bassey, Nathaniel, 193
Bauman, 29–30, 221
Bayreuth African Studies Series, 232
BBC, 32–33, 114
beauty contests, 45
beauty shop, 55
Becher, 222
Bediako, 112, 222
Beefeater, 149
Behavioural Sciences, 226
Belem, 38
beliefs
  cultural, 208
  millennialist, 108
  political, 7
  religious, 67, 124, 127, 149, 189, 204
  younger generation African
      Pentecostal, 210
Beliefs & Values, 223, 228
beliefs and practices, xii, 1, 7, 37–39,
    127, 137, 144, 147, 152, 187, 208
beliefs and praxis, 137, 144, 155, 165,
    167, 177, 188, 203–5, 208, 210,
    218
Beliefs and Praxis in African Churches,
    208
believers, born-again, 39

Believe TV, 105
believing, 43
Bellah, xi, 222
Benneh, 52
Berger, xi, 222
bible, 4, 12, 14, 77, 106, 139, 146, 152,
    182, 206–7
Bible-centred, 118
biblical, 49–50, 77, 89, 144, 159, 172,
    201, 217
biblical explanation, 188
biblical jargon, 154
biblical narratives, 65, 92, 171, 207
biblical patriarchs, 206
biblical principle, 93
biblical text, 153
biblical way, 188
Bill Winston Ministries, 241
Bimrose, 222
Biography, 239
Birmingham, vii, 56, 98, 223, 232–33
Birmingham City Temple, 56
birth, xii, 44, 81, 129, 155–56, 160
Bishop Climate Irungu's Kingdom
    Church, viii
Bishop Michael Hutton-Wood, 239, 241
Bisin, Alberto, 229
Blackaby, 70, 222
Black Africans in Britain, 31, 34
Black and White Christian Partnership
    and Westhill, 222
Black Caribbean, 80
Black Majority Pentecostal, 34
black man, 216
black people, 50–51, 62, 179
  young, 174
Black Roots, 227
Black Theology, 226
Black Training, 174, 240
Black Training and Enterprise Group
    (BTEG), 174, 240
Blair, Tony, 32, 211, 239
Blanc-Szanton, 8, 234
blessing, 41, 50, 93, 111, 150, 152, 220
  invoking ancestral, 242
Bloom, 25
  David E., 235
Bloomsbury, 219
Blunkett, David, 32
Bode, 79, 222

book, vii, xii–xiii, 12, 70, 153, 204–7, 209, 215–16
borders, 29, 69, 196–97
  physical, 196
Borgman, Eric, 231
Borocz, 6, 233
Bosch, 4–5, 223
Bourdieu, Pierre, 16
Bowdich, 164, 223
Boyd-Franklin, 199, 223
Bradford, 37
branches, satellite, x
Brazil, 38
Brettell, Caroline, 234
Brill, 219, 221
Brimrose, 84
Britain, contemporary, 191
Britain integration, 73
Britain part-finances, 62
Britain's Black Majority Churches, 219
Britain's Ethnic Communities, 229
Britain's prosperity, 211
British and African churches, 192
British Christianity, 187
British citizens, 74, 126
British citizenship, 59, 74
British colony, 60
British communities, vii, 124, 186, 216
British cultural context, 182
British cultural values, 117
British culture, 63, 123–24, 135, 168, 178
British economy and society, 69
British Gospel Music, 192
British government, 89
British history, 178
British institutional initiative, 119
British jobs for British people, 64
British Journal, 230, 235
British Labour Market, 222
British life, 74
British-migrant religious discourse, 84
British Minority Churches Directory, x
British mode of institutional organisation, 119
British Pentecostal, 188, 202
British perception, 181
British scene, 189
British societal values and culture, 210
British society Stewardship's services, 100
British way, 74, 128, 195, 207, 211

broadcasting, 104, 108
broadcasts, 107–8, 113–14, 116–18, 198
Brong Ahafo Region of Ghana, 152
Bruce, 13, 223
Brunton-smith, 235
Bryman, 223
Bubiashie, 148
Buddhism, 236
budgets, 64, 101, 213
  household, 101
buildings
  acquisition of, 201
  derelict, 58
  landmark, 187
  public, 201
Bulmer, Martin, 230
bureaucratisation, 13
Burgess, 186, 223
buses, church commuting, 189
business enterprise, 24
businesses, 15, 65, 95–97, 99, 120
business start-ups, 92, 98, 167
Bynner, 228

C
Caglar, 6, 198, 234
Cain, 26, 223
California Press, 231
Calvinism, 15
Calvinist, 19
Cambridge, 176, 229–31
Cambridge University Press, 229–31
Cameron, David, 33, 125
Camp, 225
Campbell, 102, 223
Canada and returned migrants, 230
Canadian Journal, 234
capabilities, 84, 179
capacities, 91, 218
capacity auditorium, 61
capital
  economic, 66, 129
  foreign, 27
capital accumulation, 9
capital assets, 28
capital investment, 28
capitalism, 15, 19–20, 236
capitalist, modern, 16
capitalist enterprise, 15
capital markets, 28

Church Documents, 240
church elders, 49
church environment, 175
churches
  average, 132
  black majority, x, 98, 100, 102, 106, 238
  city, 55
  colonial, 200
  diasporean, 48
  dominated, 103
  first African Spirit, 38
  foreign, 129
  historical, viii, 3, 84, 152, 188–89
  immigrant, x
  independent, 200
  large, xii, 54
  largest Protestant, 38
  mega, 54–55
  migrant, 1–2, 21, 66, 114
  migrant-led, 83
  multicultural, 59
  non-conformist, 187
  prophet-led, 145
  rich, 131
  self-governing, 216
  sending, 28
  specific ethnic, 185
  spiritist, 142
  spiritual, 143
  targets, 98
  traditional, 14
  transnational, 205
  white British, 112
  white majority, 84
churches approach, 182
churches contextualise, xii
churches structure, 48
churches studies, 146
churches transnational, 196
church facility, 61
church ideas, 196
church leaders, vii, 1, 60, 84–85, 94
church leadership, 129
church members, 4, 167, 193
church membership, 48
church music, 171
Church of England churches in Britain, 132
church organisations, 92, 197
church organization, 200
church services, 114, 118, 127, 134, 178,
187, 189, 194
  quiet, 186
church uniforms, 186
church way, 159
church wedding, 126
cinema halls, 3
circuit, speaking, 85
circumstances
  economic, 65
  political, 205
  social, 70, 94
cities, ix–x, 47, 61, 92
  global, 28
citizens, 34, 65, 72
citizenship, 59, 70, 225, 234
  social, 234
Civil Service, 118
civil society groups, 134
civil unrest, 30
clan, 149–50, 156
Clark, 70, 198, 224
Clarke, 224
class, 233
  first, 87
  middle, 19
class divisions, 15
Classical Pentecostal, 3, 38
class structures, 16
class systems, creating, 86
clergy, 83, 237
clients, new Pentecostal, 141
Clifford, 224
Clinebell, 139–40, 224
clips, video, 101
Coast, Ivory, 58
co-existence, peaceful, 44
cognatic descent, 156
cohabitation, 127
co-habitation, migrants practice, 124
Cohesion, 230
Coleman, 32, 224
colonialism, 50
colonial masters, 191
colonisation, 130
  prior, 27
command, perceived, 206
commercial plane, 87
Commission, Charity, 47, 118–19, 132
commission, supernatural, 206–7, 214, 217
Common Mission, 236

D
Daly, 79, 224
dance, swag, 176
Dance and Choreography in Britain, 174
dance craze, 176
Dark Continent of Europe, 232
Darwin, Charles, 14, 16
Daswani, 208
Davidson, 232
Daystar, 105
declarations
  compulsive, 145
  prophetic, 89
deities, 43, 142, 162, 192
  revered, 148
deliberate mission initiative, 45
deliverance, 162–68, 182, 208, 221
  appropriation of, 165
  subject of, 166
Deliverance Practice in Pentecostal
    Churches in Ghana, 162
deliverance process, 152
delivery, 11, 15, 161
  safe, 157
demarcation, clear, 139
demons, 152, 164, 166
Denkyira, 40
depictions, audio-visual, 109
deprivation, 86–87, 177
  social, 85
destination areas, 24
destiny, 116, 130, 143, 154
development, 8, 11, 13–14, 19, 22, 104,
    106, 111, 120, 122, 198–99, 225,
    235–36
  church's, 56
  cultural, 183
  human, 155
  personal, 71, 85–86, 91, 103, 134,
    213–14
  social, 54, 64
Development-Induced Displacement, 236
Development Tool, 234
devil, 104, 116, 152, 163–64, 181
DeWind, Josh, 234
Deya, Gilbert, 105
dialogue, 17, 139
diaspora, viii, 192, 219–20, 224, 227–

28, 232, 235
  new, 34
diasporisation, 34
Dickson, 153, 224
differences
  cultural, 124
  geographic, 23
Differential migration networks
    information, 225, 235
difficulties, 82, 87, 89, 111, 120, 125,
    173, 178–79, 206, 212, 214
  economic, 3, 173
  financial, 93
  personal socio-economic, 85
Diffusion, 234
dignity, 7
  human, 50
Dijk, 225
dilemma, cultural, 135
dimension
  multi-cultural, 129
  religious, xi, 206, 222
  spiritual, 139, 206
din pa, 157
direction, 25, 64, 85, 140, 143, 218
  divine, 145
directives, assimilationist policy, 72
discipleship, 53
disciplines
  academic, 17
  modern academic, 17
discontinuity, 42, 64, 147, 161, 167
Discontinuity of African Pentecostal
    Beliefs and Praxis, 208
Discontinuity of Ghanaian Pentecostal, 229
discourse, 91, 147, 225
discrimination, 210
  racial, 62, 235
disease, 30, 162
disenchantment, 20
diversity, cultural, 73
divination, 141–44, 235
  practice of, 141–42
divination process, 142, 145
Divine Healers Church, 171
divinities, 157
Dixon, Thomas, 14
doctrinal straitjackets, 139
doctrines, 12, 116

English test, 212
Enlightenment, 13
entanglement, theological, 147
Enterprise Group, 240
entities, 1, 12, 14, 40, 79, 99, 165,
    205
  conceptual, 18
  divine, 11
  organisational, 12
  religious, 140
  shared, 2
  spiritual, 141
Epworth Press, 233
era
  colonial, 63
  modern, 15, 17
eschatological, 116
eschatology, 116
Ethne Online Journal, 238
Ethnic & Migration Studies, 228, 230
ethnic African origins, 122
Ethnic and Migration Studies, 229,
    236
ethnic background, 5
ethnic category, 31
Ethnic diversity, 235
ethnic groups, 40, 138
ethnicity, 61, 70, 122, 225, 233
Ethnic Lens, 234
ethnic minorities, 32, 57, 62, 72–73,
    76–78, 80, 84, 100, 177, 209,
    224
ethnic minority groups, 73, 80
  largest, 80
ethnic origins, 122
ethnographic investigation, 90
ethnography, 226–27, 232
ethos, 1, 39–40
  core evangelical Christian, 100
Europe, pre-industrialised, 13
European countries, 59–60, 79
  non-English speaking, 59
European descent, 80
European Economic Area, 33
European history, 16
Europeans, 6, 216
European Social Policy, 222
European states, 79
Evangelical Presbyterian, viii
events

domestic, 169
  negative, 142
  social, 18, 155
  unfortunate, 162
evil, 41, 145, 163, 234
Ewe, 233
EWTN, 104
examination, critical, 134, 217
excellence, 50, 77, 100
exclusivity, theoretical, 22
existence, 18, 27, 42, 44, 48, 115, 205
  human, 6, 16, 22
Existing theories on migration, 206
exorcism, 39, 163, 232
experiential, 11
Expert Advice, 95
experts, 96, 125, 215
exposure, cultural, 128
External Integration strategies, 211

F
Facebook, 102
factors
  contextual, 195
  economic, 29–30
  environmental, 119
  external, 119
  global, 216
  large-scale institutional, 7
  local, 38
  political, xiii, 110
  religious, 22, 110, 206
  spiritual, 8, 201, 206–7
Factors Precipitating Migration, 21
Faith-based Organisation, 226
Faith Based Organisations (FBOs), 79
faith communities, xi–xii, 139
faith leaders, 83, 237
faiths, existing, 202
Faith World TV, 105, 243
families, 25–26, 65–66, 81–82, 123–
    24, 145, 148–50, 152–53, 156,
    159, 162–63, 169
  father's, 156–57
famine, 30, 169
Faupel, 37
FBOs and African churches, 80
FCI (Freedom Centre International),
    55–58, 62, 66, 95–96, 116,
    160–61, 240, 242

Fei, 23, 226
fellowship, 2, 46, 52–53, 190
financial hand-outs, 71, 134
financial irregularities, 132
financial planning, 166
Financial Times, 32
Firm Policies, 237
firms, 194
  capitalist, 27
  foreign, 194
First Capital, 96
Fiske, 118, 197, 225
flavour, cultural, 154
Florida timeshare, 132
flow
  international, 27
  international migratory, 23
  reverse, 6, 8
focus, 1–2, 6–8, 15, 17, 21, 78, 83–84,
    114, 116, 119, 133, 135, 138
Folklore, 235
followers, 50, 118
Fontomfrom, 168
fontomfrom drum, 168
Forced Migration, 30, 236
forces, 22, 25–26, 60–61, 112, 241
  enemy, 42
  police, 169
  supernatural, 41, 148
foreigners, 34
foreign investment, 28
  direct, 27, 111
formation, spiritual, 67
forms
  de-humanizing, 50
  organisational, 196
Forson, 163, 225
forums, immigration and nationality,
    71, 82, 134, 213
foundation, 90, 99, 226, 242
founder, vii, 45, 58, 130
founding pastor, 49
framework, 6–7, 71, 141, 186, 197
  analytical, 8
  bifurcated occupational, 26
  changing legal, 7
  conceptual, 27
  cultural, 144
  ecclesiastical, 137
  empirical, 26

  mental, 4
  theological, xi, 218
  theoretical, 6, 9, 40, 42
France, 58–60, 79
fraternity, 66, 211
freedom, 165
Freedom Centre International. *See* FCI
Free Press, 222, 225, 231, 234–36
free tuition, given, 173
Full Gospel Evangelical Ministry, 194
function, 16, 101, 140, 156–57, 161,
    169
  spiritual, 170
functional building blocks, 228
funds, 2, 29, 63, 87, 92, 97, 99, 108
funeral, 124, 129, 168
Funmati, 8, 71, 129, 213

G
Galia Sabar, xiii
Gananath Obeyesekere, 16
Ga People, 219
GDP (Gross Domestic Product), 64
Geertz, Clifford, 16
generation
  older, 210
  third, 35, 81, 210–11
  younger, 167–68, 210–11
Georgiadis, 69, 229
Gerloff, 2, 7, 120–21, 226
Germany, 59–60, 90, 232
Gerrie, 3, 235
Gerrie ter Haar, xiii
Ghana
  churches in, 163, 171, 173, 216
  government of, 96, 131
  rural, 226
Ghanaian-Akan culture, 126
Ghanaian and African Pentecostal
    church practices, 155
Ghanaian-British identity, 135
Ghanaian churches, 60, 185
Ghanaian churches in London, 61
Ghanaian communities, 62, 198
Ghanaian congregation, 48–49
Ghanaian context, 39–40
Ghanaian culture, 135
Ghanaian highlife musician, popular,
    172
Ghanaian Indigenous Communities, 40,

44, 168
Ghanaian indigenous context, 43
Ghanaian Indigenous Cosmologies,
40, 44
Ghanaian languages, 59
Ghanaian Migrants, 59, 220, 230
Ghanaian Migrants in Germany, 232
Ghanaian Pentecostal Diaspora, 225
Ghanaian Pentecostalism, 221, 225
Ghanaian Pentecostals, 35, 40, 42, 45,
154, 158, 163–64, 229
Ghanaians, average, 66
Ghanaian TV stations, 105
Ghana Presbyterian Church, 180
Ghana's New Christianity, 226
Ghana's premier, 45
Ghana Wesleyan Methodist church, 180
Giddens, Antony, 16
Gifford, 42, 78, 226
Gift Aid, 101
gifts, monetary, 101
Gilbert Deya Ministries, 105
Gilded Age, 12
Glaniel, Gladys, 83
Glick Schiller, 6
global affairs, 112
global appeal, 103, 110
Global Christianity, ix, 198, 234, 238
Global Context, 219
global impact, 203
global influences, 203
Global Introduction, 228
globalisation, 29, 67, 102, 149, 191,
197–98, 219
Globalised African, 226
globalised units, 218
Globalization of Pentecostal, 233
global labor market, 233
Global Mission, 227
Global Pentecostalism, 35–36
Global Perspective, 227
global playing field, 199
global power geometry, 200
Global Processes, 227
global religious market, 218
Global Revival Ministries, 194
global social field, 97
Global Society, 222
Global South, ix
Global Spread, 220

Gocmen, 79, 226
God
house of, 52–53, 115, 131
people of, 52–53
power of, 54, 113
servant of, 140, 146
word of, 14, 139, 146–47, 166, 181
God in Yoruba Belief, 227
gospel, 4, 6, 28, 50–51, 55, 175–76,
181–82, 186, 190, 193, 200, 203
Gospel Church, 232
gospel music, youthful rap, 193
government, 12–13, 31, 33, 69–70, 72,
74, 96, 99, 119, 125, 145, 212
government policy, 32, 215
Gross Domestic Product (GDP), 64
groups
choreography, 173
civil, 73
religious, 95, 120
growth, ix, 30, 48–49, 60, 67, 80, 84,
140, 193–94, 214, 224
Guardian, 65, 132–33
Guardian's research, 132
Guildford Press, 223
Gulbrandsen, 7, 215
Gunther, 232
Gustav, 226, 233
Gyekye, 116, 226

H
Hackett, 108, 118, 196–97, 226
Hagin, Kenneth, 108
Hammersley, 226
Hanciles, x, 226
Handbook, 235
Hand-book of International Migration,
234
Hardill, 79, 221
harmony, 44
Harper, 222
Harrassowitz Verlag, 219
Harris, Wade, 37
Harris J, 227
Harvey, 18
headquarters, 51, 131
healers, traditional, 41
healing and deliverance, 164
heaven, 19, 90, 93, 188
Hegel, 16

immigration
  illegal, 201
  transnational, 9
Immigration and Citizenship in
  Europe, 234
immigration forums, 126
immigration generation, 229
immigration policy, 32, 65
Immigration Policy Debate, 31
Immigration Reconsidered History,
  231
immigration rules, 214
immigration status, 49, 83, 103
  settled, 86
immigration strategies, 69
implications
  ethical, 193
  social, 16
  spiritual, 125
incantation, 149
income, 26, 93, 97, 131
income inequality, reducing, 28
incorporation, 6, 9, 22, 26, 90, 233
  nonethnic immigrant, 234
India, 37–38
  religions of, 15, 236
Indian, 80, 161
Indiana University Press, 224, 226
indicator, 66, 138
indigenes, 4, 39
indigenous, 42, 138, 144, 158, 160,
  162, 170, 204, 208
  competing, 163
Indigenous African Beliefs, 137
indigenous Akan context, 157
indigenous ceremonies, 160
indigenous communities, 44
  largest, 40
indigenous cosmology, 39–40, 43, 67,
  189
Indigenous Cultures, 173, 220
indigenous deities, 149
indigenous forbearers, 161
indigenous framework, 159
Indigenous Libation Practice, 148
indigenous libation prayer, 154
indigenous music, 171–72
indigenous priests, 164
indigenous proverbs, 44
indigenous religions, 39, 43, 137–38,

140–41, 143–45, 147–48, 153–
  55, 162–66, 170–72, 182–83,
  198, 202, 204
  adherents of, 148, 155, 164
  practices of, 138, 163
indigenous religion's adherents place,
  152
indigenous religions exorcise, 164
indigenous religions libation prayer,
  152
indigenous religions practitioners, 153,
  198
indigenous rituals, 149
indigenous values, 44
indigenous worldview, 41
individuality, 44, 225
individuals control, 147
individual's fortune, 165
industrialisation, 12–13, 19
Industrial Revolution, 13, 15
infant, 152, 156–58
influenza epidemic, 38
information
  historical, 25
  new, 205
information dissemination, 100
infrastructure, 66, 187
infusion, cultural, 180
initiatives, xi–xii, 71, 75, 79, 83, 100,
  103–4, 110, 114, 134, 203–5,
  209, 212–14
innovation, 98, 234
insider perspective, 17
Inspiration Network International, 105
institutional organisation, 119
institutions, 13, 70–71, 102, 179, 206
  pre-tertiary educational, 47
  religious, 205
instructions, 14, 53, 140, 146, 152, 159
integration, xi, 1–2, 6–9, 19–21,
  69–79, 103–4, 116–17, 174, 177,
  185, 211–14, 217, 230, 238–39
  agents of, 72, 84
  defining, 72–73
  idea of, 6, 72–73
  internal, 205
  migrant community approaches, 75
  natural form of, 76–77
  politicians approach, 75
  processes of, xii, 133

process of, 8, 19, 21, 71, 77, 122, 133–34, 178, 204, 211, 218
  social, 199
  tool of, 129, 138
  word, 70
integration agenda, 2, 113, 212
integration efforts, 103
integration initiatives, 215
  internal, 205
integration point, 129
integration policies, 178
  governmental, 204
integration strategies, 45, 67, 79, 185, 214
  internal, 7, 213, 215
  internal micro-level, 204
  non-deliberate, 67
Integrity Music, 192
intention
  economic, 28
  religious, 32
Interdisciplinary Journal, 227
interdisciplinary understanding, 7
intermediaries, human, 41
internal initiatives, 6, 79
International Bulletin, 226–27
International Central Gospel Church. *See* ICGC
international competitiveness, 32
International Handbook of Migration, 224
International Journal, 226
International Labour Migration in West Africa, 220
international migration, 6, 8, 21–25, 27–30, 230, 232, 234
International Migration Review, 233
international migration strategy, 25
International Migration Systems, 228
International Review of Mission, 221, 226, 236
International Studies in Demography, 230
International System, 233
internet café, 55
Internet Church, 223
Interpreting Contemporary Christianity, 227
interventions, socio-theological, xi
Introduction, celebratory, 121

Introductory Level, 99
investment opportunities, 96
investments, 27, 96–97
invocation, 150, 152, 170, 192–93, 209
İpek, 226
Irish Christian family, 62
Irish School, 83, 237
Islamic culture, 16
Israel, xiii, 234
ITV, 114
IZA Discussion Paper, 224

J
Jackson, 227, 235
JAI Press, 225, 235
Japan, 37
Jeffreys, George, 188, 239
Jenkins, ix, 73, 227, 237
  Philip, ix
Jennings, 192, 227
Jesus, Junior, 172
Jewish tithing, 94
jobs, 64–65, 82, 84, 115, 132, 163, 169, 174, 179, 212
  minimum-wage, 24
  undesirable, 33
  white-collar, 24
Johnson, ix, 227, 238
Jolin, Annette, 230
Jorgensen, 227
Joseph Rowntree Foundation, 224
Jossey-Bass, 234
Journal, 220, 223, 228–30, 235
Journal of Beliefs, 223, 228
Journal of Black Studies, 219
Journal of Computer-Mediated Communication, 223, 227
Journal of Contextual Praxis, 226
Journal of Economic Literature, 223
Journal of European Social Policy, 222
Journal of Labor Economics, 228
Journal of Pentecostal Theology, 233
Journal of Religion in Africa, 225–26, 230–31, 237
Journal of Social Issues, 230
Journal of Social Policy, 224
Journal of Vocational Behavior, 222
Joy 99.7FM, 47
Juergensmeyer, 17, 228

K

Kalu, viii, 29, 194, 219, 227–28
Kanda Fellowship, 46
Kasinitz, Philip, 234
Kate, 176
Katz, 25, 228
Kay, 228
Keely, Charles B., 233
Kent, 56–57, 61
Kenya, 58
Kenyan, xii–xiii
Kenyan Church, viii
Kete, 168
  dancing, 169
Al-Khawarizmi, 16
KICC (Kingsway International
    Christian Centre), viii, 105, 130,
    132, 243
KICC TV, 105
Kietzmann, 102, 228
Kiev, 4
Al-Kindi, 17
Kingdom of God, 50
Kingsley Larbi, vii
Kingsway International Christian
    Centre (KICC), viii, 105, 130,
    132, 243
Klaus Koschorke, 219
Klear TV, 105
Knibbe, Kim, 5
knowledge
  hidden, 143
  secret, 147
  spiritual, 141
knowledge base, 215
Koforidua, 130, 148, 198, 220
Kok Pharos, 236
Komla Dumor, 47
Korankye-Ankrah, Sam, 52
Korea, 37–38
Koser, 230, 237
kra, 157
Krause, 2, 6, 8, 200, 213, 228
Kristine, 228
Kritz, 6, 228, 233
Kuha, 235
Kumasi, 130, 148, 216
Kuusisto, 179, 228
Kwaku Bonsam, 148

L

Labi Siffre, 62
labor, 23, 221, 233
Labor Economics, 228
labourers, unsung Pentecostal, 37
labour market, 26, 224
Lagos, 38, 220
Lake, John G., 36
Landes, 13, 229
  David, 12
landscape, changing, 191
Lang, Peter, 219
Langman, xi, 222
language
  libation prayer, 182, 208
  national, 59
language divisions, 121
Larbi, xiii, 37, 41, 138, 229
Larteh-Akuapem, 148
Latin America, ix–x, 39, 224
latinised name Avicenna, 16
Layder, 229
Leach, 93–94, 229
leaders
  accomplished spiritual, 142
  excellent, 63
  political, 62
  raising, 49
leadership, 40–41, 52, 55, 57, 60–61,
    63, 83, 85–86, 90–91, 128–29,
    232, 235
  elitist, 77
leadership experience, 224
leadership growth consultancy, 46
leadership positions, 214
Leadership's Teaching, 93
leadership training, 53, 71, 82, 84, 134,
    213–14
Leadership Training Seminars, 85
left-liberal political groups, 32
legislation, supportive, 125
Lehikoinen, 102, 229
lenses, political, 94
Leroi, 213
Leslie, 222
levels
  cultural, 76–77
  maintaining high, 84
  multiple, 22
  new global, 197

Migration Studies, 229, 233, 236
migration theories, 7, 21, 28, 92, 110, 208
Migration Theory and Research on International Population Movements, 233
Migratory Processes, 224
military dictator, 172
military junta, 56
military regimes, 34
ministers, 49, 52, 66, 83, 191–92, 237
ministries, 4–5, 48–51, 53–58, 61, 66, 101, 109, 180, 186, 192, 224
ministry gift, 146
ministry group, 54
Minority Ethnic Christian Affairs, x
minority-ethnic people, 83
minority group, predominant, 201
minority perspective, 17
mission, 4–5, 21, 29, 52, 90, 100, 221, 223, 226–28, 232, 235–36
  neglected, 5
  reverse, 5, 28, 48, 78, 181–82, 200, 236
Missional Leadership, 238
missionaries, 29, 37, 220
  early, 42–43
  early Christian, 164
  early twentieth-century protestant, 143
  western, 37
Missionary Research, 226–27
mission orientation, 5
mission statement, 49, 52–53
mission strategy, 5
Mitchel, 105, 231
mmrane Dompo, 157
models
  economic, 23
  internal, 214
  neoclassical microeconomic, 25
Modern Communication, 227
modernism, 14, 19
modernity, 12, 20, 109–11, 219, 221, 231
Modern life, 12
Modern Media, 229
Modern World, 223

Mona, 16
Mona Kanwal Sheikh, 238
mo nananom ntɛm deɛ yɛ samaran, 150
mo nananom sɛ mone, 150
money, extort, 181
monotheism, 43
  diffused, 43
Moral Economy, 225
Morrison, 188, 232
mother, 123, 156, 158–59, 161
motivation, viii, 26, 65–66, 85, 104
motives, 29–30, 74, 79, 103, 113, 135, 165, 192, 197–98
Mouton, 226
movements
  charismatic, 228
  international, 24–26
  larger global, 196
  migratory, 7
  new, 144
Movements and Migratory Processes, 224
Mphahlele, 148, 222
multicultural, 22, 180
multiculturalism, 122, 239
multicultural pendulum, 127
Multi-cultural Pendulum, 121
Multicultural Racisim, 233
Mundely, 94
Munk, 237
Munroe, 91, 232
  Myles, 86–87, 241
Murie, 231
Murphy, 222
music, 168, 170–76, 190, 192–93, 202, 227
  fontonfrom, 168
  pirated, 193
  rap, 172, 175, 210, 240
  rap-style, 175
  secular, 176
  traditional, 168
  western, 171
  western pop, 175
musical equipment, 173
musical instruments, 173
Musical Quarterly, 227
music and dance, 168–73, 175–76, 182

music genres, 174–75
    contemporary, 210
Muslims, viii
mythological, 11

N
Nakaba, 171
name, umbrella, 51
naming ceremonies, 129, 155–56,
    158–59, 161, 182, 208
    traditional, 159
Naming Drama, 219
Nana Kwaku Bonsam, 120, 198
nananom mma wɔn anim nguase,
    150
narratives
    scriptural, 139, 146
    verifiable, 207
Narrative Theology and Pentecostal,
    233
Nassau, 241
national attention, 186
national average, 174
National Democratic Congress, 172
National Identity, 230
nationalist ideologies, 216
nationalists, 216
nationalities, viii–ix, 58–59, 82, 180
    predominant, viii
Nationality Act, 211
nationality forums, 71, 82, 134, 213
National Statistics, 33
nation building, 123
nations
    developed, 22, 30
    receiving, 30, 64–65, 206
    western, 115
nation's Pentecostal church circles,
    192
nation states, 70
Nation-States, 9, 222, 234
    single, 90
natural disasters, 30
naturalisation, 74
natural progression, 93
nature
    interwoven, 115
    multifaceted, 22
    prophetic, 235
    transnational, 106

unverifiable, 187
Nature and Nurture Combination
        Determining African-British
        Religious Identity, 117
negro spirituals, 170
neighbourhoods, good, 97
neoclassical, 23, 25–26
Neoclassical Economics, 22
Neoclassical Economic Theory of
    Migration, 23
neoclassical model, 23
neoclassical orthodoxy, 7
neo-Pentecostal, 106
Neo-Pentecostal Churches, 107, 171,
    220
net migration, 32
networking, ix, 71, 76–77, 120–21,
    225
    social, 66, 234
networks, 2, 7, 61, 76, 120, 197
    dynamic, 236
    maintaining, 70
New Africa Diaspora, 219
New Economics Theory of
    Migration, 25
New Focus for Migration, 236
New York, 222, 225, 230–31, 236
New York University Press, 228
Nexgen, 98–99
Nexgen Initiatives Limited, 98
Nieswand, 8, 90, 97, 232
Nigeria, 37–38, 58, 108, 176, 193,
    196, 220, 223, 226, 232
Nigerian, xii, 98, 228
Nigerian Church, viii
Nigerian churches, 185, 227
Nigerian migrant, 39
Nigerian music pirates, 193
Nigerian Pastor and founder of
    KICC in London, 130
Nigerian Pentecostal, 39
Ninian Smart, 11, 16
Nketiah, 170
Nkonyane, Daniel, 38
Nnwomkoro, 168
non-believer, 114
non-Christians, 113
non-Ministerial Government
    Department, 118
norms, cultural, 122

Nova Religio, 219
nsa
  asase yaa, 150
  nananom nsamanfo, 150
  wohu nsa nso a kasɛ, 157
nuances, xii, 67, 218
  cultural, 208
  distinctive, 39
nurturing people, 86
Nyame, 157
Nyankopon, 157

O

Obadare, 29, 219
obscurity, 185, 220
observers, critical, 66
Obuotabiri, 148
Oded Stark, 225, 235
odinsifo, 41
Odulele brothers, viii
Oestreich, 85, 234
offerings, 93, 108, 132
Ohene-Apraku, Sam, 58, 242
OHTV, 243
okomfo, 41, 147
Okorocha, 42, 115
okyeame, 158–59
Older Migrants in Europe, 236
Old Kent Road, 186
O'Leary, 70, 222
olive oil, 43, 166
Olive TV, 105, 243
Olodumare, 227
Olofinjana, ix, 232
Olupona, 228
Olympics, 99
O'Malley, Joseph, 230
Omanhene, 170
oman yi yie dee, 150
Omenyo, 143, 232
Omokodu, Alex, 105
Online Religion in Nigeria, 223
onpe abusua yi, 150
Onyankopɔn, 42
Onyinah, xiii, 163–64, 232
Open Heavens TV, 105
Oral Roberts, 108
Orbis Books, 234–35
organisation
  charitable, 5

civil-society, 33
customer service, 178
economic, 26
learning, 86
non-governmental, 31, 134
not-for-profit, 98
religious, 28
organisational hierarchies,
    formalised, 118
organisation and vision, 49, 67
orientation, 9, 106, 200
  cultural, 124, 127, 182
  religious, 118, 121
origin countries, 28
origin influence, 204
Origins of Pentecostalism, 220
Orozco, 33
orphanage, 29
orthodoxy, 32
  traditional religious, 14
oscillations, 122, 127
oscillations of religious and social
    convictions, 121, 127
Osofo Komfo Damoah, 198
outlook, theological, 117
outreach, international, 6
ownership, 169, 201, 243
own-shared cultural understanding,
    30
Oxford, 223, 231
Oxford Economic Papers, 222
Oxford Handbook of Religion and
    Violence, 228
Oxford University Press, 220, 223,
    228–31, 237
Oyakhilome, Chris, 105

P

Pacific Rim, 39
packaging, 107, 112
Painkiller, 235
Pajo, 31, 232
Pakistani, 80
palm oil, 200
pan-african, 7
Pan-Africanism, promoted, 130
pan-Africanist, 131, 216
Pan-Africanist disposition, 216
Pan-Africanist ideals, 217
pan-Africanist wave, 130

Pentecostal traditions, 158, 171
Pentecostal understanding, 2
Pentecostal worship, 193
people's perspectives, 16
perception changes, 216
perception discourse, 177
perceptions, 111, 127, 167, 181, 188,
        191, 211, 236
    broadcasting industry, 113
    negative, 181
    shaping society's, 20
    traditional African, 40
Perez Chapel, 131
permission, planning, 187
persecution, political, 3, 31
Persistence of Traditional Religious
        Beliefs, 225
person
    black, 50
    conservative British, 124
personal charisma, 106
Personal Development and
        Leadership Training Seminars
        and workshops, 85
personal development events, 90
personal development initiatives, 90
Personal Giving, 129
perspective
    broader, 205
    evangelical, 163
    socio-political, 127
    socio-theological, 204
    spiritual, 125
    theological, 77, 144, 148
Petras, 27, 233
phenomenon, viii, x, xiii, 13, 18–19,
        38, 41, 105–6, 111, 191, 198,
        202, 205
Phillips, Trevor, 73
philosophical lineages, 102
philosophy, 49–50, 76–77, 107, 230
    deliberate, 77
    guiding, 77
pictures, 109, 191
pioneers, 36, 130
Piore, 27
places migration, 26
places of origin and settlement, 71,
        122, 138
planning permission issues, 61

plantations, 171
platform
    multimedia, 54, 209
    noise-making, 198
    public media, 148
    social networking, 196–97
    terrestrial TV, 104
pluralistic, 84
PMP, 99
PNDC (Provisional National Defence
        Council), 56
Pneuma, 228
Pnina, 225
Pobee, 149–51, 153, 233
Points Based System, 212
Poirier, 147, 233
police academy, 169
policies, 70, 73–75, 133–34, 177,
        212, 230, 236
    assimilationist, 74
    asylum, 32
    existing, 73, 213
    governance and social, 224
    macro level, 75
    public, 34, 72, 177
    shaping, 75
Policy Implementation, 236
policy initiatives, 74–75
    national level, 213
policy makers, 73–76, 78–79, 134,
        178, 212
policymakers, 28
political insecurity, 9
political loyalties, 9
political rallies, 172
Political Science, 230
politicians, 73, 75–76, 78–79, 125,
        133–34
politics, 74, 206
    international, 238
Politics of Religious Networking,
        219
polity, 40, 221
popularity, 165, 175–76
population, 64–65, 114, 123, 164,
        193, 224, 230
    white majority, 70
    world's, 30
Population Studies, 220
Portes, 6, 27, 233

progenitors, 15
programmes, xi–xii, 9, 71, 82–84,
    105, 109, 113–14, 134, 210, 212,
    214–15
  broadcast, 105
  interventionist, 76
  religious, xi, 71, 113–14
  social welfare intervention, 79
Project Management, 99
project managers, 99
projects, 5, 50, 66, 84, 91–92, 100,
    108–9, 129, 131, 178, 182
  community development, 100
  community-wide, 217
  major church, 111
  nation building, 9
proliferation, 134, 171
promotion, 103, 109, 113
property, 58, 62, 65, 97, 217
  acquired, 61
  first, 96
  landed, 97, 217
prophecy, 146
prophetic actions, 141, 147
prophetic consultation, 139, 141,
    144–45, 182, 208
  practice of, 144–45, 147
Prophetic Consultation in Britain, 143
Prophetic Consultation in Ghana, 142
prophetic counselling places, 140
prophetic ministration, 43
Prophetic Phenomenon, 232
prophetism, 143
prophets, 6, 29, 142–46, 165
Prophet Uebert Angel, viii
prosperity, 78, 88–89, 191, 220, 231
  prolonged, 32
prosperity dimension, 78
prosperity message, 39, 78
protection, 150–51
Protestant-Pentecostal animation ain
    Ghana, 231
Provision of Personal Development
    and Leadership Training, 84
provokes, 146
psychotherapeutic techniques, 139
public perception, 177–78, 180, 236
Public Perception Discourse, 177
Pune, 37–38
purposes

asylum, 31
  economic, 28
  humanitarian, 182
  intervention, 170
  religious, 29
Pyongyang, 37–38

R
Race Equality Strategy, 237
races, 50, 61, 95, 160, 229
  mixed, 208
racial backgrounds, 85
Racial Equality, 32, 73
Racial Studies, 227, 229, 235–36
Racism, 9
radio, 51, 72, 107, 199, 207
Rainham, 61
Ranis, 23, 233
ranks, social, 31
Rap, 176
rate tax, basic, 101
rational explanation, 13
rationalisation, 20
rationalism, 13, 20
Rawlings, 173
raw materials, 29
reality, xi, 17, 22, 40, 110, 113, 157,
    222
  perception of, xiii, 18
reason
  historical, 191
  medical, 156
  socioeconomic, 125
Recent British Policy, 230
receptions, virtual, 178
recognition, 63, 70–71, 76–78, 91, 98,
    107, 179–80, 183, 191–92, 207
  cognitive, 142
  community's, 78
  lack of, 178, 183
recorded Audio CD, 242
Redeemed Christian Church of God,
    105, 219, 223, 243
Reed-Danahay, Deborah, 234
refuge, 30–31, 35
refurbishment, 62
regions, cultural, 30
register, edited electoral, 190
Rehoboth Foundation, 242
reinvigorate, 188

Robin, 234
Rogers, 111, 234
Rojan Eati, 223
role, 13, 15–16, 41–42, 70–71, 123,
    125, 153, 156, 158, 173, 176,
    213, 217
  diminished, 14
role models, 174, 178–79, 183, 207,
    211
Role of Faith-based Organisation in
    Social Welfare, 226
Role of Spatial Practices and Locality,
    228
Romania, 39
roots
  misplaced theological, 77
  religio-cultural, 111
Routeledge, 225
Routledge, 221–22, 224, 229–30
Row, 222
Royalhouse Chapel, 54–55
Royalhouse Chapel International,
    51–52, 66, 238
rules
  democratic, 172
  spiritual-moral, 125
rules migrants, 133
Ryan, 85, 234

S
Sabar, 234
sacred places, 3
sacrifice, 41, 142, 150
Sage Publications, 227, 235, 237
salvation, 19, 229
Samson Ayorinde, 105
Samson Kwaku Boafo, 56, 58
Sankofa Publishing Company, 226
Sarkodie, 176
Sassen, 27–28
Saul, 144, 146
Sawyerr, Harry, 153
Scalon, Paul, 239
Schanton, 215
schemes
  educational scholarship, 47
  social insurance, 129
Schiller, 2, 70–71, 197–98, 215, 222,
    234
scholars, ix, 1–2, 4, 16, 28, 70, 78,

140, 163, 188, 208
  socially-minded, 16
scholarships, 53
school times, 171
Schreiter, 234
science laboratory, 46
sciences, vii, 14, 17, 234
  social, 13, 17, 19, 229
scientists, 12, 16
  social, 14, 17
Scotland, 33, 57
Scott, 77, 234
screen, projector, 101
scriptures, 89–91, 93, 95, 115, 133,
    144–48, 163, 182–83, 201,
    207–8, 236
  practices in, 144, 147
  use of, 139
sea, 169
seats, senior pastors, 106
Second World War, 31, 211
secret place, 77
sectors, third, 79
secular counsellors, 139
secularisation, 17, 19, 223, 231
Secularisation Paradigm, 235
secular musician, 176
secular-spiritual therapist, 141
secular therapists, 139–40
security, social, 60–61
Sedgewick, Henry, 14
Seeing Minorities, 236
segregation, 235, 238
self-actualisation, 214
self-financing, 129
Senge, 86, 234
sermons, 9, 31, 46, 50, 88, 95, 112,
    114, 116, 160, 166
  motivational, 103
servant, 144
services
  financial, 96
  funeral, 199
  multiple, 194
sessions, 90, 96
settled communities, 122, 206, 213–
    15, 217
  new, 215
settled status ruptures, 9
settlement, 8–9, 71, 122, 133, 135,

98, 103, 187, 189–90, 195, 197
aggressive, 190
church organisation, 192, 202
deliberate, 66, 210
effective, 26
innovative, 189
internal, 71, 211
stratification, 207
social, 232
structures, functional, 118
students, 34, 46, 81, 193–94, 238
Studies in Forced Migration, 236
Studies in World Christianity, 219,
221, 232
Sturgis, 76, 235
style, 87, 172, 187, 192–93, 196
sub-culture, 167
sub-Saharan, 108
sub-Saharan Africa, viii, 24, 37, 69,
79, 81, 141, 186, 216, 221
success, 55, 66, 71, 76–78, 88–89, 109,
134, 188, 212
succession planning, 168
Sumrall, Lester, 130
sumsum, 142–44, 147, 171
sumsum sore, 38
Sunyani, 152
supernatural, 207
supernatural encounter, 52–53
Superstitions, 223
supervisor, vii
supplications, 151, 154, 170
support
economic, 213
welfare, 177
support networks, 9, 78, 129, 214
suprareality, 113
Supreme Being, 42, 157, 172
Supreme God, 148, 152
Swain, 225
Swatson, John, 37
systemic failure, 180
systemisation, 235

T
Tabernacle, Faith, 36–37
Talal Asad, 16
Tambiah, Stanley, 16
Tani, Grace, 37
Taoism, 236

target audience, 51, 104, 113–14
Taylor, 13, 23–25, 30, 235
TBN, 104
technological revolution, 196
Tedlock, 142, 235
Telegraph, 176
Telelvision Culture, 225
Televised Charismatic Christianity,
237
television programmes, 116
Tema metropolis of Ghana, 47
Ter Haar, 4–5, 208, 235
terminologies, 13
testimonies, 88, 114–15, 167
musical personal, 172
Thaddeus, 234
theatres, 186–87
theological basis, 188
theological change, 205
Theological Controversy, 144
theological discourses, existing, 207
theological ideas, 15
theological interpretation, 77
theological issues, vii
theological position, 147
Theological Studies, 222
theology, 16–18, 20, 102, 108, 147,
197, 223–24, 236
theology metamorphoses, 108
Theoretical Milieu, 1
Theoretical Perspectives, 233
Theoretical Reflections, 230
Theoretical Sociology, 231
theories, 7–9, 22–23, 25, 28, 65, 206,
208, 229
capitalist, 20
dual labour, 65
micro, 23
migration systems, 6, 65
neoclassical, 26
orthodox, 223
segmented labour market, 223
social, 15
transnational, 8, 65
world systems, 22, 27, 65
Theories of International Migration,
230
Theorizing Transnational Migration,
234
theory's prognoses, 26

third generation migrant groups, 81
Thomas Nelson Publishers, 230
Thompson, Cindy, 173
Thorne, 139–40, 235
Tiemoko, 237
time
  feudal, 15
  pre-colonial, 33
  scheduled, 61
tithes, 93, 108, 132
tithing, 93–94
Tobago, 88
Todaro, 23
  Michael P., 227
Tokugawa Religion, 222
Tomasi, 233
tongues, 36, 127
tools, 2, 19, 71, 78, 86, 134, 138,
    176–77, 185
  socio-economic, 78
top job placements, 2
Traditional African religions, 116
traditions, 37, 39, 82, 152, 155–56,
    158, 173
  black church, 222
train, 47, 93, 103–4, 112, 134
training, 78, 84, 95–97, 99, 104, 134,
    168, 170, 215
training initiatives, 84
training programmes, 100
train people, 99–101
transformation, 117, 187, 203, 219–20,
    222
  spiritual, xiii, 18
transmigrants, 9, 208, 234
transnational appeal, 91
transnational discourse, 115
transnational engagements, 215
transnational entities, 204
transnationalism, 121, 135, 137, 202–
    3, 215, 222, 230
transnationalism theory, 137–38
Transnational Journal of Culture, 225,
    232
transnational links, 78, 176
transnational migrant status, 206
transnational occurrence, 85, 107
Transnational Pentecostalism in Africa
    and Latin America, 224
transnational perspective, 70, 106, 133

Transnational Perspective on
    Migration, 234
transnational point, 198
Transnational Religious and Social
    Dynamics in Africa, 219
transnational status, xi–xii, 1–2, 8, 63,
    67, 71–72, 166, 174, 176, 186,
    215
transnational statuses, 40, 185, 204
transnational ties, xi, 105, 135, 203,
    217
  maintaining, 97
  strong, 126
transnational transcendence, 224
Transsubjectivity, 225
trend, modern, 109
Trinity Baptist Church, 29
Trinity College Dublin, 83, 237
trustees, 100, 120, 132
Tschannen, 13, 235
Tsypylma, 232
Tufnell Press, 228
Turner, 200, 236
TV, 72, 104–5, 107–8, 117, 199, 207,
    243
TV broadcasting, 107
TV stations, 104–5, 243
Twereduapɔn Onyankopɔn Kwame,
    150
Twi language, 40
Twitter, 102

U
UCB TV, 105
Uche, 193
Uganda, 58
UKBA, 69
UK Border, 177
UKET, 100
UK Home Office, 34
UK Labour Force Survey, 224
Ukraine, 4, 39
UK taxpayers, 101
UK World Evangelical Church, 243
understanding
  contemporary, 140
  emerging, 29
  theological, 110
Understanding Mediated Faith, 229
Understanding Voluntary Return, 237